George Albert Smith, George A. Smith

Correspondence of Palestine Tourists

Comprising a series of letters by George A. Smith, Lorenzo Snow, Paul A. SChettler,

and Eliza R. Snow of Utah

George Albert Smith, George A. Smith

Correspondence of Palestine Tourists

Comprising a series of letters by George A. Smith, Lorenzo Snow, Paul A. SChettler, and Eliza R. Snow of Utah

ISBN/EAN: 9783337191566

Printed in Europe, USA, Canada, Australia, Japan

Cover: Foto ©Andreas Hilbeck / pixelio.de

More available books at **www.hansebooks.com**

CORRESPONDENCE

OF

PALESTINE TOURISTS;

COMPRISING

A SERIES OF LETTERS

BY

GEORGE A. SMITH, LORENZO SNOW, PAUL A. SCHETTLER, AND ELIZA R. SNOW,

OF UTAH.

MOSTLY WRITTEN WHILE TRAVELING IN

EUROPE, ASIA AND AFRICA,

IN THE YEARS 1872 and 1873.

Printed at the Deseret News Steam Printing-Establishment

SALT LAKE CITY, UTAH TERRITORY.

1875.

INDEX AND CONTENTS.

LETTER I.
Instructions—Going to Europe and Asia Minor—Openings for the Gospel—Palestine to be Dedicated—Return of the Jews—Fulfilment of Prohecy. 1

LETTER II.
At Washington—Visit to the Departments—The Presidential Election—The Epizootic—Interview with President Grant—Passports for Europe. 2

LETTER III.
Traveling by Steam—Departure from Salt Lake City—Good By—The Plains—The Missouri Bridge—Thunder Storm—In a Palace Car—Arrival at Chicago. 4

LETTER IV.
Visiting Relatives at Fountain Green—Sisters of Joseph Smith, the Prophet—At the Birthplace of Joseph and Hyrum Smith—The Epizootic—Fitchburg—At New York. 6

LETTER V.
Riding Five Days and Five Nights—Arrival in New York—Members of the Company—Missionaries for Europe. 8

LETTER VI.
On the Ocean—Sea-sickness—At Davenport—At Buffalo—Niagara Falls—The Railroad Suspension Bridge—Crossing to Canada. 9

LETTER VII.
Nearing Queenstown—Departure from New York—Rain and Wind at Sea—Sea-sickness—Headwinds—Smooth Sea and Fair Winds—"Crossing the Atlantic," a Poem by Miss E. R. Snow. 11

LETTER VIII.
On Terra Firma—Ben Butler—At the St. Nicholas Hotel—West Point—Interview with Officials—A Drive Round Central Park. 15

LETTER IX.
At Liverpool—Visit to the Workhouse, It Covers Nine Acres of Ground—The Shoemakers' Quarters—Picking Oakum—Paupers do not Like Work—Their Sleeping Rooms—Apartments of the Female Inmates—Tea and Bread and Butter—The Laundry—The Childrens' Apartments—"Poor Little Forsaken"—The Hospital—The Dining Room—The Church—Monument to Agnes Jones—The Vagabonds' Apartment. 18

INDEX AND CONTENTS.

LETTER X.
Crossing the Hudson—Visit to West Point—Trophies of War—Putnam's Fort—Tete-a-tete with a Student—Information about Palestine—Leave New York. ... 23

LETTER XI.
On Board the "Minnesota"—First Sight of the Ocean—Arrival in Liverpool—Dense, Interminable Fog—Leave for London—English Railway Cars—No Sleeping Cars—English Rural Scenery—Poem, "London," by Miss E. R. Snow. ... 24

LETTER XII.
A Conference—Passed Queenstown—Arrival at Liverpool—Scattering of the Members of the Party—Arrival in London—The Albert Memorial—The Princess Theatre—Houses of Parliament—Under-ground Railway—Attend Meetings—George J. Adams and the Holy Land. ... 28

LETTER XIII.
In London—Full Description of the National Monument—The Grandest Monument in the World—One Hundred and Eighty Feet High—Its Construction—Mass of Concrete—Substructure of Brick—The Podium—One Hundred and Eighty Marble Statues—The Tabernacle—Lofty Spire set with Thousands of Gems—Embossed Globe—Statue of Prince Albert—Faith, Hope, Charity and Humanity. ... 30

LETTER XIV.
Description of the Tower of London—When Built—Queen Elizabeth's Armory—Cell of Sir Walter Raleigh, Ralstone, &c.—The Horse Armory—Coats of Mail and Weapons of Different Ages—Torture Rooms—Ann Boleyn—Earl of Essex—Lady Jane Grey—Executioner's Axe—Instruments of Torture—Regalia and Jewel House. ... 34

LETTER XV.
A Week in London—Sight-seeing—Visiting—Attending Conference—Theatres—Crystal Palace—The Grand Aquarium—Tower of London—"Man's Inhumanity to Man"—Going to Rotterdam. ... 38

LETTER XVI.
At Rotterdam—Programme of Travel—Antwerp—Brussels—Paris—Lyons—Marseilles—Nice—Genoa—Turin—Milan—Venice—Bologna—Florence—Rome, &c. ... 40

LETTER XVII.
Amsterdam—The Hague—Haarlem—Description of Rotterdam—Jews, Catholics, Protestants—Canals—Church of St. Lawrence—Public Schools—Fighting Old Ocean—Windmills and Steam Engines—Calamity at Dort—The Hague Described—Mode of Keeping Back the Waters—The Museum—Masterpieces of Dutch Painters—"The House in the Wood"—An Evening with the American Minister. ... 41

LETTER XVIII.
Sight-seeing in Liverpool—Arrival in London—Albert Memorial—Houses of Parliament—Westminster Abbey—Nelson Monument—Crystal Palace—Theatres—Rotterdam—Table d'Hote—Visit to a Moravian Settlement—The Hague—The Japanese Museum—Visit to the American Minister—Haarlem

INDEX AND CONTENTS.

PAGE.

—The Cathedral and Grand Organ, Imitation Thunderstorm—Meeting with Saints—Amsterdam—Its Museum—The King's Palace—Visit the Navy Yard—Leave for Rotterdam—Cross the Maas—Enter Belgium—Catholic Marriage Ceremony—Programme of Travel. 46

LETTER XIX.

Sea-sickness—Rotterdam—Among the Moravians—The Canal System—The Utrecht Cathedral—Beautiful Trees—Struggle for Mastery between Land and Sea—The Hague—"House in the Wood"—Evening with Mr. Gorham and Lady—Haarlem—A Shot by the Spaniards—"Bible Hotel"—King's Palace—Navy Yard—Building Iron-clad Monitors—The Cemetery—Meeting with Saints—Baptisms—Enter Belgium—Antwerp Cathedral—Paintings and Tomb of Rubens. 51

LETTER XX.

At Haarlem—Its Former Struggle with Spain—Two thousand People Executed—Church of St. Bavon and its Wonderful Organ—A Dutch Wedding—The Inventor of the Art of Printing—Amsterdam—A City on Piles Built on a Salt Marsh—Amsterdam Sapped and Mined by a Formidable Army of Worms—Canals—A City Containing One Hundred Islands and Two Hundred and Eighty Bridges—The Museum—A Palace on Piles—The Council Chamber—Clipping Iron Plates—Diamond Cutting—Charitable Institutions. 55

LETTER XXI.

Journey to New York—Crossing the Atlantic—London—The German Ocean—Rotterdam—House and Statue of Erasmus—Queen's Palace—The Old Bible Hotel—Shipbuilding—A Dutch Burial Ground—Antwerp—The Cathedral—Church of St. Jacques—Tomb of Rubens—Field of Waterloo. 60

LETTER XXII.

In Brussels—A Tour in Holland—Its Geographical Divisions—Naval and Mercantile Marine—Colonies—The Executive—The Legislature—Modes of Travel—Brick Roads—Canals—Annual Expense of Dykes—Lofty Buildings Cleanliness—Mirrors in the Streets—Church Chimes—A Singular Custom—Births and Marriages—Dutch Country Houses—Gigantic Windmills—"Polders," how Produced—Public Schools. 63

LETTER XXIII.

Brussels—Hard-worked Women—Feeding Horses with Coarse Bread—Field of Waterloo—Monument of the Prince of Orange—A Saying of Joseph Smith—A Genuine Relic of Waterloo. 68

LETTER XXIV.

Antwerp, Its Maritime Trade—Cathedral of Notre Dame, Its Wonderful Chimes—The Museum—A Masterpiece of Rubens—The Royal Palace—Brussels, Paris in Miniature—Cathedral of St. Nicholas—Selling Wax Candles—A Catholic Devotee—A Singular Marriage Ceremony—Royal Operatic Theatre—National Palace—Hotel de Ville—Monument to Counts Egmont and Horn. 70

LETTER XXV.

Paris—Visit to Versailles—Bois de Boulogne—St. Cloud—Attend the National Assembly—French Glory, Bruises and Scars—Interview with the President of the French Republic. 75

LETTER XXVI.

Paris—Destruction of the Commune—Palace of the Louvre—Relics of Napoleon First—Napoleonic Rule in France—French Aristocracy—Magnificent Improvements—Champs Elysees—Garden of the Tuileries—Garden of the Luxembourg—The Palace of Versailles—The Finest Hall in the World—Memories of Louis XVI—Le Grand Monarque—An Aristocratic Gambling Saloon—Bed-chamber of Three Queens—Fifty Miles of Parks and Gardens—Extract from the Paris "American Register"—Poetry—"Farewell to Paris." 79

LETTER XXVII.

Brussels—Theatre Royal—Church of St. Michael and Gudule—Visit to a Lace Factory—Houses of Parliament—Hotel de Ville—Waterloo and the Farm of Hougomont—Arrival at Paris—Call upon the American Minister—Visit to Palaces—Notre Dame—Opinion of Utah Silk—Visit the Common Schools—Go to Versailles—Bois de Boulogne—Visit the President of the French Republic—Arrival at Lyons—Silk Factories and Cocooneries. 86

LETTER XXVIII.

The Religions of France—Marriage A Civil Contract—The Concordat—Convents in Paris—The Educational System—Number of Births in Paris—Illegitimacy—Working classes—Paupers—Prisons—The Supreme Power, Where Vested—The Standing Army. 91

LETTER XXIX.

From Paris to Lyons—Burgundy and its Wines—Famous Towns—Fontainebleau—Lyons and Its Silk Industries—Thirty-one Thousand Silk Looms—Weaving Portraits—Beautiful Marseilles—An Amphitheatre 1,800 Years Old—Roman Relics—Olive Plantations and Vineyards—The Mediterranean. 96

LETTER XXX.

London Conference—Visiting the Poor—"Work Their Lives Out to Keep Life In"—Rotterdam—Dutch Cleanliness—Political Economy in Holland—Brussels and its Carpets and Lace—Waterloo—Continual Rain—Twenty Miles of Tunnels—Alpine Railroads—European and American Railways. 100

LETTER XXXI.

Reflections—Members of the Party—Birthplace of Columbus—Religion on Continental Europe—High Mass—The Cathedral at Genoa—Approaching Marseilles—Orange and Lemon Groves—The Mediterranean—European Apples. 105

LETTER XXXII.

At Venice—Railroad Track on Artificial Ground—Gondolas—A City Without Horses—A Glass Factory—News From Home—Death—Consolation. 108

LETTER XXXIII.

Shores of the Mediterranean—At Venice—Genoa—Statue of Columbus—The Cathedral St. Lorenzo—The Chain That Bound John the Baptist—Desecration of the Sabbath—Start for Turin—Milan—The Arcade—Cathedral of Our Blessed Lady, the Grandest Religious Edifice in the World—Magnificent Marble Statuary—Statue of St. Bartholomew—Attend High Mass—Arrival in Venice, the City of Waters. 110

LETTER XXXIV.

Venice—A Railroad on Piles—A City without Horses, Cabs or Omnibuses—Gondolas—Sailing Along the Streets—Method of Building—The Grand Canal—Three Hundred and Six Bridges—The Rialto—The Armenian Monastery—Former Residence of Lord Byron—A Mad-house—National Arsenal—Ancient Arms—Trophies of War—Flayed Alive—Terrible Method of Execution—The Republic—Last of the Doges—Mercantile Marine. ... 115

LETTER XXXV.

More about Venice—Historical Reminiscences—Administration of the Doges—Destruction of the Republic—Vandalism of Napoleon—Curious Method of Burial—Popularity of Victor Emanuel—Old Palace of the Doges—Senate and Council Chambers—Bridge of Sighs—House of Shylock—Residence of Othello—Palace of Desdemona—Dwelling Place of Marco Polo—Remains of St. Marc the Evangelist—Columns of Solomon's Temple—Granite Slab from Mt. Tabor—Slab from the Prison of John the Baptist—Ancient Tombstones, &c. 120

LETTER XXXVI.

Architectural Appearance of Venice—Ancient Customs—Fires—Plague and Pestilence—Council of Ten—Traitor Beheaded—Instruments of Torture—Bridge of Sighs—Bologna—An Arcade with 700 Arches—Leaning Towers—Florence, the Most Beautiful of Italian Cities—Paintings and Sculpture—A Wonderful Cabinet of Gems and Works of Art. 125

LETTER XXXVII.

Visit to an Infant School—Singing—Exercises in Reading and Writing—Lunch Time—Excellent Order—Medicine and Beds for the Sick, &c. 130

LETTER XXXVIII.

Bologna—House of Galvani, Inventor of the Galvanic Battery—University of Anatomy—Florence—Railroad through the Apennines—A Tunnel Two Miles Long—Damage by High Waters—Rome—The Forum—Triumphal Arch of Titus—Ruins of Heathen Temples—The Colosseum—Arch of Constantine—Famous Churches—Aqueduct of Nero—St. Anthony's Day, Blessing Horses and Asses—Pio Nono—Italian Unity—Victor Emanuel Denounced. 133

LETTER XXXIX.

At Rome—Ruins of Ancient Temples—Excavating the Forum—The Holy Staircase—Arch of Titus—The Colosseum—St. Anthony's Day—Palaces of the Emperors—Ruins of Caligula. 135

LETTER XL.

Rome and its Population—The Seven Hills—Purchase of Real Estate by Napoleon III—Excavations by the Government—The Forum—Anthony and Julius Cæsar—Where Virginius Stabbed his Daughter—Famous Obelisks—Temple of Venus—The Tarpeian Rock—Dimensions of the Colosseum—Visits to Cathedrals—St. Peter's—A Call on the American Minister. 138

LETTER XLI.

Leave Venice—A City with One Hundred and Thirty Churches—A Famous University—Villa of King Victor Emanuel—Leaning Towers—Road over the Apennines—" The Garden of Italy "—At Florence—Pisa—The Campanile—The Basilica—Rome—Ancient Ruins—Beggars—Santa Scala, or Holy Staircase—Aqueduct of Nero—The Apollo Theatre—Palaces of the Cæsars—The Pantheon—Capitoline Hill—Prison where St. Peter and St. Paul Were Confined—House of Rienzi—Column of Pius Antoninus—The Chamber of Deputies—The Sixtine Chapel—Cemetery of the Capuchins—Visits to Famous Localities and Places—The Quirinal—The Appian Way—Tombs of Celebrated Romans—Tumuli of the Horatii and of the Curatii—Circus of Romulus—The Vatican—Baths of Caracalla—Golden House of Nero—Statue of Moses. 113

LETTER XLII.

Go to Turin and Venice—A Hotel in Water—A City Without Carriages—Famous and Curious Glass Manufactures—Bridge of Sighs—Bologna, Florence and Pisa—At Rome—Cemetery of the Capuchins—Burial Place of Five Thousand Monks—Arches, Chandeliers and Candlesticks of Human Bones—Palace of Victor Emanuel. 149

LETTER XLIII.

Description of the Vatican—Decorations of Michael Angelo—"The Last Judgment"—Anecdote of Paul III and Michael Angelo—The Appian Way—Remains of Seneca—Baths of Caracalla—A Much Venerated Chapel—Footprint of the Saviour—Obelisks—Forum of Trajan—Statue of St. Peter—Constantine Embracing Christianity—Naples—Herculaneum—Pompeii—Mount Vesuvius. 153

LETTER XLIV.

Cathedral of St. Januarius—Beggars and Peddlers—Excavations of Pompeii—Villa of Diomede—Villa of Cicero—Inn of Albinus—Vestals of Narcissus—House of Sallust—Bread Baked 1,800 Years Ago—Ancient Baths—Temple of Fortune—Temples of Jupiter and Mercury—National Museum—Relics of Pompeii—Herculaneum—Ascent of Vesuvius. 158

LETTER XLV.

City of Naples—Dwellings of the Poor—Beggars—Pompeii—The Earthquakes of Anno Domini 63 and 79—Excavations and Relics—Herculaneum—The Museum of Naples—The "Secret Cabinet"—Ascent of Vesuvius—Pliny the Elder—Thirty-four Volcanic Eruptions—The "Hermitage"—From Naples to Brindisi—Hardworking Women—Turkish Towns and Villas—Corfu—Olive and Grape Culture—Religious Service in a Greek Cathedral—No "Grecian Bend"—Take Steamer for Alexandria. 160

LETTER XLVI.

Railroad Ride Across Italy—At Foggia—A Filthy Hotel—A Night in a Railway Station—Brindisi—Arrival at Corfu—Mementos of Venetian Rule—Services in a Greek Church—Holy Water—Kissing Pictures of Saints—A Political Meeting—A Man Killed—Take Steamer for Egypt—Alexandria—Pompey's Pillar—Cleopatra's Needles—A Mahommedan Cemetery—Wailing for the Dead—A Mussulman Gala Day. 165

LETTER XLVII.

Leave Naples—Arrival at Foggia—On Board the "Trebisonda"—Cross the Adriatic—Corfu—Visit a Greek Church—Embark on the "Saturno"—Correcting False Impressions—The Ionian Islands—Reach Alexandria—

INDEX AND CONTENTS.

	PAGE.
Crowds of Arabs, Turks, Greeks, Copts, Armenians, Syrians, &c.—Mahommedan Passover—Summer Gardens and Palace of the Viceroy—Cleopatra's Needles.	169

LETTER XLVIII.

Rome—Excavations by Napoleon III—Naples—Pomp and Beggary—Thousands of Homeless People—Ascending Vesuvius—Brindisi—Corfu—Women "Beasts of Burden"—Embark on the "Saturno"—"Sunrise on the Mediterranean"—Alexandria. 172

LETTER XLIX.

In Cairo—Description of Alexandria—People of Various Nationalities—Riding on Asses—Arab Runners—Turkish Dresses—Veiled Ladies—Cleanliness of the Mussulmen—Washing and Prayer—The Mahommedan Hegira—Mourning for the Dead—A Famous Greek Church—Joseph's Well—The Pyramids—The Sphinx—Gardens and Palace of Gizeh—Marriage Festivities. 176

LETTER L.

Leave Alexandria—Cross the Nile—Irrigation—Method of Cultivation—Arab Mounds—Primitive Mode of Dressing—A Famous Mosque—Joseph's Well—Cairo—Church where Joseph, Mary and Jesus Tarried—The Oldest Mosque Known—Visit to the Khedive's Gardens—A Drive to the Pyramids—Backsheesh—The Sphinx—Religious Services by the Dervishes—Marriage of the Khedive's Children—City of Heliopolis—Temple of On—Fountain of the Sun—A Famous Sycamore Tree. 181

LETTER LI.

Cairo—Mosque of Mahomet Ali—Joseph's Well—The Khedive's Festivities—Visit a Coptic Church—A Sheik Hanged—Hieropolis and City of On—The Place Where Moses Was Educated—Virgin Mary's Sycamore Tree—Salt Well Miraculously Sweetened—Plain of Heliopolis—Defeat of the Mamelukes—Egyptian Hotel Accommodation—Land of Goshen—Suez—Where the Israelites Crossed the Red Sea—An Arab Village. 185

LETTER LII.

Tour of Egypt—Love of Children among the Egyptians—Divorce and Marital Infidelity Rare—Turkish Mosques—The Turkish Sabbath—The Copts—Lack of Education—Mahommedan Schools—Sobriety and Honesty Among Mahommedans—Male and Female Attire—Religious Sects—Modes of Worship—The Dervishes—Visit to a Dervish Place of Worship—Hotel Accommodations in Alexandria—Agriculture and Irrigation—A Steam Plow in Egypt—Suez and the Red Sea—Leave for Jaffa. 190

LETTER LIII.

Leaving the Land of Egypt—Going to Jaffa—Land of Goshen—City of Bubastis—Suez—Mount Sinai—At Kantarah—Lake of Menzaleh—The Suez Canal—Port Said. 195

LETTER LIV.

Near Jaffa—The Martyrs' Tower—Plains of Sharon—Battle Ground of David and Goliath—Church of the Holy Sepulchre—St. Stephen's Gate—Valley of Jehoshaphat—Sacred Relics—Centre of the Earth. 197

INDEX AND CONTENTS.

LETTER LV

View of Jerusalem—Solomon's City Wall—Hole " Made by the Saviour's Elbow "—Crowds of Beggars—Mourning Women. 199

LETTER LVI.

Leave Port Said—Jaffa—Mussulman Customs Officials—Travelling Arrangement—The Oldest Seaport in the World—Place where the Ark was Built—Jonah's Place of Embarkation—House of Simon the Tanner—Mahommedan Funeral Ceremony—Plains of Sharon—The Martyrs' Tower—A Night in the Desert—Start for the Holy City—Battle Field of David and Goliath—Resting Place of the Ark of the Covenant—Rose of Sharon—St. George's Church—Mount Zion—Mount of Olives—In Camp Before Jerusalem. 201

LETTER LVII.

On the Mediterranean—At Jaffa—Cheap Oranges—Visit a German Colony—Arimathea—Hills of Judea—Valley of Ajalon—Lydda of the Acts—Kirjath-jearim—Mount of Olives—The Holy City—Camp by the Jaffa Gate—Church of the Holy Sepulchre—Where the Saviour was Scourged—Judgment Hall—Place of the Crucifixion—Valley of Jehoshaphat—Garden of Gethsemane—Tomb of Zacharias-Jacob's Well—Solomon's Pools—Bethlehem—Church of the Nativity—Dead Sea—Ruins of Jericho—Elisha's Fountain—Gilgal—Christ's Hotel—Mosque of Omar—Judgment Seat of Solomon—Tomb of Aaron's Sons—Pool of Bethesda 206

LETTER LVIII.

Land at Jaffa—Orange and Lemon Orchards—German Settlements in Palestine—Valley of Ajalon—Ancient Battle Field—Church of the Holy Sepulchre—Start for the Dead Sea—Famous Localities Mentioned in the Scriptures—Novel Water Vessels—Bethlehem—Monastery of Mar Saba—Brook Kedron—The River Jordan—Ruins of Jericho—Mountain on Which the Saviour was Tempted—A Bedouin War Dance—Bethany—Church of the Ascension—Backsheesh—Mosque of Omar—Saddle of Mahomet—Mount Moriah—Garden of Eden—Sacred Cradle—Foundations of Solomon's Temple—Visit to the Chief Rabbi—Ancient Parchments. 217

LETTER LIX.

Suez—Red Sea—Port Said—On Board the " Vesta "—Anchor off Jaffa—Passports Demanded—Commencement of Tent Life—House of Simon the Tanner—Travelling to Jerusalem—Plains of Sharon—Valley of Ajalon—Valley of Elah—Mount of Olives—Church of the Holy Sepulchre—Tomb of Rachel—Bethlehem—Dead Sea—Jordan—Jericho—Gilgal—Bethany—Mosque of Omar. 226

LETTER LX.

One Day in Jerusalem—Rachel's Tomb—Description of the Pools of Solomon—Birthplace of the Saviour—Church of the Nativity—Grotto of the Nativity—Altar of the Innocents—Studio of St. Jerome—Bedouin Arabs—The Shepherds' Field—Convent of Mar Saba—Skulls of the Dead—An Ancient Palm Tree—River Jordan—Rencontre with Bedouins—Description of the Dead Sea. 229

INDEX AND CONTENTS. xi

PAGE

LETTER LXI.

Visit to the Jordan River—Sacred Localities—Singular Custom Among the Christians of Palestine—Fountain of Elisha—Valley of the Jordan—Brook Cherith—Plains of Jericho—The Jericho of To-day—Entertained by Bedouins—Bethany—Residence of Mary and Martha—Tomb of Lazarus—Garden of Gethsemane. 236

LETTER LXII.

Topography of Jerusalem—Hill of Evil Council—Mizpeh—Mount of Olives—Valley of Jehoshaphat—Hinnom and Kedron—Absalom's Pillar—Siloam—Mosque of Omar—Solomon's Temple—Hill of Zion—Tombs of the Holy City—Mount Moriah—Worship of Moloch—Scarcity of Water in Jerusalem—Political and Financial Condition of the Jews—Place of Lamentation. 244

LETTER LXIII.

Sacred Localities—The Stone of Unction—The Holy Sepulchre—The Chapel of the Angel—Hill of Calvary—The Hole in which the Cross was Planted—House of Pilate—"Behold the Man"—The True Cross—Opposition Gardens of Gethsemane—Rivalry of Christian Sects—A Terrible Massacre—Fighting Among Christian Zealots Prevented by Turkish Guards—Christianity Despised by Jews and Mahommedans. 249

LETTER LXIV.

Robbers' Glen—Bethel—Ancient Shiloh—Jacob's Well—Joseph's Tomb—Mount Gerizim—Ancient Shechem—Ancient Samaria—Tomb of John the Baptist—Dothan—Plains of Esdraelon—Mountains of Gilboa—Spring of Jezreel—Suite of Rooms of Joseph and Mary—Dining Room of the Saviour and his Apostles—An Assyrian Chapel—Mount Carmel, Nain—Church of the Annunciation—Assyrian Pilgrims. 254

LETTER LXV.

Church of the Holy Sepulchre—Sacred Localities—Religious Services on the Mount of Olives—Dedication of the Land of Palestine—Hospice of the Knights Templars—Trades Among the Arabs—Arab Cookery—Visit to the Chief Rabbi—Valley of Hinnom—The Gibbeah of Saul—Bethel—Robbers' Glen—Mosque of Shiloh—Jacob's Well—Mounts Ebal and Gerizim—Sychar—A Gala Day—Dothan—Valley of Esdraelon—Mount Tabor. 259

LETTER LXVI.

Farewell to Jerusalem—A Gala Day—Arab Agriculture—Nablous, Ancient Shechem—Among Ferocious People—Avengers of Blood—Cultivation of the Olive—Samaria. 264

LETTER LXVII.

A Famous Scripture Locality—A Village of Robbers—The "Fountain of Gardens"—The Battle Field of Palestine—Mounts Tabor and Hermon—Nazareth—The Holy Grotto—Workshop of Joseph—Table of Christ—Arab Ploughs—Cana of Galilee—An Arab School—Sea of Galilee—Tiberias—Bedouin Spinsters—Residence of Mary Magdalene—Serenaded by Bedouins—Backsheesh. 270

INDEX AND CONTENTS.

LETTER LXVIII.

Services in a Greek Church—Personal Cleanliness and Mean Dwellings of Turks and Arabs—Nazareth—Armenian Pilgrims—Hills and Plains of Galilee—Arab Villages—Communism—Novel Method of Churning—From Alexandria to Cairo—Sea of Galilee. 276

LETTER LXIX.

Cana of Galilee—Ancient Stone Jars—Jotapa—A Memorable Battle Field—Tiberias—Sea of Galilee—Ancient Ruins—Chorazin—Bethsaida—Site of Capernaum—Lake of Gennesareth—At Dan—Cesarea Philippi—Burial Place of Nimrod—Castle of Subeiteh—Damascus—Visit the American Consular Agent—Mosque of St. John—Interview with Abd-el Kader. 279

LETTER LXX.

Leave Jerusalem—Bethel—The Robbers' Glen—Ruins of Shiloh—Jacob's Well—Gerizim and Ebal—Shechem—City of Samaria—Church of St. John the Baptist—Dothan—Valley of Jezreel—Endor—Nazareth—Church of the Annunciation—Cana of Galilee—Dwelling place of Joseph and Mary—Tiberias—Where Nimrod was Buried—Cesarea Philippi—Damascus. 287

LETTER LXXI.

Start for Beyrout—At Damascus—An Excellent Road—Massacre by Turks—Rain—At Kob Elias—Arrive at Beyrout—Sacred Relics—Monkish Rivalry—Physical Contrast Between Arabs and Jews—Silk Culture—Groves of Figs, Oranges, Olives and Dates. 292

LETTER LXXII.

Sea of Galilee—Tiberias—A Daughter of Juda—Visit Jewish Residences—Human Beings and Asses Dwelling in one Room—The Cleanest Town In Palestine—Mouth of Jordan—Chorazin and Bethsaida—Ruins of Magdala—A Ramble on the Sea Shore—Mount Hermon—Damascus and Its Forty Thousand Dogs. 296

LETTER LXXIII.

Leave Damascus—The only Wagon Road in Syria—Fine Scenery—Mountains of Lebanon—Beyrout—Finish of Camp Life—On Board the "Mars"—Island of Cyprus—Rhodes—Patmos—Scio—Smyrna—Lesbos—Tenedos—Dardanelli—Abydos—Gallipoli—Sea of Marmora—Golden Horn—Constantinople. 299

LETTER LXXIV.

Damascus—Reception Rooms of a Prince—River Abana—At Dimas—Large Flocks of Goats—In Camp on the Anti-Labanon Mountains—The Scenery of Lebanon—Contrast Between Art and Nature—Beyrout—Silk Industry—Entertained by Turks—Adieu to Tent Life—On Board the "Mars." 302

LETTER LXXV.

Four Days at Constantinople—Visit the German Minister—Embark on the "Mars"—Arrive at Athens—Famous Grecian Ruins—Religious Toleration. 306

LETTER LXXVI.

At Athens—Plains of Attica—Hill of Mars—Galilee—Scriptural Reminiscences Fountain of Dan—Cesarea Philippi—Damascus—An Unfortunate Architect. 312

INDEX AND CONTENTS. xiii

PAGE.

LETTER LXXVII.
Leave Constantinople—Piræus—Classical Ruins—The Greek Parliament—The Acropolis by Moonlight. ... 321

LETTER LXXVIII.
Beyrout—Protestant College and Schools—Embark for Constantinople—Island of Cyprus—Mount Olympus—Sea of Marmora—Arrival at the Turkish Metropolis—Leave for Athens—Greek Independence Day. ... 324

LETTER LXXIX.
Palestine Tour Completed—Beyrout—Constantinople—Reminiscences of Crimean War—The Piræus—Athens, Ancient and Modern. ... 330

LETTER LXXX.
Sunday at Sea—The Austrian Lloyd Steamers—An Immense Ship of War—Leave for Verona—The Quadrilateral—Field of Solferino—Tomb of Romeo. 333

LETTER LXXXI.
At Athens—Classical Ruins—Peculiar Customs Among the Greeks—Funeral Ceremony. ... 336

LETTER LXXXII.
Brigandage in Greece—The Classical Ruins of Athens—Leave the Piræus—The Austrian Lloyds—At Trieste—Verona—Ancient Roman Amphitheatre—The Tyrol—Munich. ... 342

LETTER LXXXIII.
Constantinople—Island of Syra—Athens—The Acropolis—The Areopagus—Visit the American Minister—Trieste—Verona—Munich. ... 346

LETTER LXXXIV.
The Nile—Heliopolis—Goshen—Red Sea—Holy Places—Sea of Galilee—River Jordan—Mountain of the Temptation. ... 349

LETTER LXXXV.
At Munich—Visit a Kindergarten—Employments and Pastimes of the Children—Contrast between Children of Germany and France—Convenience of the Kindergartens. ... 351

LETTER LXXXVI.
Munich—Visit a Royal Palace—Statue of Bavaria—Imperial Wedding—Vienna—The Arsenal—Summer Palace—The Great Exhibition. ... 353

LETTER LXXXVII.
Stormy Weather—No Beggars—Royal Marriage—Instruments of Torture—Visit the American Legation. ... 359

LETTER LXXXVIII.
Principal German Cities—The King's Palace—A Famous Glass Factory—Glass Window Curtains—Visit the Universities—Marriage Festivities—Vienna and Its Great Exhibition—"No Place Like Home." ... 361

LETTER LXXXIX.

At Vienna—Berlin—The Royal Palace—A Large Banquet Hall—Beautiful New Chapel—Monuments—Visit the U. S. Minister—Freedom of Parliament—Multitudes of Soldiers—Unhealthy Moral Condition of Berlin—Hamburg—Church of St. James—In London Again. ... 365

LETTER XC.

Leave Vienna—Bad Weather—Berlin—The Thier-Garten—Bismarck and Moltke—Prussian Ladies—Hamburg—The Hollanders—A Land of Soldiers. 370

LETTER XCI.

In London—Attend Conference—Russian and Turkish Baths—Visit to Topesfield—Visit From the Marquis of Sligo. ... 374

LETTER XCII.

On the Atlantic Ocean—Hamburg—London Conference—Leave for Liverpool—Embark on the "Wisconsin." ... 376

LETTER XCIII.

At St. Louis—Fine Scenery—Visit Relatives. ... 379

TELEGRAMS.

Telegrams from Salt Lake City and Evanston. ... 382

LETTER XCIV.

Home Again—Reception by Friends. ... 383

LETTER XCV.

Salutation to the Ladies of Utah. ... 384

CORRESPONDENCE

OF

PALESTINE TOURISTS.

LETTER I.

Instructions—Going to Europe and Asia Minor—Openings for the Gospel—Palestine to be Dedicated—Return of the Jews—Fulfilment of Prophecy.

SALT LAKE CITY, Utah Territory,
October 15th, 1872.

PRESIDENT GEORGE A. SMITH:

DEAR SIR:—As you are about to start on an extensive tour through Europe and Asia Minor, where you will doubtless be brought in contact with men of position and influence in society, we desire that you observe closely what openings now exist, or where they may be effected, for the introduction of the Gospel into the various countries you shall visit.

When you go to the Land of Palestine, we wish you to dedicate and consecrate that land to the Lord, that it may be blessed with fruitfulness, preparatory to the return of the

Jews in fulfilment of prophecy, and the accomplishment of the purposes of our Heavenly Father.

We pray that you may be preserved to travel in peace and safety, that you may be abundantly blessed with words of wisdom and free utterance in all your conversations pertaining to the Holy Gospel, dispelling prejudice, and sowing seeds of righteousness among the people.

BRIGHAM YOUNG,
DANIEL H. WELLS.

LETTER II.

At Washington—Visit to the Departments—The Presidential Election—The Epizootic—Interview with President Grant—Passports for Europe.

METROPOLITAN HOTEL, Washington, D. C.,
November 2nd, 1872.

MRS. BATHSHEBA W. SMITH:

MY DEAR WIFE:—Elder Feramorz Little and myself called upon several heads of Departments, and other gentlemen with whom we are acquainted, but found that Secretaries Fish and Delano, and most of the others had gone to their respective States to look after the Presidential election, and be ready to vote next Tuesday.

More than half the horses in Washington are disabled by the epizootic, and but few street cars and conveyances are moving, making it difficult to get conveyances.

We called at the White House, where we expected to meet our acquaintance, Gen. Babcock, but he was absent with the rest. We sent in our cards to the President, and were almost instantly admitted into the Reception Room. On our entrance he arose and gave us each a cordial shake by the hand, and motioned us to seats. We told him we were about to visit the Old World, and wished to commence our journey by paying our respects to the Chief Magistrate of our country. He enquired after the material progress of Utah, her railroads, and her iron and coal mines, and said that we should manufacture our own iron, instead of buying it from abroad. We told him that we were doing so to a limited extent, but would be compelled to purchase railroad iron from abroad until we could form connections between the iron and coal regions, which were generally at a distance from each other, and it would require time, and the construction of railroad lines to connect them. We gave him some account of our progress in the manufacture of woollen goods and other necessaries, in which he seemed interested. When we arose to retire, I tendered him our thanks for the interest he had taken in our affairs in getting the Engelbrecht case before the Supreme Court before its regular order, and obtaining a decision which had released us from many embarrassments, and placed us right before the country.

The interview was a pleasant one, although President Grant was suffering from the effects of a violent cold.

We have obtained our passports from the State Department, and expect to sail from New York by the Guion line on the 6th, as our party have arranged to meet us at the St. Nicholas Hotel, New York, on the 4th.

Affectionately, your husband,

GEORGE A. SMITH.

LETTER III.

Traveling by Steam—Departure from Salt Lake City—Good' By—The Plains—The Missouri Bridge—Thunder Storm—In a Palace Car—Arrival at Chicago.

CHICAGO, Illinois, October 30th, 1872.

EDITOR WOMAN'S EXPONENT:

DEAR LULA:—Traveling with steam velocity is productive of sudden changes, my home is already considerably in the distance.

I left Salt Lake City on the morning of the 26th; was accompanied to Ogden by several prominent ladies, where I met my brother, Lorenzo Snow, of Brigham City, with whom I traveled. President G. A. Smith, with others of his party, started on the 16th. We shall meet them in New York.

On board the train for the east I bade "good by" to very many dear friends of Salt Lake and Ogden cities, who waited on the platform to see us off, and, at 6 p. m. of the 3rd day, arrived at Omaha.

In crossing the plains, I frequently drew the contrast between the present and the past, and could hardly realize the present to be a living reality. To travel with ease, devoid of fatigue, in three days, a distance which a few years ago required more than three months of weariness and privations to accomplish, is certainly a very great change.   *   *   *
I took an earnest glimpse of the beautiful, stupendous bridge as we crossed the Missouri River. It is a piece of workmanship worthy of a critical daylight observation.

We left Council Bluffs in the midst of one of those thunder-storms so common to that locality, beyond the necessity of artificial irrigation. It was 9 o'clock at night, but what were the night and the storm to us! Instead of pitching tents and circling beneath a dripping roof, we were comfortably seated in a palace car and travelling at an almost incredible speed. So much for the blessings of God on the march of improvement. These night travels cheat us of many pleasurable scenic views, a tax which time-saving naturally brings.

At the Bluffs we took the Rock Island route to Chicago, and arrived at Davenport, where we breakfasted, and took a hasty view of the stirring, beautiful place, with the railroad bridge—one in progress of erection—all curiosities to one as little acquainted with railroads as myself. The scenery from Rock Island to Chicago is variegated, and as seen while passing, as we did, at times at the rate of nearly a mile per minute, is very delightful, one characteristic worthy of notice, being the freshness of verdure in comparison to what we had previously passed.

We arrived here last evening at 4 o'clock, and the missionaries to Europe left on the 5 o'clock train for New York. *   *   *   My health is good, and my heart full of gratitude. Sister Mercy R. Thompson joins in love to all our good sisters.

ELIZA R. SNOW.

LETTER IV.

EXTRACT FROM A LETTER TO PRESIDENT YOUNG.

Visiting Relatives at Fountain Green—Sisters of Joseph Smith, the Prophet—At the Birthplace of Joseph and Hyrum Smith—The Epizootic—Fitchburg—At New York.

NEW YORK CITY, November 1st, 1872.

Brother W. D. Fuller accompanied me here, and did his best to make me comfortable. Brother Feramorz Little went to St. Louis from Omaha. I went to Chicago by the Burlington road, switching off to visit Colchester and Fountain Green, at which places I found three sisters of the Prophet Joseph Smith, whom I had not seen for twenty-five years. They were very glad to see me. Sophronia McClarry is a widow, residing with her daughter, Maria Stodard, who married a man named Woolley. Catherine is living on the place that you furnished her means to purchase, and is apparently the happiest woman I have seen on the journey. Her place is a piece of timber land, which your last bounty enables her to increase to twenty acres, and as in all her life she has never been able to enjoy a home of her own for a single hour, her gratitude to you seems unbounded.

Arthur Milliken rents a house at Colchester at nine dollars per month, and spends his time weighing coal for the railroad company, for which he receives a regular salary. His boys are at work digging in the mines, and the family are living quite comfortably. I did not fail to tell them that they ought to be in the mountains, striving to build up Zion.

I took the Grand Trunk Railroad through Canada to Boston, stopping one day in St. Lawrence County and passing through the towns in Vermont where Joseph and Hyrum Smith were born, and through the town in New Hampshire where my father was born.

While at Boston business was much paralyzed by sickness among the horses, the streets being silent. A few yoke of oxen were all that could be seen, moving express wagons.

I spent the Sabbath with the Hon. Alva Crocker, M. C., of Fitchburg, Mass., whose family took every pains to make us comfortable, and he exhibited to us to the best advantage the wonderful manufactories of that place. His kind feelings towards our people, so often manifested in Congress, are repeated by him whenever opportunity offers. He wishes to be remembered to you.

Brother Feramorz Little and family arrived in New York to-day, all well. They have had an agreeable visit, among others, with Malcolm Little's family.

I was glad to learn that the brethren expecting to accompany me had started and that Brother Schettler was also to arrive here in time to cross the sea with us. I am very glad of this, as I do not wish to remain long in the damp climate of England, and I shall be in favor of crossing the channel as soon as consistent.

Brother Thomas Taylor and daughter arrived to-day. Brother Feramorz Little and myself go to Washington by the night train. We have seen Brother Spencer Clawson, he is well and in good spirits. Brother Staines is very busy outfitting small parties of emigrants who have unexpectedly made their appearance.

GEORGE A. SMITH.

LETTER V.

Riding Five Days and Five Nights—Arrival in New York—Members of the Company—Missionaries for Europe.

St. Nicholas' Hotel, New York City,
1 a.m., November 6th, 1872.

Editors Salt Lake Herald:

I arrived here yesterday morning at 7 o'clock, after a ride of five days and five nights, and was very busy all day arranging for our passage to Liverpool. Our company consists of Elders George A. Smith, Lorenzo Snow, George Dunford, Anson Call, Feramorz Little, Miss Eliza R. Snow, Miss Clara S. Little, Mrs. Mary R. Thompson, Mrs. Mary A. Fielding and myself, also a number of our missionaries who are going to Europe, but whose names I have not been able to ascertain. We intend to leave at 9 a. m. to-day, on board the *Minnesota*. Elders Thomas Taylor, Jacob Weiler and W. D. Fuller are returning home. We are all well and anticipate a pleasant time. You will hear from me again after we arrive in England.

Very truly yours,

PAUL A. SCHETTLER.

LETTER VI.

On the Ocean—Sea-sickness—At Davenport—At Buffalo—Niagara Falls—The Railway Suspension Bridge—Crossing to Canada.

STEAMER "MINNESOTA," 800 miles from Liverpool,
November 15th, 1872.

MY DEAR MISS GREENE:

Here I am in the midst of the ocean. We embarked, as we had anticipated, on the 6th. The sea was calm and sailing pleasant till towards night, when the winds became too strong for the sails—they were all furled, which produced a rolling motion of the vessel, conducive to sea-sickness with some of the passengers. We have had considerable rough weather, but now all is calm. I have experienced a slight touch of that disquieting malady called sea-sickness, just enough to make my appetite inexpensive for two or three days, and to cause a little cleansing of the stomach for my future benefit.

The short period of time since leaving my Mountain Home has introduced me to much that has been interesting; my health has been good, and thus far my endurance of the fatigue (if anything I have experienced is worthy to be called such) has been beyond my expectations. · * * *

On entering Davenport I remarked that they could not run street cars there, but I was mistaken, for presently I saw one despite the narrowness of the streets, some of which are very handsome. Davenport is a pleasant, stirring town, but, like all other towns and cities I have seen since I left Salt Lake, it seems destitute of sufficient land to give elbow room to the streets.

We stopped two hours in Buffalo—a rainy morning, but I wanted to see Buffalo and took a long ramble for that purpose. From Buffalo we went to Niagara—crossed into Canada on the new suspension bridge, over which the railroad trains pass, to view the Falls; and, after witnessing those scenes of nature in her display of the grand and beautiful, we recrossed on the old bridge. From descriptions from various sight-seers, my imagination had been whetted to an appreciative idea, so far as the majestic grandeur of the scenery is concerned; but its beauty—so chaste, so indescribably delicate—I had not anticipated. In fact, without actual, personal view, I never could have comprehended such a harmonious combination of power and delicacy. Imagine for a moment a body of water falling in a magnificent volume to a great distance, and forming in its descent a mantle of pure, sparkling white, of ever changing folds, over a robe of the most delicate shade of green that either the dye of art or of nature can produce—at times the green appearing as if approaching the surface—at other times seen obscurely—the chaste and beautiful snowy white ever preponderating; while from the depths below springs are constantly ascending, apparently as far as the eye can reach, and then dropping in heavy mists on the ever humid surroundings. But after so many able pens have descanted upon this subject, it seems like folly for mine to attempt it. I leave it, after drawing the conclusion that Mark Twain was induced to speak indifferently respecting this celebrated curiosity, lest he should be suspected of doing or thinking for once like somebody-else.

As yet I have had but little opportunity for writing, the passage being rough makes it difficult.

E. R. SNOW.

P. S. Still pleasant, and all right.
Nov. 17, 180 miles from Queenstown.

LETTER VII.

Nearing Queenstown—Departure from New York—Rain and Wind at Sea—Sea-sickness—Headwinds—Smooth Sea and Fair Winds—"Crossing the Atlantic," a Poem by Miss E. R. Snow.

STEAMSHIP "MINNESOTA," November 16th, 1872.
At Noon, 2,554 Knots from New York.

EDITORS SALT LAKE HERALD:

The sea being very calm to-day, I think I cannot do better than pen you a few lines, to be mailed on our expected arrival at Queenstown on Monday morning, the 18th inst. We left pier 46 in New York at 9.45 a. m. on the 6th inst., bidding adieu to Messrs. Staines, John W. Young and lady, Bishop Thomas Taylor and Messrs. Jacob Weiler, S. B. Young and W. D. Fuller, the former having done all he possibly could to make us comfortable on our passage over the Atlantic.

As soon as we had passed Sandy Hook it commenced raining and a heavy breeze was swelling our sails. The consequence was that Miss Clara S. Little and Mr. Anson Call soon felt the effects of being afloat, and during the night and the two following days all of us, Mr. Dunford excepted, followed suit. We made pretty good time, our log book showing 263, 270, 260 and 258 knots for the first four days, and after recovering a little from the first attacks of sea-sickness, we commenced to enjoy our meals up to the 12th, when the wind shifted towards the east, and during about thirty-six hours we had to contend against heavy head-winds, which made the steamer roll and pitch tremendously, and not only turned our stomachs inside out, but tossed about and upset everything that was not very securely fastened in the saloon and in our small staterooms.

President George A. Smith had a pretty hard time of it, as he could hardly turn over in his berth; but with the rest of us the contrary was the case, as we were continually rolled from one side to the other, and had to brace ourselves against some part of the berth to prevent our being pitched out. Miss E. R. Snow has stood the voyage and sea-sickness so far, as well as any of us, and has given us a good deal of intellectual enjoyment. Mr. Call had to suffer the most, but he is getting over it now. Since the 14th we have had pretty fair wind, and to-day the sea is remarkably smooth. All are well now and in good spirits, and we pass away the time in reading in different guide books and making our plans for future journeyings.

As I informed you before, our excursion party now consists of seven, viz.—President George A. Smith, Elders Lorenzo Snow, Feramorz Little and George Dunford, and Miss Eliza R. Snow, Miss Clara S. Little and myself. Mrs. Mary R. Thompson and Mrs. Mary A. Fielding are travelling with us to England; also Elder Anson Call, who is going on a short mission. The names of the other missionaries on board are John I. Hart, Mark Lindsey, John Martin, Wm. Parker, Wm. Bircumshaw, Thomas Snarr, Hugh S. Gowan and Henry B. Wild with wife and child. They are all well.

I enclose you a copy of a nice little poem written by Miss Eliza R. Snow, entitled "Crossing the Atlantic," a copy of which she presented to our captain, who highly appreciated it.

Very truly yours,

PAUL A. SCHETTLER.

CROSSING THE ATLANTIC.

Written at Sea by Miss Eliza R. Snow, of Salt Lake City, Utah.

We're on the "Minnesota,"
   A ship of "Guion Line,"
Which boasts her Captain Morgan,
   The gen'rous, staunch and kind.

Amid the heaving waters
   That form the liquid plain;
With four and twenty draft feet
   The steamer ploughs the main.

I'm gazing on the ocean
   As on the deck I stand,
And feel the cooling breezes
   With which the sails are fanned.

By sunlight, star and moonlight,
   And tranquil evening shade,
The ever varying features
   Of ocean I've surveyed.

At times with restless motion,
   As if her spirit grieves—
As tho' her breast were paining,
   Her mighty bosom heaves.

And then, vast undulations,
   Like the rolling prairies spread;
With wave on wave dissolving,
   With tumbling, dashing tread.

Upon the deep, dark billows,
   Broad, foaming whitecaps rise,
And sprays in dazzling beauty,
   Shoot upward to the skies.

'Tis now a plain, smooth surface,
   As tho' in cozy sleep
Were wrapped each wave and billow
   Upon the briny deep.

But hark! The Captain orders
  The furling ev'ry sail;
Storm clouds and head-winds rising
  Portend a coming gale.

Anon all Neptune's furies
  Are on the steamer's path;
We mount the deck to witness
  The ocean in its wrath.

The scene! What pen can write it?
  What pencil's art could show
The wild, terrific grandeur
  Which reigns around us now?

The waving, surging waters,
  Like battle armor clash;
Tumultuous waves upheaving
  With foaming fury dash.

The steamer mounts the billows,
  Then dips the space below;
And bravely presses onward,
  Tho' reeling to and fro.

We're sailing on the ocean
  With wind and sail and steam;
Where views of "terra firma"
  Are like the poet's dream.

The God who made the waters—
  Who made the solid land,
Is ours—our Great Protector,
  Our life is in His hands.

Subservient to His counsel—
  Confiding in His care—
Directed by His wisdom,
  There's safety everywhere.

LETTER VIII.

On Terra Firma—Ben Butler—At the St. Nicholas Hotel—West Point—Interview with Officials—A Drive Round Central Park.

LIVERPOOL, England, November 19th, 1872.

EDITOR WOMAN'S EXPONENT:

MY DEAR LULA:—I am now on "terra firma," but so highly elevated that I almost claim to be filling an aerial position, being located on the fourth floor in the "North-Western Hotel," a spacious building. The room I occupy, in company with Mrs. Thompson and Miss Little, fronts St. George's Hall, said to be the largest edifice in the city.

In my last, I left you with the Falls of Niagara. I do not recollect anything of special interest occurring between there and New York, unless the presence of Hon. Ben. Butler should be so considered. Not having seen him, I felt considerable interest when it was announced that he was on the train, and to my entire satisfaction, he entered the car in which I was riding, and seated himself where I had a good view of his ample phiz. As we arrived at towns by the way, the citizens, no doubt having been apprised of his coming, were out in masses, to whom he delivered electioneering speeches, which were listened to with the usual enthusiasm of such occasions. For my part, I feel to respect any man who possesses sufficient independence of character, in this age of political bribery, to speak as he thinks—which I believe Ben Butler does.

We arrived in New York on Sunday morning; it was

raining, but luckily for us, the beautiful depot afforded us shelter, while, after considerable delay, a carriage (probably the property of some unpopular infidel) was procured to carry ourselves and our baggage to St. Nicholas' Hotel. The fact of our arrival on the Sabbath was the cause of delay; this very religious people have plenty of cabs and hacks to receive strangers on other days of the week, which strongly reminds me of a class of religionists referred to in New Testament history. I am now speaking in general terms—there are very excellent people living in New York, I know several, although my knowledge is very limited.

St. Nicholas' Hotel is a splendid establishment—it contains 600 rooms and accommodates from ten to eleven hundred occupants. It is freely ventilated, and so warmed with pipes running in various directions as to keep an equilibrium of temperature. Water is conveyed to and from the rooms in pipes, so that you are not stinted—you can wash yourself and rinse too, if you choose. The whole establishment is lighted with gas, and you can have as much light as you please; yet I think there is an extra charge if you keep it burning all night. What I consider an enormity is the charge of one dollar per day for fire, however small it may be; and then the porter graciously expects a small fee for his condescension in making it for you. But that is all very well—he is so obliging and does it so much better than any one else.

I stayed three nights in New York—spent two days in the city and one in visiting Willard Young at West Point. In company of President George A. Smith, my brother and Brother Dunford, I went to the office of the Notary Public, the kind and affable Mr. None, before whom I solemnly subscribed to my allegiance to the United States Government, etc., according to due form of law, and he made out my application, which he promised to send to Washington for my passport, which I expect to meet in London on my arrival.

In conversation with Mr. None, Brother Smith spoke of his rejection from the Philadelphia Convention, on account of his religion, when Mr. None exclaimed, emphatically, "How ridiculous!" He expressed much pleasure on meeting President Smith, saying he was the first official of our people with whom he had met. We then called on the "Consul General of the German Empire," Mr. Roesing, where we met the very gentlemanly Mr. Schleiden, member of the German Parliament. Both these gentlemen had visited Salt Lake, where they made Brother Smith's acquaintance. They spoke of their visit in the highest terms.

Through the kindness of Brother J. W. Young, I enjoyed a pleasant turn around Central Park; and here, amid its shades, fountains, equestrian statues, etc. etc., I leave you for the present.

ELIZA R. SNOW.

LETTER IX.

At Liverpool—Visit to the Workhouse, It Covers Nine Acres of Ground—The Shoemakers' Quarters—Picking Oakum—Paupers do not Like Work—Their Sleeping Rooms—Apartments of the Female Inmates Tea and Bread and Butter—The Laundry—The Childrens' Apartments—"Poor Little Forsaken"—The Hospital—The Dining Room—The Church—Monument to Agnes Jones—The Vagabonds' Apartment.

LIVERPOOL, England, November 20th, 1872.

EDITOR DESERET NEWS:

Through the blessings of kind Providence, we have safely crossed the Atlantic, and are now in Liverpool.

All are in good health and excellent spirits. We were twelve and a half days crossing the ocean, and were well pleased with the steamer *Minnesota* and its accommodations. The captain, James Morgan, we found to be a kind, affable, and intelligent gentleman. We anchored in the Mersey on the 19th, at 1 a. m. Early next morning President A. Carrington and son, accompanied by Elders J. G. Bleak and G. F. Gibbs, joined us on board; and through the hospitality of the Captain we breakfasted together.

Presuming that you have been posted, through other sources, concerning our tour thus far, I will proceed to give you a brief sketch from my journal, of "Two hours in a Workhouse."

Liverpool embraces many objects of curiosity and interest, among which is its celebrated workhouse. Through the interest of some friends and the courtesy of Mr. Teasdale, the Deputy Governor of the establishment, I had an opportunity, in company with Elder J. G. Bleak, of visiting these magnificent premises. An area of nine acres is covered by this enormous pile of buildings, being nearly one half mile in circumference. In 1868 its inmates numbered 5,000. At present the number is reduced to 2,300, all of whom are recognized as paupers. They are admitted into this institution by virtue of their citizenship in Liverpool parish, and their entire inability to provide their own living.

The management of this workhouse is under the supervision of a committee elected by the people of the parish, and is conducted on the most economical principles, but in no sense approaching a point of self-sustaining. It is supported principally by city taxation, with slight assistance by appropriations through the influence of some member of the British Parliament, who has taken it, I believe, as a kind of pet child, under his protection. In the year 1871 its expenses amounted to about $700.000. It consumes, in the winter season, coal, averaging per week 120 tons. Cost of provisions consumed by the paupers in 1869 was estimated at $100,000. The expenses, the same year, for educating pauper children, were nearly $5,000.

Mr. Teasdale conducted us through the various departments explaining, and answering our many inquiries. The first building we entered embraced the quarters appropriated to shoemakers, consisting chiefly of aged men, who were busily engaged and appeared contented. The boots and shoes, when made, were given to the inmates of the establishment as their necessities demanded. In the next department men were picking oakum; in another, others were picking to pieces and preparing material for stuffing cushions, sofas, &c. I asked Mr. Teasdale whether this business, together with others in which the paupers were engaged, could not be made lucrative. He said that, as a general rule, the paupers were disinclined to labor, and exercised considerable ingenuity to avoid work; furthermore, that a large majority of them were aged, sickly, and broken down in body and mind, that they were compelled to labor, more for a moral effect and to retard others from unnecessarily crowding the institution, than for any pecuniary advantage. In the course of my conversation with this gentleman, I discovered that the managers of the workhouse kept in view the idea that paupers were naturally inclined to avoid work ; but the interests of the institution demanded that it should be rendered impossible. We examined their sleeping apartments. They were extraordinarily neat and tolerably well ventilated. They were all furnished with good bedsteads and good comfortable beds, made of soft material, with clean bedding in abundant supply. The sleeping rooms contained, each, about thirty-two single beds, arranged in rows on each side, the rows being about fifteen feet apart.

We visited the buildings and apartments appropriated to the women. We were ushered into a spacious room, where I viewed with astonishment a most indescribable scene. With a feeling of profound respect, I uncovered my head. Two hundred tidily dressed, venerable appearing, gray-haired matrons, seated on benches of two rows extending the whole length of the extensive apartment, were plying their needles, knitting stockings in solemn silence. What a spectacle! Some of these unfortunate mothers of men once moved in the circles of wealth and fashion, ere the cruel floods of adversity engulphed them beneath their seething billows.

We were conducted into other buildings and apartments for women. In one of these about twenty paupers were seated around a table enjoying their tea with bread and butter. We passed through a lengthy hall containing numerous rooms, in each of which were two single beds and a coal grate, designed for two women, who were furnished weekly with provisions, instead of having it dealt out daily, according to general regulations. We visited the washing and drying departments, where a battalion of women in a fog of steam were engaged in washing immense quantities of sheets, shirts, blankets, etc., for the entire institution. They had an ingenious arrangement for drying by the application of steam. We were conducted into the apartment for cutting garments, another for making them up. We also visited one appropriated to pauper children, where we saw a nice lot of them, some very pretty and intelligent looking, all clean and well dressed, and many of them orphans, some entirely ignorant of their parentage, being foundlings. I noticed with peculiar interest one lovely infant, which had recently been found one stormy night, abandoned. Poor little forsaken! Why not have waited or sought your path into life by way of Utah, where you would have been recognized and appreciated?

We next visited the hospital department. Two hundred and seventy were on the sick list, mostly very elderly people. The hospital consisted of numerous rooms with an average of thirty single beds. Many of the invalids had been confined to their beds for several years, their diseases affording no prospects of recovery. In a frame a record is suspended over each sufferer, giving name, age, with date of reception into workhouse, nature of disease, and how treated and dieted. Excellent nurses are provided for these sufferers.

The largest dining hall seats 800. In this, every Sabbath, Roman Catholic service is performed. An Episcopal church constitutes a portion of this mass of buildings; it is well seated and has a fine organ.

I noticed, as a matter of curiosity, a marble statue representing an angel with extended wings. It was carved at Leghorn and placed here to honor and perpetuate the memory of Agnes Jones, a wealthy lady, daughter of an Irish Colonel. This estimable and philanthropic woman devoted her large fortune to the relief of the poor, and while administering to the sufferers in this institution she contracted a contagious disease, of which she died at the age of thirty-six years. A beautiful epitaph is inscribed upon her monument, written by the Bishop of Derby, and also lines with deep expression by Florence Nightingale.

Finally we came to apartments appropriated to vagabonds. Here philanthropy exhibited itself upon a higher plane. A bath, supper and breakfast, could be obtained by any vagrant outside of Liverpool parish. To obtain these benefits, the participant must enter the register's office, have his name registered, then be conducted to the bath-room, where he undergoes a thorough process, to wit, stripped, soaked, soaped, and scrubbed, and having his clothes replaced, is served to a dish of soup, then admitted to a clean cot for the night. For these services he is required to render compensation in labor in the morning, after which he receives another dish of soup and departs. This department is never crowded.

We were introduced to Mr. Wilkie, the Governor of the Workhouse, with whom we had an interesting interview. On our leaving he politely proffered to send to my address written information on any point I might wish in relation to the institution.

My "Two hours in a Workhouse," constitutes a very interesting item in my experience.

LORENZO SNOW.

LETTER X.

Crossing the Hudson—Visit to West Point—Trophies of War—Putnam's Fort—Tete-a-tete with a Student—Information about Palestine—Leave New York.

LIVERPOOL, England, November 20th, 1872.

EDITOR WOMAN'S EXPONENT:

MY DEAR LULA:—In my last, I left you at Central Park in New York. Early next morning, (5th of Nov.,) in company of Brother Feramorz Little, Sister Little, Clara S. Little and her little brother Frank, also Brother Spencer Clawson, I took the cars for West Point, where we arrived at 10 a. m., after crossing the beautiful Hudson River on a steam ferry-boat.

West Point is a delightful point. The natural scenery is variegated and imposing. Having one hour to while away before we could have an interview with the object of our visit, Mr. Willard Young, we strolled around the premises, viewing the objects of interest, and some things, which to us, promoters of peace, were not particularly interesting. Great numbers of cannon, of various forms and sizes, were to be seen in different places—some from Mexico, others from the Crimea, preserved as specimens; also a portion of the ponderous iron chain which the Americans stretched across the Hudson, in the Revolutionary war, to impede the British ships. I admired the beautiful green area, with its fine shade trees, surrounded by rugged hills; on the top of the highest, in the distance, Putnam's Fort is to be seen, which is said to remain precisely as the veteran General, whose name it bears, built, and left it. The next hour was very pleasantly spent in a *tete-a-tete* with the young military student, whom we found in good health and spirits, and returned to New York at 4 p. m.

That evening Mr. Richardson and lady called on us; he has been a traveller in Palestine and gave us much interesting information respecting it. Before we left New York, the number in the hotel, from Utah, amounted to twenty.

ELIZA R. SNOW.

LETTER XI.

On Board the "Minnesota"—First Sight of the Ocean—Arrival in Liverpool—Dense, Interminable Fog—Leave for London—English Railway Cars—No Sleeping Cars—English Rural Scenery—Poem, "London," by Miss E. R. Snow.

LONDON, England, November 24th, 1872.

EDITOR WOMAN'S EXPONENT:

DEAR LULA:— I wrote you from Liverpool up to our last evening in New York.

On the morning of the 6th we went on board the steamer *Minnesota*, and, through the kindness of Brother W. C. Staines, were very comfortably quartered, and soon launched forth into the Hudson and from thence into the broad ocean.

I saw the ocean for the first time, and was in nothing so disappointed as its color, which is, when calm, dark, very dark, yes, positively black, and to me appeared like a mass of lava. I wanted to look at it poetically, and watched intently for "blue waves," or even "green waves," but to no purpose, except when the waters were stirred, then, beneath the white foam, the blue, and more particularly the green, were observable. I was but little sea-sick, and although our passage was rough, I enjoyed it. It was raining when we arrived in Liverpool on the morning of the 19th. The Northwestern Hotel, where we stopped, is a finely constructed building, with many accommodations, but is conducted altogether too ceremoniously to consult convenience and comfort. We stayed two days in the dense, interminable fog of Liverpool, where they have more light by night from gas than the sun affords them by day.

The first day I spent in writing, with a very agreeable and interesting visit to the sanctum of President Carrington; on the second, a severe cold prevented my visiting the workhouse, as I had anticipated, a sketch of which my brother Lorenzo has written to the *Deseret News*.

We left Liverpool for London by train at 9 a. m., and arrived at 2 p. m.—two hundred and three miles. The cars in England, instead of being open from end to end and the seats all in one view, as in America, are petitioned into boxes containing two seats, the first-class seating six persons, three on each seat, face to face; and the second-class eight, four on each seat. These compartments open only on the outside, so that there is no communication between the different sections. Here the distances are so short compared with those of America that sleeping cars are not in use.

I was delighted with the appearance of the country between Liverpool and this city. Even at this sterile season of the year it is picturesque, and must be very, very beautiful when the fields, which are enclosed by scrupulously neat hedges, are clothed with fresh vegetation.

With this brief letter, I will enclose a poem I have just written, entitled

CORRESPONDENCE OF

LONDON.

Far, far away from our dear native land,
In England's great Metropolis we stand;
Where art and skill—labor and wealth combine
With time's co-operation in design
Of superstructure's bold and beauteous form,
With all varieties of strength and charm.

Here massive columns—stately towers, arise,
And lift their spires in greetings to the skies;
Fine parks and gardens, palaces and halls,
With sculptured niches—frescoe-painted walls;
Where no expense is spared to beautify,
Nor time, nor toil, to captivate the eye.
We saw, and viewing, courteously admired
The master strokes by Genius' hand inspired.

To "New Westminster Palace" we resort,
Where the Chief Justice holds his august court;
'Twas then in session, and the Exchequer too—
In wig and gown—a grand, imposing view!
The House of Lords and Commons too, we saw,
But not those grave expounders of the law.

With deferential thought we fixed our gaze,
There, in the "Prince's Hall," where face to face
On either side, on carved projections stood,
With features varied as in life's warm blood,
White marble statues, from the sculptor's hand,
Of British Statesmen, men who could command
The power of eloquence—the force of mind,
A mighty nation's destinies to bind—
Chatham, Pitt, Granville, Walpole, Fox, beside
Others who're justly England's boast and pride.

We visited the "Abbey," where repose in state
The effigies of many good and great,
With some whose deeds are well deserving hate.
Group'd in the "Poets' Corner," here, we found,
With rich, artistic sculpture trophies crown'd,
The mem'ries of the muse's world-renowned.

In some compartments where old massive stones
Comprise the flooring, lie their mouldering bones,
And we with reverential footsteps tread
Above the ashes of the illustrious dead.

Great London City, mart of wealth and power,
Home for the wealthy—charnel for the poor!
And here, amid its boasted pomp and pride,
Some faithful Soldiers of the Cross reside—
A few choice spirits, whom the watchman's care,
By humble search, found scatter'd here and there,
"Like angels' visits, few and far between,"
As patient gardeners sep'rate clusters glean.
They barter earth's allurements and device
To gain the "Pearl" of great and matchless price,
And what to them the honors, pride and show,
That perish with their using, here below?
Their hopes are high—their noble aims extend
Where life and peace and progress never end;
Where God's own Kingdom Time's last knell survives,
Crowned with the gifts and powers of endless lives.

ELIZA R. SNOW.

LETTER XII.

A Conference—Passed Queenstown—Arrival at Liverpool—Scattering of the Members of the Party—Arrival in London—The Albert Memorial—The Princess Theatre—Houses of Parliament—Under-ground Railway—Attend Meetings—George J. Adams and the Holy Land.

LONDON, England, November 24th, 1872.

EDITOR DESERET NEWS:

DEAR BROTHER:—Having just returned from the conference held to-day, at East India Dock Road, to our boarding house, I feel like dropping you a few lines. We passed Queenstown on the 18th inst., at 4 a. m., and reached Liverpool on the 19th at 1.30 a. m. Brother Carrington with his son Brigham, Brothers Bleak, Gibbs and a few others, came alongside the *Minnesota* in a tug boat at 7 a. m., to bid us welcome, and we were very glad to meet them. After taking breakfast with them, we went ashore, soon got through with the examination of our luggage, and drove to the "North Western Hotel," opposite St. George's Hall, where we found good and comfortable quarters, and felt thankful to be on *terra firma* again. We spent the rest of the day and the day following partly at "42" and partly in attending to business matters and making other preparations for our further journey.

Brother Dunford went to Trowbridge, Wilts, to visit his friends, and Sister Thompson, who is still with us, went to Preston for the same purpose. Thursday the 21st, at 9.15 a. m., Brothers George A. Smith, Lorenzo Snow and Feramorz Little, and Sisters Eliza R. Snow, Clara S. Little, Mercy Thompson, and myself took train for London where we arrived at 2.30 p. m. and put up at Mr. Cook's boarding house, opposite the British Museum, which is a very quiet place. Brother Junius Wells met us at Willsden Junction and is now stopping with us.

On the morning of the 22nd a few of us called at Mr. Cook's office, but his son was out of town, and we intend to meet him to-morrow and see if we can make any satisfactory arrangements with him. We have seen several parties who have been travelling with his coupons, and under his arrangements, who speak very favorably of him. About noon we drove to the Albert Memorial in Hyde Park, which is a very fine specimen of art and workmanship, but as the weather was very wet and unpleasant we gave up the further part of our programme for that day, and returned to our lodgings. In the evening five of our party, with Brother George Crismon, visited the Princess' Theatre, and saw "Hamlet" performed in very fine style. Yesterday we visited the Houses of Parliament and Westminster Abbey, Westminster Bridge, and thence, per under-ground railway, to Charing Cross and Trafalgar Square. The evening we spent writing up our journals.

This morning at 8.45 we drove to the Conference meeting house, East India Dock Road, five miles distant, and had two highly interesting meetings, at 10 a. m. and 2 p. m. Most of the Elders made short remarks, and President George A. Smith and Elder Lorenzo Snow delivered very interesting discourses to the Saints and to quite a sprinkling of strangers, who were present.

At the close of the meeting George J. Adams, of former notoriety, came on the stand to see President George A. Smith, and gave us an invitation to call on him, in order to give us some useful information in regard to the Holy Land, where he has resided.

We are all well and in fine spirits.

Yours truly,

PAUL A. SCHETTLER.

LETTER XIII.

In London—Full Description of the National Monument—The Grandest Monument in the World—One Hundred and Eighty Feet High—Its Construction—Mass of Concrete—Substructure of Brick—The Podium—One Hundred and Eighty Marble Statues—The Tabernacle—Lofty Spire set with Thousands of Gems—Embossed Globe—Statue of Prince Albert—Faith, Hope, Charity and Humility.

LONDON, England, November 28th, 1872.

EDITOR DESERET NEWS:

In company with President Smith and party I visited the Prince Consort National Monument. It is situated in Kensington Gardens, in the central part of the Metropolis. It is designed to perpetuate the name of Prince Albert, also to show the high estimation in which he was held by the British nation, likewise to represent allegorically, by sculpture and Mosaic pictures, the arts and sciences which he fostered, and to point to some of his important undertakings, the Great National Exhibition being the foremost.

For grandeur of design and excellency and beauty of workmanship I believe it excels every other structure of a commemorative character in any part of the world. In approaching it I was struck with astonishment by its beauty and magnificence. A vast column, covered from base to pinnacle, with beautiful sculptures, rich carvings, embossed and Mosaic work of the most elegant description, beautiful foliage of beaten metal, fine enameling, the whole being set out in artistical order with twelve thousand gems sparkling like stars in the firmament.

This monument, including the foundation, rises one hundred and eighty feet above the surrounding ground, terminating in a large ball, embossed, supporting a magnificent cross. It commences with a mass of concrete sixty feet square, seventeen feet thick, overlaid with two courses of thick stone; upon this is erected a substructure of massive brick work, upon which the great column is based. The base of this column or "podium," as it is termed, is about twelve feet high, surrounded by one hundred and eighty marble statues about six feet in height, representing men of all ages, distinguished in the arts and sciences. This podium, built of massive blocks of granite, forms the foundation for the "Shrine" or Tabernacle, a vast canopy about fifty feet high, richly ornamented, beneath which, upon a lofty pedestal, will be placed the colossal statue of the Prince. This Tabernacle is supported by four clusters of pillars of finely polished granite of various colors. Several of these pillars are two feet in diameter, held together, in part, by an ornamental band of bronze set with polished "gem-like stones;" and in part are cemented by a dove-tail groove to the central core, around which they cluster. The Tabernacle is terminated by four gables ornamented with Mosaic pictures and decorated with carvings and enamel work and polished gem-like stones, some of them nearly four inches in diameter. Upon this tabernacle is reared a lofty spire of cast iron work, ornamented in the most magnificent style and set with thousands of gems. Out from this Tabernacle, near its angles, arise four small structures built in imitation, in many respects, of the principal one, being enriched and highly ornamented from base to pinnacle. This column, or spire, the same as the Tabernacle which forms its base, is surrounded with statues at successive heights, standing in its ornamented niches, and at their angles.

Four of these figures, standing in niches above the base of the spire, are eight and a half feet high, the four at the angles are seven and a half in height; far above them, the spire is flanked by statues six and a half feet high, representing angels; and still higher, other figures six feet in height with a like representation. These sixteen statues are all of copper.

This lofty spire is crowned with a magnificent globe, beautifully embossed, supporting a great cross highly ornamented.

A vast pyramid of granite steps surrounds this monument. The total length of these steps is equal to two miles and a half, and the number of steps is eighteen hundred and three. Several of the blocks of granite in the base of the column and in the pillars weigh fifteen tons each; the working of each of these stones occupied twelve men sixteen weeks. The iron girders which bear the spire weigh twenty-three tons, and the weight resting upon them is two hundred and ten tons. The spire is made of iron built up in stages and bolted together; the girders are of wrought iron. The gems and inlays are formed of vitreous enamel, spar, agates and onyxes, more than twelve thousand in number; two hundred of these are *real* onyxes, many of them nearly four inches in diameter.

The general features of the design are thus delineated: The Prince is to be represented by a colossal statue seated upon a lofty pedestal beneath this magnificent canopy; around and above him are gathered in series and in groups the most beautiful works of man, illustrating the arts and sciences which he promoted, and the subjects to which he devoted his attention. Upon four large pedestals, composed of blocks of granite, at the outer angle of the steps, the four quarters of the globe are represented by groups of marble statues. Upon the pedestal forming the angles of the podium, or base of the Tabernacle, are groups of marble statues illustrative of Agriculture, Manufactures, Commerce and Engineering. Again, still above, on pedestals of polished granite, are statues in bronze, representing Astronomy, Chemistry, Geology and Geometry. Above these is another set or order of bronze statues representing Rhetoric, Medicine, Philosophy and Physiology. The four sides of the podium contain one hundred and eighty marble statues, representing eminent artists in Printing, Sculpture, Architecture, Music and Poetry. From the base to the roof of this Tabernacle, the whole range of arts and sciences is illustrated. The column above is devoted to illustrating Virtue and Religion. The four statues in the niches of the spire, point to the Christian virtues—Faith, Hope, Charity and Humility. The four figures at the angles represent the moral virtues—Fortitude, Prudence, Justice and Temperance. The four angels above them are in attitudes signifying resignation of worldly honors, while those above, surrounding the base of the cross, are in attitudes as if desiring celestial happiness.

Here, I will close my sketch of this curious and wonderful specimen of intellectual and physical effort, so happily and beautifully displayed in this magnificent monumental structure.

LORENZO SNOW.

LETTER XIV.

Description of the Tower of London—When Built—Queen Elizabeth's Armory—Cell of Sir Walter Raleigh, Ralstone, &c.—The Horse Armory—Coats of Mail and Weapons of Different Ages—Torture Rooms—Ann Boleyn—Earl of Essex—Lady Jane Grey—Executioner's Axe—Instruments of Torture—Regalia and Jewel House.

LONDON, England, November 30th, 1872.

EDITOR DESERET NEWS:

If one wishes to indulge in melancholy or the sympathetic, he should visit the "Tower of London," and devote an hour or two in examining its mouldering records and crumbling inscriptions, pointing to heart-rending scenes enacted in past ages within its dark and gloomy walls.

In company with President Smith and others of our tourists, I visited this place, although not for the purpose above mentioned.

It is a sombre mass, consisting principally of antique walls, gates, portcullis, bastions, moat and twelve towers. None of the excellency, beauty, splendor and grandeur is exhibited in these structures as is seen in Prince Albert's Monument. Simplicity and solidity are characteristics of its architecture; I was impressed with no other, with the exception of oppressive gloominess.

About thirteen acres are enclosed by the moat surrounding the Tower and a double line of walls and bulwarks encircles inside the moat, with a street running between, except on the south.

The White Tower, or citadel, the most important edifice, occupies the central part of these premises. It is one hundred and sixteen feet by ninety-six, and ninety-two in height, with walls fifteen feet in thickness. It was built in the latter part of the eleventh century, nearly eight hundred years ago, and is a specimen of Norman architecture. It is divided from base to summit into various compartments by walls seven feet in thickness. The smallest apartment is now occupied by what is termed Queen Elizabeth's armory. On one side of this room, formed in the wall, is a cell eight feet by ten, without light except at its entrance—formerly the prison of Sir Walter Raleigh, Ralstone, Fane and Culpepper. Above this apartment is St. John's Chapel, another specimen of Norman architecture. A chaplain was formerly engaged to perform service here for about twelve dollars per annum. The most spacious room on the upper floor, in former ages was used by the king as a council room, where their courts were held. It is said to have been here that, when the council was assembled, the Duke of Gloucester demanded Lord Hastings' immediate execution. This chamber and the banqueting room are used at the present time as depositories for small arms. Great artistical skill is displayed in the arrangement of some of these arms and their implements, in form of floors, aquatic plants appearing in streams of water, luminous stars and the sun rising in splendor.

We were conducted to the Horse Armory, which is nearly one hundred and fifty feet in length by thirty-four in breadth, filled with objects of curiosity and historical interest. There were equestrian figures, others on foot, dressed in armor of different periods embracing over two and a half centuries. It is curious to trace the development of the idea relating to armor and weapons, as exhibited in the multitude of those specimens. The conception in its perfect development, in regard to armor, was strikingly illustrated by a full suit on a life-sized effigy of Henry the VIII, mounted on a horse.

This suit of armor was made of plated metal artistically arranged in sections overlapping one another, and turning upon pivots so as to afford the body, head, neck and limbs free motion, without exposing any portion. It is ponderous, weighing, as nearly as I recollect, about one hundred and twenty pounds. This armor is elaborately worked—inlaid with gold and very beautiful. We were shown a rough suit he wore at the age of eighteen, which weighed ninety-two pounds.

The first specimens of armor manifested the idea as rather confused: leather cut in pieces in the form of fish scales and sewed on cloth or deer skins. The next stage of development appears in a specimen made of small rings of steel sewed on to the same material. Again, in the beginning of the thirteenth century, a higher point of development was reached—armor was constructed of vast quantities of small rings intersecting one with another so as to form a connected garment. After this, another improvement was introduced—mixed chain and plate being worn on the arms and legs. And thus invention progressed to its full development as represented at the period of Henry the VIII.

We saw various specimens of weapons invented at different periods, commencing with the cross-bow, the spear and battle axe, exhibiting step by step successive improvements represented in the matchlock, improved matchlock, flintlock, improved flintlock, percussion lock, improved percussion, double-barreled gun, improved double-barrel, revolving cylinder, cylinder improved, until we have reached the most perfect weapon now known.

The twelve towers of this fortress were erected, principally, in the early part of the thirteenth century; some of them, however, were built about the close of the eleventh century. The strange scenes enacted in past ages, beneath these frowning battlements, form a dark and bloody page in English history. Observing the multitude of objects bearing distinct marks of those terrible events, my mind was almost overpowered with sad and gloomy reflections. In these dark and loathsome dungeons, kings and queens, after having been divested of their crowns and robes of royalty, were forced to make their ignominious abode.

These walls bear traces of having echoed the sighs and groans of illustrious men while gasping for life beneath the bloody instruments of horrid torture, also of princes and nobles having been thrust into these dungeons and ended their lives by means shrouded in mystery! Tradition speaks of secret passages, of torture rooms and hidden recesses within and underneath these walls where I stood. Many eminent personages left inscriptions upon their prison walls, which yet remain—sad mementoes of themselves and their sufferings, Queen Ann, having enjoyed a few years of pomp and splendor, basking in the smiles of Henry the Eighth, was forced to exchange queenly habiliments for the prison costume, in which she passed from this loathsome captivity to the executioner's block. Queen Elizabeth's favorite, the Earl of Essex, the pride of the English court, was immured within one of these towers previous to being beheaded upon the scaffold. The beautiful, amiable and accomplished Lady Jane Grey was incarcerated here. "Jane," engraved by Lord Dudley, her unfortunate husband, on the stone walls of his prison, which I saw, reminded me forcibly of the melancholy circumstance. Two princes, sons of Edward the Fourth, while suffering captivity in what is termed "the bloody tower," were secretly murdered, and afterwards their bodies found mouldering beneath its walls.

We were shown the executioner's axe, the heading block, thumb-screws, iron collars and other horrid instruments for human torture. We were conducted to a small enclosure, surrounded with iron pailings, where many illustrious men and women of distinction and royalty had been privately executed.

Omitting many objects of interest, perceiving my letter becoming lengthy, I will close by noticing the "Regalia" as a strange contrast with what has been described. The "Jewel House" is a building of modern construction, within the enclosure of these ramparts, and contains the "Crown Jewels." There is a magnificent display of crowns, diadems and sceptres embellished with pearls, rubies, emeralds, diamonds and sapphires, together with Edward's staff of beaten gold, over four feet in length, added to which are the "swords of justice," temporal and ecclesiastical, and the pointless "sword of mercy."

LORENZO SNOW.

LETTER XV.

A Week in London—Sight-seeing—Visiting—Attending Conference—Theatres—Crystal Palace—The Grand Aquarium—Tower of London—"Man's Inhumanity to Man"—Going to Rotterdam.

LONDON, England, November 28th, 1872.

EDITOR DESERET NEWS:

We have been in London one week. We have divided our time among the various occupations of resting from our voyage across the sea, sight-seeing, visiting the brethren, calling upon gentlemen who have visited Utah, attending London Conference with the Saints, and a concert got up by them, studying to obtain information concerning the further progress of our journey, attending theatres, etc.

Our several calls, without exception, have been pleasant and agreeable.

On the 26th we spent the day very pleasantly in the Crystal Palace, in company with President Albert Carrington, Elders John B. Fairbanks, Brigham Carrington, David O. Calder, Erastus W. Snow, Samuel S. Jones, Junius F. Wells, Elijah A. Box, James G. Bleak, George F. Gibbs, Charles H. Wilcken, Newell Clayton, John Neff, Anson Call, Mark Lindsey, David Cazier, John Bennion, missionaries from Utah, Brother Scofield of the Manchester Branch, Sister Mercy R. Thompson, President Lorenzo Snow, and his Sister Eliza R., Feramorz Little and his daughter Clara, Paul A. Schettler, Thomas W. Jennings, visiting and examining the curiosities that have been collected in this magnificent structure. It would require weeks, perhaps months, to make even a partial examination of the specimens of nature and art that are here on exhibition, including statuary, paintings, numerous varieties of machinery, clothing, furniture, rare plants—native and exotic, representations of different nations in their native surroundings, etc.

The Aquarium exhibited here, presents to the eye specimens of the mysteries of the deep. A considerable variety of fish, in all stages of existence, moving in their own element, carefully fed and nourished, is a recent addition of much interest. Most of the same party visited the "Tower of London," rife with gloomy historic reminiscences, and when we left we mutually felt like exclaiming with the poet, "Man's inhumanity to man."

We are making arrangements to leave England for Rotterdam on the 30th.

Yours, etc

GEORGE A. SMITH.

LETTER XVI.

At Rotterdam—Programme of Travel—Antwerp—Brussels—Paris—Lyons—Marseilles—Nice—Genoa—Turin—Milan—Venice—Bologna—Florence—Rome &c.

NEW BATH HOTEL, Rotterdam, Holland,
December 5th, 1872.

GEORGE Q. CANNON, ESQ., SALT LAKE CITY,

DEAR BROTHER:—My time is so completely occupied in attending to the business and traveling arrangements of our party, that it is impossible for me to send you further correspondence, but Brother Lorenzo Snow kindly volunteered to attend to it.

We are all well, enjoy ourselves very much, and intend to leave here for Antwerp to-morrow at 10.10 a. m. On the 8th inst. we shall reach Brussels, and at Paris we intend to make a stay from the 11th to the 18th inst., at Lyons the 20th, Marseilles 24th, Nice 25th, Genoa 27th, Turin 29th, Milan Jan. 1st, 1873, Venice Jan. 3rd, Bologna Jan. 9th, Florence 10th, Rome 16th to 24th, Naples 26th to 30th, from Brindisi to Corfu Jan. 31st, Alexandria Feb. 7th, Cairo 23, Jaffa 26th, Beyrout March 23rd, Constantinople March 31st, Athens April 5th, Trieste April 19th. Should we stay six weeks in Palestine instead of four weeks, the last four dates will be two weeks later each.

Remember us kindly to Presidents Young and Wells, and to all inquiring friends.

Yours truly in the Gospel.

PAUL A. SCHETTLER.

LETTER XVII.

Amsterdam — The Hague — Haarlem — Description of Rotterdam — Jews, Catholics, Protestants—Canals—Church of St. Lawrence—Public Schools—Fighting Old Ocean — Windmills and Steam Engines — Calamity at Dort—The Hague Described—Mode of Keeping Back the Waters—The Museum—Masterpieces of Dutch Painters—"The House in the Wood"—An Evening with the American Minister.

AMSTERDAM, Holland, December 5th, 1872.

EDITOR DESERET NEWS:

We, President Smith and party, are now located at "Old Bible Hotel" in the city of Amsterdam. We reached Rotterdam, Sunday, 1st December, having left London the previous evening. Tuesday we visited the Hague, Wednesday resumed our journey for this place, calling a few hours at Haarlem, and arrived here in the afternoon.

I now make a few extracts from my journal, beginning at Rotterdam. Our Hotel is pleasantly located—fronting a beautiful quay extending one and a half miles, bordering an extensive harbor, bearing on its placid bosom ships of the largest tonnage from the four quarters of the globe.

The city of Rotterdam is situated on the river Maas; it is the second commercial city in Holland, numbering one hundred and twenty thousand inhabitants, Jews, Catholics and Protestants. It is intersected by numerous canals of sufficient depth to accommodate large ships, which discharge their valuable burdens into the very heart of the city, producing stir and life truly wonderful, which render the same very picturesque. A city filled with canals—floating ships in all directions—to strangers presents a romantic appearance, exciting surprise and admiration. These canals are crossed by numerous drawbridges. The city is remarkably clean and orderly, considering its immense commerce and business. We visited the church of "St. Lawrence," containing several splendid marble monuments of Dutch heroes, bearing old Dutch inscriptions, which I regret to say baffled our best linguists. It has a magnificent organ with three key boards, seventy-two stops, four thousand and sixty-two pipes, the largest being thirty-two feet long and seventeen inches in diameter. This organ is supposed, by some, to equal if not surpass the famous instrument at Haarlem. The tower of this church is two hundred and eighty-eight feet in height; its summit affords a fine view of Dutch scenery —canals bordered with trees, country houses, straight avenues, broad arable fields, green pastures and meadows, forming a plane with no perceptible inclination; also numerous windmills, in motion, in every direction.

Rotterdam has several public schools. We saw eleven hundred children belonging to one of them of from four to eleven years of age. We remarked that their countenances failed to exhibit those characteristics of health and longevity observable in the children of our Utah schools.

The Hollanders possess indomitable energy and perseverance. By untiring industry, towns and cities have been built upon trembling morasses, lakes and seas rolled from their beds giving place to cultivated fields, green pastures and beautiful meadows. Portions of seas and lakes have been intersected and surrounded by dykes or embankments and the water pumped out by steam engines and windmills. This reclaimed land is intersected by canals and sects at suitable distances, taking advantage of every perceivable inclination, dead levels being the characteristic of the country, and yet the most formidable enemy a Dutchman has to combat. The main canals are continued through the country to some river, inlet or the ocean. In every instance the surface waters from a lower plane are conducted, into canals running on a higher elevation, by windmills and steam engines, carrying an immense amount of surplus water, which is constantly gathering, especially in rainy seasons, out from these reclaimed districts. This process imposes a heavy tax on the wisdom and patience of the irrepressible Dutchman, initiating him imperatively into the practice of the mysteries of hydraulics. In Utah, we labor to secure water for our lands; here, the removal of it, and the preservation of life and property from its overflow, is a national work, which involves an almost infinitely greater amount of toil and expense. The least neglect in their operations exposes the country to devastation. In the province of Dort, in the fifteenth century, seventy villages were overflowed and one hundred thousand inhabitants destroyed.

From Rotterdam we proceeded to the Hague, containing one hundred thousand inhabitants. It is the most elegant, beautiful and fashionable town in Holland. It possesses no internal resources or advantages of commerce, but to the presence of the Court, and of numerous nobles and diplomatists, who make it their residence, it chiefly owes its aristocratic and prosperous appearance. Many of its streets are broad and handsome, bordered with beautiful trees; its buildings lofty and substantial. A magnificent basin of water in the central part of the town, with an ornamental island and flocks of white, graceful swans, is the most fashionable locality.

The Hague and its environs are so flat that the waters in the canals are destitute of fall; this difficulty, however, is overcome by artificial arrangement. A steam engine on the Duenny pumps fresh water into the canal, by which an imperceptible current is formed, carrying a flow towards Rotterdam, where it is pumped into the river Maas.

The Museum attracted our attention. It contains a fine

collection of curiosities in the lower part of the building, and in the upper a picture gallery comprising specimens by the most celebrated Dutch painters. I was so delighted with the beauty and artistical display that I invested in an opera glass. Our attention was attracted to a painting by Rembrandt, representing a school of anatomy, possessing rare merit and beauty of design and execution. This wonderful picture was purchased for about thirteen thousand dollars, by King William the First. It represents Professor Tulp, surrounded by his anxious pupils, in the act of dissecting a corpse. The subject perhaps is not very agreeable, but all of the figures, the expression of their features, the death appearance of the corpse, the whole was brought out with such profound skill as to invest the painting with an irresistible charm.

Paul Potter's far-famed "bull," regarded as the gem of the whole collection, also rivetted our attention. The French carried it as a trophy to Paris and placed it among their pictures in the Louvre, and considered it worthy to rank as fourth in point of value. The Dutch government offered Napoleon twenty thousand dollars for its restoration. We were conducted through various departments appropriated to objects of curiosity of various descriptions. I will merely notice a model house constructed by order of Peter the Great with the intention of taking it to Russia to present to the Empress a view of the interior of a house in Amsterdam. This model is reported to have cost about twelve thousand dollars, and to have occupied twenty-five years in its completion.

We visited the Queen's palace, called "The House in the Wood," very romantically situated in an extensive park. We were conducted through the principal apartments. The palace contains some excellent paintings, and magnificent silk tapestry of exquisite needle work done by Chinese and Japanese, representing birds of their country with their brilliant plumage, etc. This tapestry, we were informed by our conductor, was presented to the Stadtholder, William the Fifth, by the Emperor of Japan.

After many expressions of admiration, and, by request, having inscribed our names in the Queen's register, we proceeded to Scheveningen, a fashionable resort upon the sea coast, and enjoyed a splendid drive, passing through groves of majestic oak, elm and linden.

While at the Hague we called on Mr. Gorham, the American Minister, who received us very cordially and insisted on the whole party joining him at tea and spending the evening, which invitation was accepted by President Smith in behalf of the party. Our interview in the evening with Mr. Gorham, and his wife, a very intelligent, affable and accomplished lady, was agreeable and entertaining, and will ever be associated with the pleasant recollections of our visit to the beautiful Hague.

LORENZO SNOW.

LETTER XVIII.

Sight-seeing in Liverpool—Arrival in London—Albert Memorial—Houses of Parliament—Westminster Abbey—Nelson Monument—Crystal Palace—Theatres—Rotterdam—Table d'Hote—Visit to a Moravian Settlement—The Hague—The Japanese Museum—Visit to the American Minister—Haarlem—The Cathedral and Grand Organ, Imitation Thunder Storm—Meeting with Saints—Amsterdam—Its Museum—The King's Palace—Visit the Navy Yard—Leave for Rotterdam—Cross the Maas—Enter Belgium—Catholic Marriage Ceremony—Programme of Travel.

HOTEL DE L'EUROPE, Antwerp, Belgium,
December 6th, 1872.

EDITORS SALT LAKE HERALD:

You will certainly think that my letters are few and far between, but I have been so much engaged with our travelling arrangements, that I really could not find time to write ere this.

We arrived in good health and spirits at Liverpool; spent two days there in looking around the city and preparing ourselves for our further journey; left for London, Nov. 21st, at 9.15 a. m., and arrived at Euston Station at 2.30 p. m. We put up at Mr. Thomas Cook's boarding house, No. 59 Great Russel Street, opposite the British Museum, where we were comfortably quartered. During our nine days stay in London we visited the Albert Memorial in Hyde Park, the Houses of Parliament, Westminster Abbey, Trafalgar Square with the Nelson Column, The Union Bank, Sydenham Crystal Palace, Dr. Anger's College in Regent Park, and Dr. Jabez Burns and his Baptist Chapel. President George A. Smith and myself also called at Mr. Hepworth Dixon's, but we did not find him at home. Of the principal theatres we visited Covent Gardens, Drury Lane and Princess'. On the day which we spent at Sydenham Palace we were accompanied by President Albert Carrrington and about a dozen Elders, some from the Liverpool office and others who had come to see us. Saturday, the 30th, at 9.55 p. m., we left per train for Harwich, where we arrived at 12.30 a. m. on December 1st. We went on board the steamer *Richard Young*, left Harwich at 2.30 a. m., and arrived after rather a rough passage at Rotterdam at 2.30 p. m., put up at the New Bath Hotel, *onder de boompjes*, as the Dutch call it, and enjoyed the first *table d'hote* after the European plan, having from eight to ten different dishes served at intervals of about ten minutes. This gives to almost every epicure a chance to find something that will tickle his palate, and we all much preferred it to the American "bolting" system. Six of our party stopped at Rotterdam to see the sights, and to witness the enormous amount of business which is transacted here every day in receiving and shipping merchandise from and to all parts of the world. The greatest vessels can go right in front of the warehouses in the heart of the city. Holland imports most of the productions of its possessions in raw material, and after manufacturing them ships the surplus to other countries.

President George A. Smith and myself left Rotterdam the same evening at 6.40 for Zeist, a Moravian settlement near Utrecht, where some of my relatives reside. We reached there at 9 p. m., and after providing for the comforts of President Smith at the hotel of the place, I went to see one of my uncles, Mr. E. C. Martin, who with his wife received me in the most cordial manner. Next morning President Smith and myself were shown through Mr. Martin's extensive factory of white china, heating stoves and house ornaments of burnt clay. We then visited the "house of the brethren," where the unmarried men of the Moravian Church live, and went through a number of their stores, where they sell all kinds of merchandise, partly of their own manufacture. each diff·rent kind of goods in a separate room, which is unlocked for each visiting party, and locked again as soon as they leave that room. The outside door of the building is also locked, and if a person wishes to make purchases he has to ring the bell to be admitted. We then visited some of my old friends, and one of them, Mr. Muller, though being sick, had us immediately ushered into his room, and introduced us to his family. This gave President Smith an opportunity to see these people in their own houses, and learn more of their habits than he could have done otherwise. We also visited another uncle of mine, Mr. Adolphus Menzel, who received us very cordially; and he speaking English tolerably well, President Smith had about an hour's conversation with him. His oldest daughter, Emilia, about eighteen years old, is quite an intelligent girl, speaking English, French, German, and Dutch, and playing the piano very well. Mrs. Martin took us in the afternoon in a carriage to Utrecht, and we passed many fine country seats, farmhouses, meadows, etc.; she was only sorry that we could not stay longer, but she and my uncle were exceedingly pleased with the visit of President Smith, and I know that this visit will have good results. We thence took rail to Rotterdam, and after visiting the fine old Cathedral, met our friends again, all well and enjoying themselves.

Next morning, December 3rd, we took train for the Hague, the residence of the King of Holland, and visited the Japanese Museum, and the Picture Gallery, with the celebrated paintings, "The Bull," by Paul Potter, and "Anatomical Lessons," by Rembrandt. Then we called upon the American Minister, Mr. Charles T. Gorham, Bellevue Hotel, who received us very kindly, and invited all of us to take tea with him at 8 p. m., which we did, and spent a very pleasant evening with him and his lady. In the afternoon we also visited the celebrated "House in the Woods"—Dutch "t'huis ten bosh"—the residence of the Queen of Holland, where we saw some very fine paintings by Rubens and his scholars, and other objects of art. From there we drove to the fishing village of Scheveningen, the Grand Bazar, and back to our hotel. Next morning we departed for Amsterdam, and stopped two hours at Haarlem, where we visited the Cathedral which contains the large organ, that has 5,000 metal and 2,000 wooden pipes and sixty stops. We had it played for an hour. Among other pieces, the organist treated us with the imitation of a thunderstorm, which, as the Dutch say, is played so effectively that the milk in all the neighborhood turns sour. At 1.10 p. m. we arrived at Amsterdam, the capital of Holland, where we met Elder S. Van Dyke, who now labors in this mission, and he informed us that he had made arrangements for a meeting with some ten or twelve Saints at 10 p. m., as several had to work till nearly that hour. President George A. Smith, and Brothers Little, Dunford and myself attended, and we had a good little meeting at Elder W. T. De Groot's house, an excellent spirit prevailing. We all spoke a short time, and I translated for the other brethren. President Smith blessed and reconfirmed the native priesthood, and we administered to some of the sisters who were afflicted. The rest of our party did not go with us, because they suffered from severe colds, but Sister Eliza R. Snow called to see some of them the next forenoon, which gave them much satisfaction. Immediately after our arrival in Amsterdam we visited the Museum and the palace of the King, on the square called "the Dam." The celebrated Exchange Buildings are also situated on the same square. On the morning of the 5th we drove through the city and visited the navy yards, called the "Marine," where we saw some powerful machinery used for the building of monitors; shears that cut iron plates of half an inch thickness as if they were sheets of paper; and punches that went through inch plates of iron as if they were nothing but pasteboard.

At 2.30 p. m. we left for Rotterdam by a shorter route, and arrived at 4 p. m. Friday, the 6th, at 10 a. m., we crossed the river Maas, on the other side of which we took train for Antwerp, which we reached at 1.10 p. m. At the station where we entered into Belgium we had our luggage examined. Soon after our arrival we visited the Cathedral, which contains many of Rubens' celebrated paintings, and also the vault in which he and his two wives are buried. In going from there to the Church of St. James we passed through the Exchange, which is a very handsome building.

BRUSSELS, Belgium, December 8th, 1872.

At 1.18 p. m. we departed for Brussels, where we arrived after one hour's ride, and called upon the American Minister, Mr. J. Russell Jones, but he had not yet returned from the United States, and was not expected before Christmas.

In the evening we took a stroll through some of the finest streets of the city and visited some large bazars and arcades, where merchants keep their goods displayed under brilliant gas-light to the best possible advantage. This morning we visited a Catholic church and witnessed the ceremonies, which were highly interesting to some of our party who had never seen them.

Our programme is: To visit the battle field of Waterloo to-morrow; leave for Paris on the 11th; stay at Paris till the morning of the 19th; at Lyons from the 20th to 22nd; at Marseilles from 23rd to 24th; reach Nice the 25th; Genoa 26th; Turin 29th; Milan January 1, 1873; Venice from 3rd to 8th; Bologna 9th; Florence 10th to 13th; Pisa 15th; Rome 16th to 25th; Naples 26th to 30th; Brindisi 31st of January, and leave same evening per steamer for Corfu; arrive at Alexandria February 7th; Cairo Feb. 23rd; arrive at Jaffa

February 26th, where we commence our Palestine tour on horseback till we reach Beyrout, March 23rd. Thence we go per Austrian Lloyd steamer to Constantinople, to reach there March 31st, Athens April 5th, and back to Trieste, April 19th, 1873. Should we, however, prolong our Palestine tour from thirty to forty-two days, the last four dates will be two weeks later each, because steamers leave Beyrout every two weeks on Monday. We are all enjoying good health. I intend to write you again before leaving Paris, if time permits.

PAUL A. SCHETTLER.

LETTER XIX.

Sea-sickness—Rotterdam—Among the Moravians—The Canal System—The Utrecht Cathedral—Beautiful Trees—Struggle for Mastery between Land and Sea—The Hague—"House in the Wood"—Evening with Mr. Gorham and Lady—Haarlem—A Shot by the Spaniards—"Bible Hotel"—King's Palace—Navy Yard—Building Iron-clad Monitors—The Cemetery—Meeting with Saints—Baptisms—Enter Belgium—Antwerp Cathedral—Paintings and Tomb of Rubens.

Antwerp, Belgium, December 6th, 1872.

President Brigham Young:

Most of our party suffered discomfort from sea-sickness in crossing the German Ocean. I was sick about eight hours. I lay on a lounge about two-thirds as broad as I am. I turned over occasionally to keep my balance. As soon as our party were fairly settled at the Bath Hotel at Rotterdam, I started with Elder Paul A. Schettler to visit his relatives at Zeist. They belong to a settlement of Moravians, a sect of Christians who came to Holland from Germany in 1745, in order to obtain religious liberty. They purchased sufficient land from the "Lord of Zeist" to build their houses and church and a place for burying their dead.

The fine brick meeting house, erected in 1745, is still sufficiently large, which indicates that their numbers are not increasing.

Although they came from Germany, they have lived in Holland until they are thoroughly Dutch. Their houses and grounds are very neat and clean. They have canals leading from the main canal of the kingdom to all their business houses. This is the case throughout Holland, canals answering the place of roads in other countries.

Brother Schettler's relatives and friends were very glad to see him, and treated him with marked kindness and respect; seemed glad that I accompanied him. One of his uncles and one cousin spoke a little English, which was very gratifying to them and especially so to me. One of his aunts, a very intelligent lady, who has six children and one grandchild, seemed very anxious to talk. She took her carriage and carried us several miles to see the Cathedral at Utrecht. Her husband showed me through his extensive establishment for manufacturing porcelain stoves, and ornaments of burnt clay. I regarded my going with Brother Schettler as a fortunate circumstance, as it gave me an opportunity of becoming acquainted with some of the people of Holland at their own firesides. I was surprised at the number of beautiful trees which are growing in rows by the sides of the canals, and in small groves. Most of them are very beautiful. I recognized the basswood and the beech, although the bark looks greener than in the American woods.

Most all of the land appears to be but a few inches above the sea, and a good many thousand acres are lower than the sea, and are only drained by pumps run by windmills, which raise the water to higher levels, and run it off to the sea, it is then kept out by immense embankments. This would seem rather precarious—living lower than the German Ocean—when we consider that only a few hundred years ago half a million people were drowned by the overflow. Much of the country then overflowed has not yet been reclaimed.

On the 4th inst. we visited the Hague, the capital of Holland, examined its museum, and enjoyed a drive to the Queen's Palace, known as the "House in the Wood." We then drove to the sea shore, and on our return stopped at the Bazar. In the evening all called on the American Minister, Honorable Charles T. Gorham, who invited us to spend the evening and take tea. We accepted the invitation, and were introduced to Mrs. Gorham, a very pleasant and agreeable lady. We next went to the Cathedral at Haarlem, an immense pile. By paying thirteen florins we were privileged to hear the mammoth organ for an hour. It is truly a wonderful instrument, containing 5,000 metal pipes, and it is said 2,000 more of wood. We saw, embedded in the wall, a cannon shot fired by the Spaniards in 1572. It is lodged near the pulpit, and was intended to kill the minister. We passed through Leyden, rendered famous in history by the vigorous siege by the Spaniards, during the revolutionary war of 1573-4, a contest between Catholicism and Protestantism, as well as between Dutch independence and Spanish tyranny. At Amsterdam we stopped at the Bible Hotel, and we visited a museum famous for its old paintings. We also visited the King's Palace, and spent about two hours in the navy yard, examining the immense machine shops and other places in which the building of iron vessels of war is carried on. We saw one new monitor afloat, so arranged that they could sink the upper deck two feet under water, all but the turret. We also saw slabs of iron plating eight inches through, one of which had several holes shot through, the ball first penetrating twelve inches of hard wood, showing that they cannot make plates that cannon balls cannot penetrate. Went through the marine arsenal, which contains a great variety of arms of various periods, many of which are now used in the Dutch navy. We drove to the cemetery. The monuments are stone slabs, polished until they are as smooth as glass; they are laid flat on the ground.

Elder Van Dyke, of Ogden city, called to see us, and Elders Little, Dunford, Schettler and myself went with him to the home of Brother De Groot, and met with a branch of the church, all of us speaking to them in turn, Brother Schettler interpreting. Brother Van Dyke has baptized twenty-seven since he came to Holland. He accompanied us to Rotterdam and stayed with us over night. We regard him as a faithful missionary laboring under difficulties.

To-day we left the dominions of his Dutch Majesty, William II, and entered those of Leopold II, King of the Belgians. We had to stop and have our trunks and satchels examined, to see if we had anything on which we should pay duty, but on the whole we regarded the officers of our new king as rather courteous than otherwise, in the discharge of a not very pleasant duty. We are now at the Hotel de l'Europe. We have visited the great Cathedral of Antwerp, remarkable for containing several original paintings by the immortal artist Rubens. We saw a man by the name of Van den Wildenberch, who has spent thirty-eight years of his life in making copies of Rubens' two master-pieces, one of the crucifixion of the Saviour, the other, taking him from the cross. Van den Wildenberch sells these at 300f. a piece. Rubens is almost the idol of Antwerp. His statues and pictures are everywhere to be seen. We went to the Church of St. Jacques, where we saw his magnificent tomb, above which hangs one of his own paintings—a portrait of himself, his two wives, one daughter, one son, and other members of his family.

Our only annoyance in regard to health is colds. The climate is damp naturally and the whole country is but a few inches out of water.

GEORGE A. SMITH.

LETTER XX.

At Haarlem—Its Former Struggle with Spain—Two thousand People Executed—Church of St. Bavon and its Wonderful Organ—A Dutch Wedding—The Inventor of the Art of Printing—Amsterdam—A City on Piles Built on a Saltmarsh—Amsterdam Sapped and Mined by a Formidable Army of Worms—Canals—A City Containing One Hundred Islands and Two Hundred and Eighty Bridges—The Museum—A Palace on Piles—The Council Chamber—Clipping Iron Plates—Diamond Cutting—Charitable Institutions.

ANTWERP, Belgium, December 7th, 1872.

EDITOR DESERET NEWS:

We arrived at Haarlem *en route* to Amsterdam, on Wednesday the 4th of December. It is a town of considerable importance, containing thirty thousand inhabitants—in former periods the residence of the Counts of Holland. In the latter part of the sixteenth century, during the Spanish war, the citizens of Haarlem, after suffering seven months' siege, in which they endured the severest hardships, were forced to capitulate. Ten thousand people on that occasion perished by famine or lost their lives in the terrible encounters of those bloody struggles. The commandant and the Protestant clergy, together with two thousand townspeople, were barbarously executed after having surrendered. Frederick of Toledo, son of the Duke of Alva, commanded the besiegers, and had given solemn assurances of life and honorable treatment. We saw traces of a striking character, still remaining as sad mementoes of the atrocious deeds.

St. Bavon, erected about three hundred and seventy

years ago, is the principal church in Haarlem. This is a magnificent structure, four hundred and twenty-five feet in length ; its nave is supported by twenty-eight massive columns, eighteen feet in circumference. This church is renowned for its famous organ, which, for a long time, has been considered the largest and most powerful in the world. It has four key boards, sixty-four stops, five thousand metal and two thousand wooden pipes; the largest of these pipes is thirty-two feet long, and fifteen inches in diameter. It is very beautiful—adorned with marble statuary, life size, and in attractive attitudes, representing personages playing on instruments of various descriptions. We employed the organist and three or four blowers to exhibit its merits. Imitations of different tones of the piano-forte, the trumpet, whistle, battle call, sacred music, closing with a tremendous thunder storm—all were executed with admirable accuracy, fully satisfying us as to its wonderful capabilities.

We saw a cannon ball which was nearly buried in the wall, having been thrown through an opposite window from a Spanish gun during the siege above mentioned.

While exploring this church for objects of curiosity, we were interrupted by the approach of a wedding party, which afforded some diversion, especially to our young tourists, who had never witnessed a Dutch wedding. The bride and groom were accompanied by a grave clerical gentleman, to whom we bowed with becoming reverence, and with smiles of our hearty approval to the happy groom and blushing bride. As we discovered nothing in the ceremonies surprisingly characteristic, I omit description.

In front of this church is a bronze statue of Coster, formerly a citizen of Haarlem, representing him as the inventor of the art of printing.

Having spent two hours in that interesting town, we took cars for Amsterdam, where we arrived about half past 3 p. m. Amsterdam is the great commercial city of Holland, numbering 275,000 inhabitants, of whom 57,000 are Roman Catholics, and 28,000 Jews. It is built over a salt marsh, upon piles driven from forty to fifty feet into the ground. We were informed that one house only, in this city, stands on any other foundation. These people apparently feel as secure upon these wooden posts as if founded on solid ground, although at one period this faith in their safety was fearfully shaken. While busied in making canals and windmills—smoking their pipes, unsuspicious of danger, the enemy in vast numbers had succeeded in securing a lodgment beneath the city and commenced mining and sapping the entire substructure—penetrating and cutting into the very heart of these underpinnings. These fearful invaders were *wood worms!* They were honey-combing the wooden piles with alarming rapidity, threatening to tumble all Amsterdam into the great salt marsh. The whole city was in consternation! Every Dutchman's ingenuity and military tactics were called into requisition to devise measures to rout the enemy. Some of the crusaders were captured while working the trenches, and submitted to the inspection of zoologists, in hopes of discovering some vulnerable point, susceptible of attack, but all to no purpose—still they were mining and sapping, boring and eating, and, by millions, doubling and quadrupling. At last, however, these belligerents ended their hostilities after the same fashion as Bonaparte's army in Russia—the Holland winter finished them. It appears that these insects had been imported by some vessel from a warm climate—the colder regions of the north compelling them to succumb and leave the honest Dutchman to smoke his meerschaum in peace and security. Living specimens of these insects are preserved in the Cabinet of Zoologists in Amsterdam, where they may be seen by the tourist.

The expense of these foundations for building frequently exceeds that of their superstructures. The neglect of proper attention to this matter is liable to result in disaster. An extensive warehouse, containing 3,500 tons of grain, was precipitated into the marsh in consequence of the inefficiency of the foundation.

The city is about nine miles in circumference—intersected by numerous canals, dividing it into nearly one hundred islands, which circumstance, in connexion with other resemblances has given it the title of the "Venice of the North." Many of these canals are very broad—flanked with avenues of tall elms, presenting a handsome and picturesque appearance, comparing favorably with the finest streets in any city we have visited. Two hundred and eighty bridges form the crossings of these canals. A reservoir about thirteen miles distant supplies the inhabitants with drinking-water, which is conveyed in pipes.

We visited the Museum, which contains many valuable paintings, chiefly the works of the old Dutch school. The finest edifice in Amsterdam is the "King's Palace," which rests on a foundation of thirteen thousand six hundred and fifty-nine piles; its length is two hundred and eighty-two feet—two hundred and thirty-five in width, and one hundred and sixteen feet high. Its tower is sixty-six feet high, containing a splendid set of chimes. The interior of the palace is grand and beautiful—its principal apartments, through which we passed, are constructed of white marble, and many sumptuously decorated. The "Council Chamber" is one hundred and twenty feet long by sixty broad over the entrance, and opposite to it we noticed flags and trophies wrested from the Spaniards and other enemies. We also visited the Navy Yard, and were conducted through the different departments of ship-building. Steamers, monitors and iron-clads were in course of erection. We were amused in viewing the operation of their ponderous and complicated machinery. By a downward stroke chunks over three inches in diameter were punched out of cold iron plate above an inch in thickness. Ponderous iron pillars were pared, polished and grooved, blocks of iron eight inches thick were turned and twisted into every desirable shape. It seemed impossible that any projectile could be forced through an eight-inch block of iron: we were, however, shown one of this description which had been perforated by a cannon ball after having passed through a covering of oak at least one foot in thickness.

The most remarkable trade in this city is that of diamond cutting, which is done almost exclusively by Jews. The stones are cut or sawed through by means of wires covered with diamond dust and polished by being pressed by the workmen against a rapidly revolving iron disk, moistened with a mixture of oil and diamond dust. This last material has proved to be indispensable in this work, as no other substance will make impressions on the diamond.

Amsterdam is celebrated for its numerous charitable institutions. It has upwards of forty designed for the benefit of the sick, aged and indigent, lunatics, foundlings and widows, all being supported by voluntary contributions. Upwards of twenty thousand poor are sustained at the expense of private individuals. We saw a number of establishments for the poor, which appeared more like palaces for the rich than dwellings for the destitute. This city, as well as many others in Holland, is famous in its liberal arrangements for educating the poorer classes. The "Society for Public Welfare," founded in 1784, by a Baptist minister, is an admirable institution, having for its object the education and moral culture of the lower classes, and extending its operations throughout the kingdom of Holland. It comprises 14,000 members who subscribe two dollars annually. It educates teachers, publishes schoolbooks, establishes Sunday schools, reading-rooms, and libraries, publishes works of literature, bestows rewards, and confers public distinctions on persons who have made themselves conspicuous by their generosity and philanthropic conduct.

We left Amsterdam, Thursday the 5th, at 2 p. m., returned to Rotterdam, which we left on the following morning, and at 1 p. m. arrived at this place.

LORENZO SNOW.

LETTER XXI.

Journey to New York—Crossing the Atlantic—London—The German Ocean—Rotterdam—House and Statue of Erasmus—Queen's Palace—The Old Bible Hotel—Shipbuilding—A Dutch Burial Ground—Antwerp—The Cathedral—Church of St. Jacques—Tomb of Rubens—Field of Waterloo.

BRUSSELS, Belgium, December 9th, 1872.

MISS MARY E. COOK:

DEAR LADY:—Six weeks and two days have elapsed since I left the "City of the Saints." In that time I have journeyed to New York—crossed the Atlantic—spent two days in Liverpool—thence to London—stopped nine days in that mammoth city of world-wide interest, and withal, so unsystematically planned, that when asked how I liked London, I invariably replied, that, were I to shape it to my liking, I should, in the first place, take it to pieces and straighten out its streets. It is impossible to describe them—in curves, semicircles, diagonals and a few in straight lines, but most of these are so abruptly intersected, that when you turn your eyes to look in the distance, the focus of sight is brought to a sudden standstill. But with all these discrepancies— its fogs and darkness, London is a grand metropolis, where, after you have seen very much, you realize that, comparatively, you have seen but little. So I felt when, leaving on the evening of November 30th, we—President Smith and party—took cabs at our hotel, "Cook's Boarding House," opposite the British Museum—then the railroad train to Harwich, where we took steamer and crossed the German Ocean—arrived in Rotterdam in the afternoon of December 1st—after dining on board and having our effects very politely examined by the custom house officer in the service of King William, while anchored in the Maas.

Rotterdam is a beautiful city—one of many and large industries. It is alive with business—full of canals, the smaller ones used for individual purposes, instead of teams and wagons, the larger ones for extensive commerce. In every part of the city, ships are either anchored or afloat, giving the whole town the appearance of a navy yard. I was very much interested here by the way of "sight seeing"— was shown the house once the dwelling of the celebrated Erasmus, also a bronze statue of him, in standing position, on an elevated pedestal, in a much frequented portion of the city.

On the evening of the 3rd we went to the Hague—visited the Queen's Palace, entitled the "House of the Woods," situated one and a half miles from the town, in a beautiful park—the drive to it is through ranges of stately forest trees. We were shown through the lovely dwellings, and invited to inscribe our names in the Queen's register. Much to our regret her Majesty happened to be in town at the time. From the Hague we went to Amsterdam, stopping by the way at Haarlem—saw and heard the world-renowned organ in the "Old Church of Bavon." I much admired its tones, especially when it most magnificently imitated a thunderstorm. In its tower I obtained a fine view of the town and its surroundings. In Amsterdam we quartered at the "Old Bible Hotel," where a large Bible is stationed in an open position directly above the public entrance. This city, though much larger, exhibits in some respects the same characteristies as those of Rotterdam and the Hague, only more so, that is, so far as shipping is concerned. Ships are made here. In company with President George A. Smith and party I went all through a monstrously large establishment of this kind in the "Dutch Marine" or Navy Yard of Amsterdam, where a new iron monitor was just launched, and where we saw the ponderous machinery at work with which the manufacture is accomplished. It was surprising to see sheets of solid iron, several inches in thickness, cut like cheese. We visited the King's Palace, which has a ball-room said to be the best in Europe—it is one hundred feet high, one hundred and twenty long and sixty in breadth. The cemetery is very neat—instead of raised or erect stones, the graves are covered with beautifully polished granite slabs laid prostrate—some of them very expensively and elaborately ornamented.

From Amsterdam we went to Antwerp, where we submitted our trunks and valises to the respectful examination of King Leopold's officers of customs; visited the great Cathedral of Antwerp—examined some of Rubens' celebrated paintings—one in particular, which is considered his master-piece, entitled "The Descent from the Cross." We also visited the "Church of St. Jacques," which contains the tomb of Rubens, over which is a painting, by himself, into which he has introduced a representation of himself, his two wives, his father and his son. From Antwerp we came to Brussels, where we arrived on the 7th. To-morrow we anticipate an omnibus ride to the field of the "Battle of Waterloo," and the next day we go to Paris.

With the exception of a little sea-sickness, and a cold taken on emerging from my steam-boat recess across the ocean, my health has been excellent, and, thus far, I have enjoyed the tour much beyond my expectations. Whatever I enjoy as a tourist, and whatever good I may accomplish, is attributable to the financiering and philanthropy of my beloved sisters, the noble ladies of Utah. This, wherever I am, is present with me. I wish to be remembered to them all in love, with a double portion to those dear young ladies who are honoring that most important position, the "Young Ladies' Retrenchment Organization." They are often in my thoughts, with my heart's earnest response—God bless them! Clara S. Little is a good, companionable girl, and I am very much at home with our party.

ELIZA R. SNOW.

LETTER XXII.

In Brussels—A Tour in Holland—Its Geographical Divisions—Naval and Mercantile Marine—Colonies—The Executive—The Legislature—Modes of Travel—Brick Roads—Canals—Annual Expense of Dykes—Lofty Buildings—Cleanliness—Mirrors in the Streets—Church Chimes—A Singular Custom—Births and Marriages—Dutch Country Houses—Gigantic Windmills—"Polders," how Produced—Public Schools.

BRUSSELS, Belgium, December 9th, 1872.

EDITOR OGDEN JUNCTION:

I am now in Belgium, after having made a brief and interesting tour through the principal cities of the kingdom of Holland. Some observations upon the general features of that remarkable country and its inhabitants, which I extract from my journal, I trust will not be uninteresting.

The kingdom of Holland is divided into nine provinces, embracing a population of three millions and a half, one third Roman Catholics and one hundred thousand Jews. On an average, each square mile is occupied by two hundred and seventy-seven inhabitants. The total area of their possessions in the East and West Indies amounts to six hundred and sixty thousand square miles, with a population of eighteen millions. The merchant fleet of Holland numbers above seven thousand vessels; two thousand five hundred of these carry on a traffic with distant parts of the world. Its army consists of sixty-one thousand men, besides thirty thousand which are distributed throughout the colonies. The Royal Navy consists of one hundred and ninety-two vessels of war of different descriptions.

The executive power consists of a State Council of twenty members, twelve of whom are nominated by the King. The legislative power comprises two chambers: the first consists of thirty-nine members elected by the provinces for a term of nine years, the second, of seventy-four members elected by the electors of the districts.

Their modes of travel by steamboats, railways and diligences, with respect to celerity, price and comfort, compare favorably with those of other countries. The roads in Holland are worthy of commendation. As stone does not abound in the country, small, well hardened bricks, one and a fourth inch thick, are employed as a substitute, forming an extremely hard surface, which is supposed to equal, if not to excel in point of excellence, that of our best macadamized. The first cost of the construction of these Dutch roads is estimated at about two thousand five hundred dollars per mile. They are but little travelled however, except by light vehicles, the main traffic being done upon their numerous canals, which intersect the country in every direction, enlivened with multitudes of barges, often drawn by small screw steamers.

The roads or streets flanking the canals are planted with trees, relieving in part the monotonous characteristic flatness of the country, and imparting to the landscape a beautiful and picturesque appearance. These canals serve, not only as means of communication between their towns and cities, but also to carry off from their arable lands, surplus water, and likewise answer in the place of hedges and walls, to enclose fields and gardens. The large canals, which are immediately connected with the sea, are closed at the point where they empty by massive floodgates, to prevent the encroachment of the sea when its level is lower than the water in the canals. The principal canals are sixty feet in width and sixty feet in depth. The great Northern Canal, connecting Amsterdam with the North Sea, is the broadest and deepest in Europe. This, however, will be surpassed by the one now in course of construction, connecting these two points by a shorter route, seventeen miles in length, and one hundred and ninety to three hundred and twenty feet in breadth, and twenty-three feet in depth.

I presume that Holland is the lowest country in the world, at least, the lowest of any in which I have travelled, the greater portion lying several feet below the sea level; much, therefore, of the security of the country depends upon dykes, or embankments. These dykes are not only required to prevent incursions of the sea, but rivers likewise, in consequence of the gradual and constant raising of their beds by alluvial deposits. Hence, one can scarcely imagine the enormous expense connected with these undertakings. The first principle to be observed in constructing a dyke is to make a massive and permanent foundation—it must be stamped and compressed to give it the necessary solidity; as much of this banking material is of such a soft, soapy, oozy nature, it requires immense patience and labor to consolidate it sufficiently.

A vast embankment was thrown up from the slimy beds in the vicinity of Amsterdam, which required forty years to settle it to a state of firm solidity. In the construction of these dykes, twigs of willows are used, interlaced one with another with elaborate skill, the interstices being filled with clay, in order to bind the whole in one solid mass. These are renewed, usually, every three years, being cultivated very extensively in all parts of the country for this purpose. The estimated annual expense of keeping these dykes in repair throughout Holland, is about two and a half millions of dollars.

Much difficulty is often experienced in forming permanent foundations for buildings. I noticed in the cities many structures of massive proportions, beautiful and magnificent, but sadly out of perpendicular, owing to imperfections of their substructures. The houses generally are lofty—built of small, red brick, the windows of imposing dimensions, and kept scrupulously clean, cleanliness being an admirable Dutch characteristic. Looking glasses are so arranged upon the outside of the windows that one can sit upon his or her cushioned chair, inside, and observe whatever is passing in the street without being seen. Some might object to this Dutch invention as a little too much one-sided amusement.

The chimes in the towers of the churches and other public buildings indicate the quarters of the hour by playing bars of some popular or operatic air, which highly amused us until its frequent repetition moderated the pleasure.

In some of the Dutch cities a singular custom prevails, viz.—fixing bulletins on their door-knockers where persons are sick, apprising their friends of their health, thus saving the trouble of knocking or ringing. The birth of a child is announced by a placard adorned with red silk and lace. The friends of the family on these interesting occasions are treated to wine and cinnamon cakes. Betrothals are celebrated by an immense consumption of "bridal sugar," or sweet cakes and spiced wine, called "bridal tears," very appropriate and amusing terms.

In passing through Holland, we frequently noticed beautiful villas and romantic country seats in the midst of parks and pleasure grounds occupied by Dutch gentry and merchants. Many of their dwellings bear inscriptions indicating the sentiments of the occupant, such as *Wel Tevreden* (Well Content); *Myn Genægen*, (My Satisfaction); *Vriends chap en Gezellschap*, (Frienship and Sociability); *Buiten Zorg*, (Without care). Many have much more lengthy titles.

Holland is full of windmills, some of which are of gigantic size, their sails often spreading one hundred feet in length. They are used for grinding corn, cutting tobacco, sawing timber, manufacturing paper and in transferring surplus water from low grounds into canals running upon higher elevations, which discharge it into the sea.

A great portion of the country has been reclaimed from rivers, morasses, lakes and seas; these "polders," or reclaimed lands are remarkably fertile, owing to various causes. In many instances during the winter season they are covered with water, thereby receiving additional vitality; the surplus water can be removed on the shortest notice. They afford an admirable and efficient system of irrigation. There are some remarkable features in the manner in which they produce these "polders." The first step in the process consists in surrounding the morass, or portion of the lake to be drained, with a dyke sufficient to prevent the admission of water from without. Then the water is removed by means of water wheels, constructed for the purpose, driven by windmills or steam engines. In some instances these lakes or morasses, to be reclaimed, are too low or deep to admit the water being at once transferred to the main canals, and conveyed off. In such cases a system of dykes, or embankments, one within another, each provided with a canal on its exterior, constituting an ascending series of levels, from the lower of which water is transferred to the higher, and finally into the main channel, whence it is carried into the ocean.

Holland is celebrated for its numerous private and public schools, and excellent arrangements for the general diffusion of knowledge among the lower classes.

We saw some of their schools, but our time was too

limited to investigate their educational system as would have been desirable.

Holland is also proverbial for her numerous charitable institutions.

LORENZO SNOW.

LETTER XXIII.

Brussels—Hard-worked Women—Feeding Horses with Coarse Bread—Field of Waterloo—Monument to the Prince of Orange—A Saying of Joseph Smith—A Genuine Relic of Waterloo.

BRUSSELS, Belgium, December 10th, 1872.

MY DEAR DAUGHTER:

We started this morning from our hotel, eight of us, in an omnibus, and drove through a considerable portion of the beautiful city of Brussels and its environs. We entered what is here termed a wood. About one half of the country is under cultivation, the remainder is covered with trees, much resembling the tall forest trees in the northern part of the State of Ohio. The open ground, except some newly plowed fields, was all green—thousands of acres covered with turnips, cabbage, kale and other vegetables. We saw women carrying large bundles of wood on their heads and one drawing a huge load of brush on a cart. Several others were guiding dogs that were attached to and drawing loaded carts. Our coachman called at an inn by the way, saying he wanted to feed his horses and give them some water. The food was slices of brown, coarse bread, which we tasted and pronounced tolerably good.

Soon after 12 o'clock we arrived at the battle field of Waterloo, where was fought, on the 18th of June, 1815, one of the most sanguinary battles recorded in history. About one hundred and fifty thousand men were engaged for about ten hours in destroying each other. They covered the country for miles with their dead, dying and wounded—both men and horses. It is said that more than thirty-five thousand men died on the field, and many died afterwards of their wounds. All of the privates who were killed in battle were buried where they fell—friends and foes, French, English, Dutch and Germans, who had slain each other, were mixed indiscriminately; and the fields where they lay are now cultivated, and we walked over them. On the spot where the Prince of Orange was wounded, in fair view of a large portion of the battle field, the Dutch government has erected a mound of earth, two hundred and forty feet high, on the top of which is a lion made of cast iron, cast in six parts, and weighing forty-eight thousand pounds. This lion is placed in a position which represents it looking towards France, which gives offence to many of the French people.

The view, from this height, of the battle field and its surroundings, is truly grand and beautiful; we enjoyed it much, although while there we were exposed to a pelting rain. While contemplating this scene, and the melancholy circumstances connected with it, my thoughts reverted to a saying of President Joseph Smith, while on an ancient Lamanite battle field, in Clark Co., Ohio, in 1834. "When a man of God is in a place where much blood has been shed, he will feel lonesome and depressed in spirits. This spot has been an ancient battle field, I know by my feelings." In a few moments we came to an immense mound of earth, sixty feet high, covering an acre of ground. This mound contained many human bones, and was, doubtless, like the Dutch monument of Waterloo, erected to perpetuate the memory and also to bury the dead of a great battle.

Our party consists of myself, Lorenzo Snow, Eliza R. Snow, Feramorz Little, Clara S. Little, Paul A. Schettler, George Dunford and Thomas Jennings.

I should have said that while we were walking over the ground on which the battle of Waterloo was fought, Thomas Jennings picked up a bullet which was lying on newly ploughed land, which is a genuine relic of the battle.

Your loving father,

GEORGE A. SMITH.

LETTER XXIV.

Antwerp, Its Maritime Trade—Cathedral of Notre Dame, Its Wonderful Chimes—The Museum—A Masterpiece of Rubens—The Royal Palace—Brussels, Paris in Miniature—Cathedral of St. Nicholas—Selling Wax Candles—A Catholic Devotee—A Singular Marriage Ceremony—Royal Operatic Theatre—National Palace—Hotel de Ville—Monument to Counts Egmont and Horn.

PARIS, France, December 12th, 1872.

EDITOR DESERET NEWS:

We arrived in the city of Antwerp, Belgium, 7th of December. It is one of the finest cities in the kingdom, embracing a population of 133,000. It is the principal seaport of the country, carrying on an extensive traffic with Great Britain and Germany. Among other objects of interest, we examined the celebrated cathedral, Notre Dame, 390 feet in length and 216 feet in width, the most magnificent gothic structure in Belgium. It was commenced in the middle of the thirteenth century, and completed one hundred years after. It is the only church in Europe that has six aisles. Its skilfully executed and elaborate carvings, numerous paintings by celebrated artists, Mosaic work of the finest description, marble statues of exquisite workmanship, gorgeous gildings, and decorations of the most costly character, altogether form a scene of great beauty and magnificence. The tower is 402 feet in height and is ascended by 622 steps. It affords a splendid view of the city and surrounding country. Its chimes are among the most complete in Belgium, consisting of 99 bells, the smallest of which is but fifteen inches in diameter, the largest weighs eight tons.

We also visited the Museum, containing a collection of 560 pictures, possessing great merit, the productions of celebrated masters. One of these by Rubens, which I consider the most perfect, particularly attracted my attention. It represents Christ crucified between two thieves; Longinus, the Roman officer, mounted on a grey horse, is piercing the Saviour's side with a lance; the penitent thief, a grey-haired man, is invoking the Saviour for the last time. In the foreground stands the Virgin mother, whom Mary, the wife of Cleophas, in vain endeavors to console. Farther back, St. John leans against the cross of the impenitent thief, weeping; Mary Magdalene on her knees, at the foot of the cross, implores Longinus to spare the sacred body of her master.

The whole is drawn with almost startling accuracy, indeed, I never saw a life scene on canvas so strikingly illustrated. The writhing agony of the impenitent malefactor, whose legs have just been broken by a Roman soldier, while on the contrary, the composed expression of the other, though worn by suffering—all depicted with such marvellous exactness impressed me for the moment with a feeling that I was witnessing the reality of this shocking scene.

Antwerp justly boasts of many public edifices of great beauty and magnificence. The royal palace, erected over 100 years ago in fantastic pompadour style, drew our attention, though perhaps failed to excite our admiration. This city has a splendid theatre, its interior handsomely decorated with paintings, and busts in marble and bronze of eminent composers and dramatists, among whom are Shakespeare, Moliere, Euripides, and Mozart. The Zoological Garden contains a fine collection of animals, which, with its garden and beautiful park, is considered one of the best in Europe.

We left Antwerp the following afternoon and arrived at Brussels in the evening.

Brussels is the capital of Belgium, the residence of the royal family, and contains a population of 170,000, only 6,000 of whom are Protestants. This city has many points of resemblance to Paris, the capital of France, so much so that it frequently is called "Paris in miniature." The majority of the citizens speak the French language; the Flemish is chiefly spoken by the lower classes.

As usual on entering Catholic cities, we paid our respects to its celebrated cathedrals, of which St. Nicholas is the most prominent. It is of Gothic structure, and presents an imposing appearance. Its interior embraces characteristics similar to other Catholic churches—images, elaborate carvings, fine marble statuary, sumptuous gildings, magnificent decorations, together with paintings in almost endless variety. Some have rather singular representations, such, for instance, as the "Expulsion from Paradise," done in carved wood, with great skill and at vast labor and expense. Among the beautiful foliage are seen all kinds of animals—a bear, dog, cat, eagle, vulture, peacock, owl, dove, squirrel, and lastly an ape eating an apple. These are surmounted by the Virgin with the Child, who crushes the head of the serpent with the cross.

In one of these churches, an old lady was holding a stock of wax candles, some of which she insisted on our purchasing, that we might burn them for the benefit of our dead friends. In another we saw a gentleman of respectable appearance doing penance in a prostrate position upon the floor of the church, before the cross and image of the Saviour, kissing the stone pavement with great fervor, and wetting it with tears. I imagined he might have committed in secret some great crime; I may have failed to do him justice.

In one of these cathedrals we witnessed a Catholic wedding which was quite amusing—the bride and groom were kneeling before the altar, a priest with sacerdotal robes, with open Bible, wax tapers, and three silver goblets of wine, was performing the marriage ceremony, reading a sentence or two, repeatedly kissing the cross and quaffing the wine, waving his hands and pronouncing Latin, while in the background a little boy in a white gown, walking to and fro, swinging slowly, then rapidly, a small censer with smoking incense, accompanied with an occasional jingle of a bell. In the evening we attended the Royal Operatic Theatre, the most noted in Brussels, and the finest and most richly finished and artistically decorated I ever visited. The parquette was furnished with cushioned chairs, elegantly made and sufficient room to pass without annoyance. Its six-tiered gallery, with elaborate carvings and splendid gildings, presented a grand appearance. I think the performances could not be surpassed.

We visited the National Palace, where the sessions of the Senate and Representatives are held, and were conducted through the various apartments. The Senate Hall is embellished with fifteen portraits of celebrated Belgians. These two halls had the appearance of comfort and convenience, rather than display.

The Hotel de Ville, the City Hall, the most remarkable edifice in Brussels, has a graceful tower of 386 feet in height: on the summit of its spire is a figure in bronze of Michael, the Archangel, eighteen feet high. A portion of this hall is occupied by the City Council of Brussels, comprising thirty-one members. We noticed some magnificent tapestry 400 years old, and a basin with the keys of the city made of beaten gold and silver 200 years ago. In front of this hall stands a magnificent monument of Counts Egmont and Horn, who were unjustly executed by the notorious Duke of Alva, June 5th, 1568. A portion of this colossal structure contains figures in bronze representing the two Counts on their way to execution. In the Hotel de Ville, we ascended by a winding staircase to the summit of its lofty tower, where we enjoyed a magnificent view of Brussels and its environs—a fatiguing luxury. Also from this lofty height may be seen in the distance the "Lion Monument," a vast mound upon the battle field of Waterloo, erected in commemoration of the great victory won by the allied powers under the Duke of Wellington.

We visited that memorable locality about ten miles distant from Brussels, spending several hours walking over the fields, still bearing traces of those bloody struggles, examining many points and localities of intense interest; but I will defer this subject for the present.

We left Brussels, Wednesday, December 11, and arrived in Paris the same evening.

LORENZO SNOW.

LETTER XXV.

Paris—Visit to Versailles—Bois de Boulogne—St. Cloud—Attend the National Assembly—French Glory, Bruises and Scars—Interview with the President of the French Republic.

Paris, France, December 18th, 1872.

Editor Deseret News:

We are pleasantly situated at the "Hotel de Petersbourg," in the beautiful city of Paris, the capital of lovely, sunny France. Too much cannot be said of the beauty and magnificence of this wonderful city. I will not attempt, at present, to describe all that we have seen of its beauty and grandeur. I have just returned from promenading some of its principal streets, viewing it in its evening splendor, lit up with thirty-two thousand gas burners.

Yesterday we visited Versailles, some twelve miles from Paris. We passed through the forest of Boulogne, admiring the delightful picturesque scenery bordering on the river Seine, passing through a variegated country until we reached St. Cloud, where we alighted from our carriages and walked over the ground where the Prussians planted their artillery to bombard the city of Paris, and where many thousands were slain during the late bloody contest. Every building, except the Cathedral, had been demolished; this was preserved by a body of Prussians, who had been stationed there through the reverential feeling, perhaps, of the Prussian Emperor.

At Versailles we enjoyed magnificent views, comprising

objects of almost infinite variety. To me, however, our visit to the National Assembly, then in session, was the most interesting, with the exception of our interview with Monsieur Thiers, the President of the French Republic, which I will describe presently. The National Assembly comprises 758 deputies, elected by their respective districts in 1871, constituting only a provisional government. How long they may feel disposed to hold office, or the vaccilating minds of the people to sustain them, the future will reveal. The political prospects of France are shrouded in fearful mystery—at any moment the most terrible scenes may burst upon the country! The National Assembly convenes in that portion of the palace formerly occupied as a theatre, when Versailles was revelling in regal pride and splendor. We owed the privilege of admission to the President of the Assembly, through the request of Monsieur Bartholemy St. Hilaire, private secretary to M. Thiers, to whom we had been introduced by Major Lorin. We were accorded seats appropriated to foreign diplomats and embassadors, an honor we appreciated and duly acknowledged. The grave, sedate, dignified, bald-headed appearance of this great body of French deputies was rather prepossessing. We spent about an hour in listening to their eloquent and animated speeches. I have alluded to Major Lorin—this gentleman distinguished himself as a French officer in the battles fought against Austria and Italy, also in many bloody conflicts between the French and Prussians. In the late war he commanded about three thousand men. On the establishment of peace only forty-seven remained; the others were either killed or disabled. The Major was covered with French glory—scars and bruises. We had formed an acquaintance with this gentleman, and while visiting Versailles he proposed to present our cards to President Thiers and procure us an audience. We accepted the proposition and drove up to the palace of M. Thiers. In a few minutes the Major returned, accompanied by the President's private secretary, who politely stated that M. Thiers would be happy to receive President Smith and party at half past nine, p. m.

We repaired to the palace at the hour designated. M. Bartholemy St. Hilaire conducted us to the reception hall and introduced us to President Thiers. He was attended by a number of distinguished French gentlemen, principally his cabinet ministers, anxious and curious to witness the interview between the President of the French Republic and the delegation from the Latter-day Saints in Utah, *en route* to Palestine. Mr. Thiers' personal appearance impressed us favorably—his dignified bearing, plain and unassuming manners, with a countenance glowing with benevolence and patriotism. He possesses the reputation of being a good English scholar, but I presume the vast crowd of business of late years has allowed him no time to practise the English language, therefore the conversation was carried on in French, Major Lorin acting as interpreter.

After the introduction, President Smith acknowledged our appreciation of the honor accorded to himself and party, in granting this interview—that we were from Utah, *en route* to Palestine to study the Bible in the land where its recorded events had chiefly transpired—that we sympathized with the President of the French Republic in the great cause he is laboring to establish—a Republic in France, and had sought this occasion of expressing our sentiments personally.

Upon this being interpreted, President Thiers replied that he was gratified with such assurances from Americans, and pleased to meet this delegation from Utah, and that he was familiar with the history of our people. President Smith remarked that we had been twenty-five years laboring under every possible disadvantage to colonize that portion of our American desert, in order to make a destitute people great and prosperous; that in connection with other objects relating to our tour, we wished to gather information and statistics of the progress of older nations, that through their experience we might more successfully benefit and improve the people we represented.

President Thiers replied that, while we remained in France, he should take pleasure in rendering any assistance we might require in the promotion of this object.

We acknowledged our appreciation of this courtesy. President Smith thanked him for favors extended to American citizens since the establishment of the French Republic.

President Thiers replied that he hoped the peaceful relations now existing between the two governments would never be interrupted.

The interview closed in the following words by President Smith—"President Thiers, God bless you."

These words inspired M. Thiers with renewed interest—he requested the Major to give a literal translation of that expression. The honesty, simplicity and earnestness in which this sentiment was delivered by President Smith, not only excited pleasurable emotion in M. Thiers, but also were visible in the features of his ministers who were now crowding around.

President Thiers cordially shook hands with President Smith and each one of our party. We then retired, repaired to our carriages and returned to Paris the same evening.

Shortly after this interview, the circumstance of our reception was published in several of the French papers.

Please accept my regards for yourself and family.

LORENZO SNOW.

LETTER XXVI.

Paris—Destruction of the Commune—Palace of the Louvre—Relics of Napoleon First—Napoleonic Rule in France—French Aristocracy—Magnificent Improvements—Champs Elysees—Garden of the Tuileries—Garden of the Luxembourg—The Palace of Versailles—The Finest Hall in the World—Memories of Louis XVI—Le Grand Monarque—An Aristocratic Gambling Saloon—Bed-chamber of Three Queens—Fifty Miles of Parks and Gardens—Extract from the Paris "American Register"—Poetry—"Farewell to Paris."

PARIS, France, December 19th, 1872.

EDITOR DESERET NEWS:

We arrived in Paris 11th December. This city contains a population of about two millions. It is situated upon a plain on both sides of the Seine. The surrounding country presents but little diversity in its physical appearance, being generally level except upon the north and northeast, where it rises into low hills. Many portions of Paris still bear traces of the vandalism and terrible destruction by the Communists in their attempt to overthrow the National Government, and several places which we visited bear witness of cruel and bloody deeds. The Palace of the Tuileries, once so famous for its beauty and magnificence, now lies in a mass of ruins, and must long remain a silent witness of the horrors of those fearful times.

The Palace Royal, Palace of the Legion of Honor, Hotel de Ville, Library of the Louvre, besides numerous other public buildings, together with many private edifices were totally destroyed. The celebrated Column Vendome, once a boasted specimen of monumental beauty, has nothing left but its foundation.

We visited the Palace of the Louvre, famous for its immense collection of paintings, sculptures, and Egyptian and Roman antiquities. This pile of buildings embraces several miles of galleries, forming fifteen distinct museums, the most extensive in the world. The galleries of paintings contain nearly one thousand eight hundred and fifty pictures, many of them by the most celebrated artists, costing immense sums of money. One of these called the "Conception," the production of Murillo, is said to have cost over one hundred thousand dollars. In the Salle de l'Empereur, we were shown some of the relics of Napoleon First—the clothes he wore on ceremonial occasions, the hat worn in the campaign of 1814, also the hat worn at St. Helena, and the handkerchief which he used on his death bed. These mementoes occasioned curious reflections. Our guide, who spoke English fluently, took this opportunity to enlighten us respecting his own opinions of the merits of the Bonapart dynasty. He said that Napoleon First accomplished much for the honor and glory of France in military achievements, but that Napoleon Third had greatly excelled him by making vast improvements of a national character—expending immense sums for this purpose—exhausting his own as well as the public treasury in furnishing the laboring classes employment. That under his reign the interests of working people had always been studied, that peace and plenty, like streams of water, had flowed in every direction. On the contrary, since the establishment of the Republic, things had taken a wrong direction—general improvement had stopped, leaving the laboring classes without employment and the means of subsistence; therefore, to the majority of the people, especially to the working classes, the restoration of the Bonapart dynasty would not be unwelcome.

The aristocracy of the French are highly educated,

whereas the lower orders scarcely possess a knowledge of the ordinary branches taught in the common schools in America, being very ignorant, and yet ambitious to acquire wealth. They are unwilling to employ time in searching into the real causes of political evils and disabilities, but in proportion as they *feel* the blessings of political prosperity or the misery of adversity they pronounce judgment upon the merits or demerits of government, or the ruling powers.

We observed many magnificent improvements made by the direction of the late Emperor. Palaces had been reconstructed and enlarged in behalf of the national interests, ornamental monuments and triumphal arches, illustrative of the achievements of the French nation. Streets had been widened and beautified, and spacious thoroughfares formed through old and crowded localities. We were told that one thousand buildings, at vast labor and expense, were removed for this purpose.

Paris abounds in spacious grounds for promenades, public gardens, and extensive parks. The Bois de Boulogne, a fashionable promenade of the Parisians, embraces an area of about two thousand, one hundred and fifty acres. We passed through a part of this on our way to Versailles. The Champs Elysees contain many delightful parterres with choice shrubs, flowers, and fountains throwing up sparkling, silvery sprays. The Garden of the Tuileries is exceedingly attractive. It has many beautiful fountains with jets and orange trees, and fine statuary. The Garden of the Luxembourg has a large octagonal basin surrounded by flower beds and grass plats, flanked by terraces, and adorned with numerous statuary. We noticed another fountain in this garden, in the form of an oblong basin, surrounded by rows of plane trees. It has three niches separated by Doric columns. The central niche contains a group of marble figures representing Polyphemus, with one knee on a rock, in the attitude of slaying Acis and Galatea. The summer season would have afforded a better opportunity for enjoying these delightful scenes, but a Parisian climate, even in winter, in "sunny France," is frequently favorable for these enjoyments.

In my last I mentioned our visit to Versailles, the National Assembly, and our interview with President Thiers, but do not feel fully satisfied without some further reference to its objects of interest and curiosity.

Eleven years were occupied in building the Palace of Versailles, for which an army of workmen were employed and immense sums of money expended in overcoming the obstacles of nature, in erecting its massive buildings, and constructing and ornamenting the gardens and pleasure grounds.

Louis XIV held his court in this palace with such brilliancy that it became the general rendezvous of the French aristocracy. It was finally converted, after many years, into a great National gallery for works of art, illustrative of the military glory of France. One of the numerous halls is called "Galerie des Glaces," the finest in the world—two hundred and thirty-nine feet long and thirty-five feet in width. In this hall, during the siege of Paris, the King of Prussia, surrounded by the representatives of all the German sovereigns, and the chief officers of his government and of the army, formally assumed the title of German Emperor.

The "Salle du Conseil" is entered from this hall, where Monsieur de Breze came to announce to Louis XVI the refusal of the deputies to disperse, and the memorable words of Mirabeau—"We are here by the will of the people, and we will only disperse at the point of the bayonet." From this hall we passed into the apartment where "Le Grand Monarque" died. It is lavishly decorated, and the furniture remains in the same condition as at the King's death. The bed is that on which he died.

We passed into the "Salon de Paix," the card-room

in which Madame de Montespan is said to have lost, in one night, over one million, six hundred thousand dollars. From this room a door leads to the bed chamber which was occupied by the three Queens, Marie Theresa, Marie Leczinska, and Marie Antoinette. At six o'clock on the morning of the 6th of October, 1789, the Queen, asleep in this chamber, was aroused by the cries of the guard that her life was in danger. Escaping from this room she hastened to join the King, whom she found in the "Salle du Conseil." They at once appeared, with their children, on the balcony of the King's bed chamber, from which he addressed the incensed and furious mob which had crowded into the court below.

The paintings and sculpture consist of representations of the most remarkable events in the history of France, especially the victories won by military valor, including those gained by Napoleon Third. The portraits are those of the admirals, constables, marshals and many other distinguished officers of different periods, who have contributed to the glory of the nation. Many of these paintings are of immense value.

The park, including the gardens, is nearly fifty miles in circumference, adorned with marble statuary of exquisite workmanship, ornamental trees, beautiful parterres and magnificent fountains.

The original cost of this royal palace, with its splendid surroundings, is reported to have been about two hundred millions of dollars. With these observations, I close the subject.

LORENZO SNOW.

FROM THE PARIS "AMERICAN REGISTER."

On Tuesday last the Mormon party, now passing through Europe on their way to Palestine, visited Versailles and were received in the evening by M. Thiers. The Hon. George A. Smith, leader of the party, gave the President a curious and interesting account of Mormonism in the United States, and stated that the sect which he represents is already composed of about 120,000 members. Mr. Smith and his party started for Lyons on Thursday, and leave that city to-day for Marseilles, where, after remaining a couple of days, they will proceed to Nice.

Although the Mormon party at present in France disclaim any other motive than that of pleasure and instruction for their proposed visit to Palestine, it is asserted by some who profess to be well informed, that they are going there to explore the ground for the foundation of a new Jerusalem. We see nothing improbable in this assumption. The people who created a paradise in Salt Lake may well aim at founding an Eden in the land of prophets.

The long interview which the Mormon elders had with the French President, the other day, has, we are informed, seriously disquieted Madame Thiers. Surely at the President's advanced time of life there is no fear of his conversion to Mormon doctrines. As Thiers was born April 16, 1797, and, consequently, will be 76 years of age in April next, we sincerely sympathize with Madame in her alarm.

FAREWELL TO PARIS.

Farewell great Paris, soon I go
   Upon the morning train;
I go where softer breezes blow
   On land and wat'ry main.

I'm going now, and as I leave
   I take a parting view,
And see the web of distance weave
   That separates from you.

Your spires that glitter in the sun
   Above "The Arch of Time,"
Are disappearing one by one:
   I hear no church bell chime.

Gay Paris, beautiful e'en now
   Bereft of much you boast;
Tho' Prussia aim'd your pride to bow
   'Twas Paris hurt you most.

War demons 'roused in foreign lands
   Can never wield the power
As when, by suicidal hands,
   Commissioned to devour.

Of all the ills of human life
   That mighty nations cursed,
The warfare of internal strife
   And carnage is the worst.

Your ruined palaces and halls,
   Scathed by fraternal hate,
Are sad mementos—each recalls
   Your folly and your fate.

M. Thiers, with wise sagacity,
   The dire result foresaw
If France, with blind temerity,
   The battle-axe should draw.

>   He now presides. Will France sustain
>   His policy of peace,
>   Or in a vortex plunge again
>   Where waste and crime increase?
>
>   Fair, lovely Paris! What shall be
>   Your future, who can tell?
>   Your lofty spires no more I see—
>   Again I say, farewell!
>
>   ELIZA R. SNOW.

LETTER XXVII.

Brussels—Theatre Royal—Church of St. Michael and Gudule—Visit to a Lace Factory—Houses of Parliament—Hotel de Ville—Waterloo and the Farm of Hougomont—Arrival at Paris—Call upon the American Minister—Visit to Palaces—Notre Dame—Opinion of Utah Silk—Visit the Common Schools—Go to Versailles—Bois de Boulogne—Visit the President of the French Republic—Arrival at Lyons—Silk Factories and Cocooneries.

Hotel de L'Europe, Lyons, France,
December 20, 1872.

Editors Salt Lake Herald:

My last letter to you was dated Brussels, December 8th. On the evening of that day we visited the finest theatre in Brussels, called "Theatre Royal de la Monnaie," and witnessed the performance of the beautiful opera "L'Africaine." Next morning we went to the largest church in Brussels, St. Michael and Gudule, containing some of Rubens' best paintings. Thence to a lace factory which employs about 3,000 women, most of whom, however, work at home and earn from one to two and a half francs per day for twelve hours work, which is very hard on the eyes. After that we went through the Houses of Parliament, which are very elegantly furnished, contain some most excellent paintings of this century, and are quite extensive, considering the size of the kingdom of Belgium. There are seats for 124 representatives and 62 senators. After lunch we went to the old Town Hall, commenced in 1402, and ascended the tower, which is 404 feet high, and from which very fine views over the city and its environs can be obtained, even to the battle-field of Waterloo; but it rained pretty hard when we arrived at the top of the tower, and consequently we saw but little.

Tuesday, the 10th, we spent in a visit to Waterloo, leaving our hotel at 9.45 a. m., and arriving there at noon. We procured a guide, who talked English with a pretty strong French accent, but who was well posted in the history of the battle, and gave us a great deal of interesting information. We visited the celebrated farm of Hougomont, where the first shot was fired at 11.30 a. m., the Lion Monument, etc., and returned to Brussels in a heavy rain shower.

December 11th we took train for Paris at 9 a. m., arrived in the capital of "la belle France" at 5.30 p. m. We put up at the Hotel St. Petersbourg, 25 Rue Caumartin, and received a number of letters from our friends at home, dated up to November 23rd, and four numbers of your semi-weekly to the same date, which President Albert Carrington had forwarded according to arrangements made with him. We all felt glad to hear from "home, sweet home," as the news was generally of a very satisfactory nature. Our first visit next morning was to call upon our Minister, Mr. Washburne. He being still absent, his son, who is secretary of legation, received us kindly, and furnished a passport to Mr. George Dunford, who was not provided with one. After returning to the hotel we took a walk with our ladies to the beautiful "Place de la Concorde," thence through the Garden of the Tuileries to the Palace of the Tuileries and to the Louvre. A great portion of the Tuileries, which were plundered and burned by the Commune, is still in ruins and presents a rather melancholy appearance. The collection of paintings, statuary and other works of art in the Louvre is very large, and it would take weeks to go through the galleries, and study everything that is exhibited. Friday the 18th, we called at the banking house of Messrs. Marcuard, Andre & Co., to whom President George A. Smith had a letter of introduction from Mr. Ralston, cashier of the Bank of California. Mr. Andre gave to President Smith a letter of introduction to Mr. Husson, General Director of the Educational Department of the District of the Seine, who also received us with much courtesy, and instructed the Superintendent of the Paris schools to show us around in all the schools of the city that we desired to visit. In the afternoon we drove to the Palace of the Luxembourg, where the legislative assembly met for about a hundred years back, but since the late war that body occupies a former theatre at Versailles. Saturday we spent a part of the day at the Church of Notre Dame, where we were shown through the treasury chamber of the church, which contains several dozen of the most magnificent gold embroidered robes, to be used by the priests of the church on certain occasions, also the bloody garments of several of the bishops of Paris, who had been shot by the Commune.

On the 15th I visited several parties who were interested in sericulture, in company of Mr. George Dunford, to whom I had letters of introduction from Mr. L. A. Bertrand, and they pronounced the samples of cocoons which I had brought along from home of very excellent quality, and expressed the opinion that this branch of industry would prove to our people an almost inexhaustible gold mine. In the afternoon some of our party visited the botanical and zoological gardens.

Monday, the 16th, the principal clerk of the Educational Department, Mr. Chasteauneuf, who speaks English pretty well, called at our hotel to take us to some of the primary schools of the city. At the first one we visited, we met the Inspector of the Paris schools, who together with Mr. Chasteauneuf exerted himself to give us all the information we desired, and accompanied us to all the places which we visited during the day. The principal of the first school, Mr. Charles Barbier, had 350 scholars under his charge, from six to about fourteen years old, and had adopted a new system, originated in his own brain, to teach history and geography, by making his scholars draw the maps of France during the different periods of history, on the walls, which they now permanently adorn, and keep that history before the eyes of his pupils. On our entrance to each different class, the scholars arose and saluted us in military manner. They receive lessons in gymnastics and military drilling twice a week, in order to prepare all the male population of France for another attack of a neighboring enemy. Their lunch time having arrived, they all repaired to a large room on the first floor, where their lunch baskets, all named and numbered, were waiting, under each boy's seat, for an attack on the half bottle of wine and bread and butter which they generally contained. Everything was clean and tidy, no scribbling, no whittling, because, as the teacher remarked, they did not allow anything of the kind. The other schools which we visited were all conducted on similar principles, one of them, conducted by a Mrs. Lecroix, having 120 little girls and boys, from two to six years of age, under her charge, who treated us to a couple of nice songs; and another school conducted by friars. Tuesday, 17th, drove to Versailles, taking a couple of English speaking guides. We passed through the Bois de Boulogne, or Woods of Boulogne, and stopped a short time at St. Cloud, to walk through a few streets and see the terrible destruction which the Prussians had made on their retreat from Paris. Our guide, having learned who we were, proposed to get us an interview with President Thiers. We rather liked the suggestion, though we were not prepared to appear in full dress, and accordingly drove up in front of the government department. Our guide went inside to make inquiries if we could be admitted, but President Thiers was engaged in a council, and sent his private secretary, Mr. I Bartholemy St. Hilaire, member of the House of Representatives, to our carriage, to tell us that he was sorry that he could not receive us now, as he was engaged, but he would be pleased to see us at 9.30 p. m. We left our cards and visited the palace, to which we were admitted through a card of Mr. I. B. St. Hilaire, on which he wrote in pencil, to facilitate our seeing the palace, the gardens, and the hall of Assembly. When this card was presented to Mr. Jule Grevy, President of the Assembly, he gave orders to seat us in the gallery of the Diplomatic Corps, facing the President and the Speaker. In the evening we called at President Thiers', and were admitted at 10.15 p. m. He was surrounded by his cabinet and members of the Assembly. President Thiers felt sorry that he could not converse in English, and our guide had to do the interpreting between him and President Smith. When we left he shook hands with all of us, and wished us a pleasant journey. President Smith wished him a hearty "God bless you."

Thursday, the 19th, at 11 a. m., we left Paris per express train for Lyons, 319 miles distance, and reached here at 10.15 p.m., stopping at the Hotel de l'Europe. To-day I called with a letter from my friend L. A. Bertrand on Mr. Jacquemet Bonnefont, dealer in seeds, who has large mulberry plantations and cocooneries in Annonay. His agent took great pleasure in taking our party to several silk establishments, where we saw the manufacture of all kinds of silk and velvet ; also the weaving of portraits. We bought a few of President Thiers, General Washington and Mr. Jacquard, the inventor of that machine. I showed him a photograph I had with me of President B. Young, and he said he would have it set up, and weave it, to be ready in about three or four months. He sells these portraits, which are 5 1-2 by 7 1-2 inches, at ten francs, or about two dollars apiece. To-morrow I intend going to Annonay, to visit the cocooneries and mulberry plantations of Messrs. Jacquemet Bonnefont & Sons, while the rest of our party will continue sight-seeing here in Lyons.

We are all in the enjoyment of good health, and nothing has occurred to mar our peace.

Yours as ever,

PAUL A. SCHETTLER.

LETTER XXVIII.

The Religions of France—Marriage a Civil Contract—The Concordat—Convents in Paris—The Educational System—Number of Births in Paris—Illegitimacy—Working Classes—Paupers—Prisons—The Supreme Power, Where Vested—The Standing Army.

Lyons, France, December 20th, 1872.

Editor Deseret News:

We left Paris yesterday morning and arrived in this city the following evening. Before I close my observations upon our visit to Paris, allow me to extract a few more items from my journal.

The religion of France is principally Roman Catholic. The Reformed Calvinistic, the Lutheran, and Jewish churches, are recognized and sustained by the State. The masses of the people, however, profess the Catholic religion, which is eminently the acknowledged religion of the Government. The principal festivals of the Catholics are observed as public holidays, when public prayers are ordered; the authorities are supposed to be Catholics, and are expected to attend these ceremonies, yet no processions are allowed outside the walls of a Catholic church in towns where there are churches of a different order of worship.

Marriage is made a civil contract, and no religious celebration of marriage is allowed until the civil contract has been entered into before the Mayor. The registers of baptisms, marriages and burials, kept by the church, are not received as evidence in lieu of the like registers, kept by the Mayor.

The Concordat, which was arranged with the Pope, by Napoleon Bonaparte on the restoration of the Christian worship, still regulates the government of the church. Its main object is to place the church entirely under the control of the state. The government nominates the archbishops and bishops, the Pope then confers the canonical honors. The bishops appoint the priests, subject to the approval of the government. No communication from the papal court, no doctrinal decision or formula can be published or taught, no council held, no change in the discipline introduced, unless sanctioned by the government. The Lutheran, like the Catholic, churches, are under the control of the state. The appointment and removal of pastors must be confirmed by the government. The same also in respect to all protestant churches in France—the state exercises more or less influence and control.

In Paris there are over thirty convents, principally of nuns, ostensibly engaged in the education of young ladies in the relief of sick and indigent persons, besides other useful employments. We saw them attending the sick in hospitals, in private dwellings, and engaged in superintending schools for the poor, which impressed us favorably in their behalf.

The national schools are also under the control of the government, and are divided into three classes or general de-

departments—" Instruction Superieure," " Instruction Secondaire," and " Instruction Primaire." These departments are governed by a Supreme Council of Public Instruction, composed of five bishops or archbishops, three senators, three councilors of state, three members of the Court of Cassation, three ministers belonging to the Lutheran Reformed and Jewish creeds, five members of the Institute, eight inspector generals and two heads of private establishments of instruction. All the members of this council are nominated by the government for one year.

About seven thousand students are now attending in the superior department. In the primary department the total number of pupils is nearly two hundred thousand. President Smith obtained an introduction to the Prefecteur General of the Department of the Seine, who courteously accorded us the privilege of visiting and inspecting these national institutions. We were conducted by the secretary and public inspector, Mr. Charles Barbier, into several departments, and examined minutely the course of studies and discipline, methods of teaching, arrangement of desks, seats, &c., and lastly their gymnastic exercises. Every explanation and facility were afforded that we required for obtaining statistics and the information we sought. The government is very strict, approaching to that of military discipline. We admired the industry and general neatness conspicuous in every department.

One of these primary schools consisted of four hundred and fifty boys, from ten to fourteen years of age, divided into branches, each numbering from seventy to one hundred, occupying separate rooms in the same building. We noticed that the seats and desks exhibited no signs of whittling propensities in the occupants. I remarked to the superintendent that I supposed his young students were prohibited penknives, upon which he ordered the school to hold up their knives, when, to our great amusement, two-thirds of the boys presented to view this article of pocket furniture; this experiment was repeated in two other departments with like results. These seats and desks had been occupied seven years without mark or blemish, a high encomium on school discipline.

On intimating our wishes to witness their gymnastics, the superintendent ordered his school of eighty boys to retire to a capacious hall, where they performed in a masterly manner several courses of exercise consisting of military evolutions. A sentiment expressed on the occasion, by President Smith, that these young gentlemen, at some future period, might be able to "put the Prussians through," was highly relished by the superintendent. In all the national schools, I think these gymnastic exercises throughout are characteristically military, giving tone to the martial spirit and military ambition of the French nation.

After spending several hours in these public schools, we returned to our hotel fully satisfied with our visit.

A few items of social statistics might be interesting. In 1869, the last census returns show the number of births in the capital to be some above 54,000; still-born children 4,500; deaths 45,872; marriages 18,948. Of the children born 15,306 were illegitimate; of these 3,059 were acknowledged by their parents.

About one half of the population of Paris are working people; 15,000 are paupers; 21,000 patients are always in hospitals, and four times as many pass through them in the course of the year. The population of the prisons is about 5,000. It is a remarkable fact, that families constantly residing in Paris, after a while become extinct.

The supreme power in France is vested in a National Assembly elected in February, 1871, during the armistice signed with Prussia for this object. M. Thiers was elected President at the sitting of the Assembly by acclamation. His powers of government depend on the will of the Assembly. The country remains without a constitution. The common routine of business is ordinarily transacted according to former usages, though not expressly confined to any particular programme.

A few days since, a petition was circulating in the cafes of Paris, requesting the members of the National Assembly to resign. The police, however, soon suppressed these proceedings.

The standing army of France is about a half million— in every part of the country we meet soldiers promenading in military costume.

The laws, usages, all the internal operations, together with the great mass of officials, previously in existence under the monarchy, still remain nearly the same. At present, the French republic does not venture upon many material or radical changes.

France receives her republic like an ancient aristocratical household its new lord, looking for no changes of servants nor lessening of fees or emoluments, neither alterations in its anciently established usages and customs.

How long this ancient house and its new lord will continue to maintain amicable relations, we leave the future to illustrate.

LORENZO SNOW.

LETTER XXIX.

From Paris to Lyons—Burgundy and its Wines—Famous Towns—Fontainebleau—Lyons and its Silk Industries—Thirty-one Thousand Silk Looms—Weaving Portraits—Beautiful Marseilles—An Amphitheatre 1,800 Years Old—Roman Relics—Olive Plantations and Vineyards—The Mediterranean.

MARSEILLES, France, December 23, 1872.

EDITOR DESERET NEWS:

Our route from Paris to Lyons lies through a beautiful and interesting country, abounding in orchards and vineyards, many of the latter being very extensive. The district of Burgundy, so much celebrated for its excellent wines, embraces an area of 224,223 acres, all in vineyards. These vines are trained upon stakes three feet high, being more thickly set than is commonly practised elsewhere. Their yield differs according to the soil and quality of the vine, some yielding as high as one thousand gallons per acre. Immense quantities of these Burgundy wines are transported annually to foreign countries. They are highly prized by amateur consumers, being considered superior to most other wines in point of flavor and delicious quality. The price of the genuine Burgundy wines where they are manufactured will average about one dollar per gallon.

The value of these products, in this district is, annually, in the neighborhood of ten millions of dollars. We were told that the longest duration of the finest wines capable of preservation does not exceed twelve or fifteen years from the season they are made; after that time they decline instead of improve. Some, however, may be kept twenty years, but such wines are considered of an ordinary quality.

Wine in France is a common beverage, as much so as cider in our Eastern States. It is always placed upon the tables, and all are supposed to be judges of its merits, and to require its enlivening influences.

We passed many towns famous in history for memorable battles fought in their vicinity, or stirring events which have occurred within their walls. Fontainebleau, about forty miles from Paris, is remarkable for the great battle fought in Feb. 1814, in which the allies were signally beaten by the French under Napoleon. We stopped but a short time at this place.

We passed many elegant mansions, beautiful country seats, chateaux and towns—some of the latter very antique, embracing ancient castles and fortifications crumbling to pieces, or lying in ruins. We also passed many lovely vales encircled in the distance by low ranges of picturesque hills covered with vineyards and olive orchards, the latter still clothed in rich green foliage. Among these romantic hills, here and there a beautiful villa appears, with its white chapel surmounted by a modest, graceful tower.

We reached Lyons on the evening of the 19th, distant from Paris about 300 miles.

Lyons is the second city of France, with a population of about three hundred and twenty-five thousand. It is celebrated for its silk manufactures; in quality and variety they are considered superior to any others in the world. In the city and vicinity there are over 31,000 silk looms. Immense numbers of laborers are employed in the business. We visited some of these establishments and were amused and interested in witnessing the skill and ingenuity manifested. Portraits, groups of people and also landscapes were woven in silk with as much accuracy in delineation of face and figure as when done by the most skilful artist with paint and brush. We purchased a few specimens of their weaving, including exquisitely beautiful handkerchiefs, portraits of eminent personages, George Washington, M. Thiers, and other distinguished individuals. We showed the proprietor of the establishment a photograph of President Brigham Young, and on his proffering to weave the portrait, President Smith made an arrangement to have a supply in readiness on our return from Palestine.

We engaged carriages and drove through the principal streets, park and suburbs of the city. We saw remains of walls, fortifications and buildings constructed in past ages by the Romans, together with other objects of curiosity and historic interest. We had a splendid view of the hills of Savoy and also of Mont Blanc, one hundred miles distant, clothed in perpetual snows.

We left Lyons by train, on the 21st, *en route* for Marseilles. We passed through many towns and cities of great antiquity, celebrated for remains of architectural relics, attesting their former greatness and splendor. In the town of Arlis is a vast amphitheatre, supposed to have been built 1,800 years ago, now lying in magnificent ruins. It is 459 feet long and 338 feet broad, it had 43 rows of seats and could accommodate 25,000 people. The walls, to a considerable extent, are broken down, together with some of its towers. In former years, during the wars, it was occupied as a fortress.

In several parts of this ancient town the ground is strewed with Roman relics, entablatures, broken down columns, &c.

We arrived in Marseilles, about 200 miles distant from Lyons, in the evening, and stopped at the Hotel du Louvre et de la Paix—a very fine establishment.

This city contains 300,000 inhabitants, and is considered the finest seaport in France. Its harbor is formed by an inlet of the sea, extending into the heart of the city, covering an extent of seventy acres, and will accommodate 1,200 vessels. We found numerous objects of interest and attraction. No finer streets can be found in any city of Europe—they are broad and many of them bordered with ornamental trees. The park is extensive and the public gardens and promenades are romantic and enchanting to lovers of cultivated nature. To fully enjoy the smiling sun and balmy air of beautiful Marseilles, and also to avail ourselves of an opportunity for gratifying curiosity and gaining information, we perambulated the city. The gardens and parks were ornamented with rich and costly shrubbery, grass plats tastefully encircled with flowers, gravel walks with beautiful borders, ornamental trees trimmed into varied forms, flowers exhaling sweet fragrance around grottoes, fountains and cascades.

On one side, at a short distance from the city, lies a vast landscape commencing with rising hills covered with terraces of equal width, planted with olive trees and vineyards, rising in regular gradation one above another, like rows of seats in an amphitheatre, beautiful country seats here and there dotting the summits of these hills, fronted with gardens and groves of the orange and lemon tree loaded with golden fruit. These ranges of hills, continuing one above another, roll away in the distance into lofty mountains, and still onward until their towering peaks are mantled in perpetual snow. Before us stretching far off beneath the encircling horizon, in calm and sweet repose, slumber the blue waters of the Mediterranean, whose broad bosom is whitened with sails from every land and clime.

We shall long remember our stroll through the parks and gardens of Marseilles, and along the sunny shore of the beautiful Mediterranean.

LORENZO SNOW.

LETTER XXX.

London Conference—Visiting the Poor—"Work Their Lives Out to Keep Life In"—Rotterdam—Dutch Cleanliness—Political Economy in Holland—Brussels and its Carpets and Lace—Waterloo—Continual Rain—Twenty Miles of Tunnels—Alpine Railroads—European and American Railways.

Genoa, Italy, December 29th, 1872.

Editor Woman's Exponent:

I attended the London Conference of the Saints with much satisfaction. In company with Mrs. Thompson, Miss Clara S. Little and Elder Junius F. Wells, who kindly proffered to escort us, I spent one day in making calls among the Saints. I told Brother Wells that I wished to see the poorest Saints in London. He said he would take us to those in lowest circumstances of any in the city, and then to those who possessed the most of this world's goods; although, he said, outside of the city are some much more destitute than those within our reach.

All whom we visited seemed cheerful and happy. We found one family in particular, destitute enough, in an upper room, reached by a dark, narrow, winding stairway, who had apparently to "work their lives out to keep life in." In a small room that I could nearly reach across, the mother and two daughters were busy at their "annual" employment, with scissors, paste, guilt trimmings, pasteboard, wire and ribbons, making boxes of all fanciful forms and sizes for a wealthy merchant who furnished the materials, and paid them at a very low figure for their work. We spent the evening at

Brother Rowe's, where we were genteelly entertained and had not only the pleasure of the society of our Palestine tourists, but of a goodly number of Missionaries from Utah.

At Rotterdam we put up at the Bath Hotel, a commodious building—everything in excellent order, and scrupulously clean. Cleanliness seems to be a characteristic with hotels in Holland; and, admitting industry to be promotive of neatness, it must also be a national characteristic. No sensible, candid person can visit this country without according to the people the credit of industry, and indomitable perseverance. Most people think they do well to cultivate the ground after it is made, but the Hollanders make much of the ground they cultivate, and when made and cultivated, it requires constant labor and expense to protect it from inundation. They must, as a matter of course, be honest, they have not time to be otherwise.

The wise policy of the Dutch brings wealth: they import raw material of every kind—manufacture it, and export it when manufactured. For instance, they purchase American lard, and then, after multiplying its value in their factories, sell it to Americans in the form of candles. I noticed women wearing ornaments of gold on their heads, which were very conspicuous—some of the size of a silver dollar and some much larger—and was informed that those ladies were wives of wealthy farmers, and that they wore these ornaments to represent their wealth.

I could not pass over this very interesting, small portion of the world, in silence; but in writing to the *Deseret News* my brother has said so much about Holland, its inhabitants, shipping, canals, etc., I shall not attempt description. Suffice it to say, I enjoyed my visit in that kingdom, immensely. Rotterdam, the Hague, Haarlem and Amsterdam, from which we returned to Rotterdam *en route* to Antwerp in Belgium, thence to Brussels, celebrated for its carpets and lace, which we saw and admired, from which place we visited the battle-field of Waterloo, and the next day left Belgium *en route* for Paris where, including one day's visit to Versailles, we spent five days very pleasantly.

Rain in unusual quantities has been the order of the day overhead and underfoot from the time we landed in Liverpool until now, with few exceptions. Large tracts of cultivated land, with fencing nearly covered, and in many instances, houses entirely surrounded with water, sometimes on one side of the railroad, at other times on both, have presented ocean scenes rather than those of *terra firma*. But with all the rains and floods we have experienced but little inconvenience, the most was in coming from Nice to this place—overflow of water had made breaches in the track, and instead of one day we were two days on the way, distance one hundred and twenty-six miles. We have met with no other detention. Some of our party estimated the length of all the tunnels in the above distance to be, at least, twenty miles. Whoever projected a railroad in this Alpine country is worthy of a gold statue for his courage and intrepidity. It is astonishing to think of the amount of labor and expense requisite for the accomplishment of this Herculean project. Most of these tunnels are cut through solid rock, and permanently arched, a protection against mountain torrents flowing in to the Mediterranean, the shores of which the railroad follows from Marseilles to Genoa, except when tunneled or cut through the many spurs of the Alps projecting into the sea.

Compared with those of England, America may boast the long stretch of her roads, but, so far as work and means are concerned, Americans should doff hats in presence of this Herculean enterprise of southern France and northern Italy.

To-morrow morning we leave for Turin.

ELIZA R. SNOW.

THE YEAR 1872.

The year is stepping out regardless of
My long, long distance from my Mountain Home.
It leaves me in Italia's "sunny clime,"
Where verdant foliage gentle breezes kiss,
And balmy zephyrs fan the evening tide.

The year now passing out has, in its course,
In lib'ral portions, meted out to me
The wide extremes of deep bereavement, and
Munificence in richly flowing streams.
Which I acknowledge freely ere we part.

All grateful reminiscences, the old,
Expiring Year inscribes indelibly
On mem'ry's sacred tablet, richly wreath'd
With choice mementos of the good produced,
Of vict'ries Truth and Justice have achieved,
Improvement's progress in the march of mind,
And every aid to poor humanity,
While its successor treads upon its heels.

Good bye old Year! We both are moving on:
You, to the cloister of the mighty past,
To join it to the future yet unborn;
I, to the far-famed land of Palestine,
Which has a hist'ry of the past, that bears,
With a momentous and eternal weight
Of destiny to all of human kind,
Upon the future, which the passing years
With hurried tread ere long will introduce
With bold, magnificent developments.

I go to place my feet upon the land
Where once the Prince of Peace, the Son of God,
Was born—where once He lived and walked and preach'd
And prayed, admonished, taught, rebuked and blest;
And then, to answer Justice' great demand
And seal his mission of Eternal Love,
Upon the cross poured out his precious blood,

Arose to life triumphant o'er the tomb;
And after being seen and heard and felt,
Ascended up to heaven; and as He went,
Those who stood looking heard an angel say—
"Ye men of Galilee, why stand ye here
Gazing to heaven? The self-same Jesus whom
Ye see ascending in like manner will again descend."

Each year that passes on
Clips from the thread of time a portion of
Its intervening length, and hurries up
The coming great and grand fulfilment of
That strange prediction, strange and strangely true.

That most momentous period, for the great
Event is fast approximating, and
The moving of the waters now, amidst
The nations of the earth, like deepest shades
Of pencil drawings, seems foreshadowing
The world's great crisis.

Human Policy
Grows tremulous, while human governments,
With tender care are fondly fostering
And feeding with their life's best nourishment,
The seeds of their own dissolution.

France
Is poising on a pivot, England rests
On her broad pedestal, but resting moves
With vacillating tendencies. The famed
Italia stands in leaning posture from
The Papal Chair to King Emanuel;
While Russia, beckoning to Austria,
To Germany, or whosoever will,
Solicits help to lift the balance
Of Power, now lying just beyond her reach.

The wires of destiny are working on
To consummate eternal purposes,
And bring results of change that must precede
"The Second coming of the Son of Man;"
When, unto him, "whose right it is to reign,"
All human powers and governments will bow.

ELIZA R. SNOW.
Milan, Italy, December 31, 1872.

LETTER XXXI.

Reflections—Members of the Party—Birthplace of Columbus—Religion on Continental Europe—High Mass—The Cathedral at Genoa—Approaching Marseilles—Orange and Lemon Groves—The Mediterranean—European Apples.

MILAN, Italy, January 1st, 1873.

MRS. JANE S. RICHARDS:

DEAR SISTER:—How very changeful are the events of human life! One year ago, the idea of addressing you from Italy at the commencement of this year would have seemed almost an impossibility. But here I am, a long distance from what to me is the dearest spot on earth—the home of the Saints of the living God. The lapse of time, since parting with you and the many dear ones associated with you in Ogden, has been a constant routine of change combined with deep interest. Our party consists of President George A. Smith, Elders Lorenzo Snow, Paul A. Schettler, Feramorz Little, George Dunford, Thomas Jennings, Miss Clara S. Little and your humble servant. So far as society is concerned, we are independent wherever we are, and enjoy ourselves as well as possible for people abroad, feeling assured of the faith and prayers of the righteous; and I assure you that I never forget a tribute of gratitude to those through whose love, kindness and generous energies the privilege of this tour is extended to me. I have, so far, enjoyed it far beyond my anticipations. Two months and one week, and I am between seven and eight thousand miles from home, having traveled through England, visited the most prominent cities in Holland and Belgium, and in

France the cities of Paris, Versailles, Lyons, Marseilles and Nice. After leaving Nice we enter the dominions of Victor Emanuel. Our first stopping place in Italy, according to our programme, would be Genoa, but in consequence of heavy rains having made a break in the railroad, we stopped one night in St. Reno, and went the next day to Genoa, the birthplace of Christopher Columbus. From Genoa we went to Turin and came thence to this place.

The national religion, we found since leaving England to be Catholic. I had never witnessed the service until in Brussels. This being New Year's Day, high mass was performed in the grand Cathedral of Milan, which we attended. The cathedral is a magnificent Gothic structure, containing fourteen chapels; it is, by many, considered the finest in the world. We were informed that the service on the occasion was of the highest order; certainly much of it was senseless form and unmeaning, though dazzling, display. I enjoyed the singing and the sweet music of the two organs, which played alternately. The Archbishop, who represented the Pope in all respects except that his hand, instead of his toe, was kissed, was most gorgeously dressed, bearing, at times, upon his head a superb mitre, and at other times, according to the requirements of the service, it was taken off by an officiate and held until again required, and then replaced. The burning of incense was profuse. Great numbers, variously attired, officiated on the occasion, and the congregation was immense. The services were performed in Latin and, it is presumable, was as little comprehended by the majority of the church members as by us. I readily understood that many of the people present were, like ourselves, spectators. But when I looked upon the congregation and saw some crossing themselves, some reverently kneeling and others bowing, first to a golden crucifix, then to the Archbishop, my heart responded—How long, O Lord, shall these, thy children, be bound in the dwarfing chains of traditional superstition and ignorance? It is true the powers of earth are shaking, but at present I can see no hope for millions of people under the training of the "Mother of Harlots," and the influence of priestcraft, but through the ordinances for the dead. Such were my reflections while I remained a spectator in the midst of a great multitude in the stately and superb Cathedral of Milan, which is described as being four hundred and eighty-six feet in length, and its total breadth three hundred and fifty feet.

As we approached Marseilles, the face of the country, which had been level, assumed a very uneven appearance, hills approximating to the dimensions of mountains, and for the first time on our route, we saw groves of olive trees, and occasionally oranges, and when we reached the Mediterranean they became very common, ornamenting the cities along the coast—the orange and lemon trees being loaded with golden fruit; some of them, very large, must have been planted long ago.

Our present location is inland from the sea, and the olive, orange and lemon have all disappeared, save as the orange is placed on our dinner table every evening for desert. On this side the Atlantic I have not seen apples that would compare with those of our mountain home—most of those we have seen are very ordinary.

January 2nd.

Yesterday was rainy, to-day, being favorable, we ascended five hundred and twelve marble steps, which brought us to the platform of the great cupola of the cathedral above mentioned, where we had a most delightful view of the whole city; and but for a fog, which encircled the distant horizon, we might have seen the surrounding chains of snow-capped mountains in the distance.

To-morrow morning we leave for Venice.

Yours with love,

ELIZA R. SNOW.

LETTER XXXII.

At Venice—Railroad Track on Artificial Ground—Gondolas—A City without Horses—A Glass Factory—News from Home—Death—Consolation.

VENICE, Italy, January 5th, 1873.

BELOVED SISTER HORNE:

We arrived here on the 3rd, the same evening I received a note with your signature attached. In acknowledging the receipt I would give expression to my feelings were it in my power to do so, but I leave you to imagine. * * * *
Venice is a very interesting city, both on account of its history and its singular location. Approaching it for a considerable distance, the railroad track is laid on artificial ground, with water on each side. When we arrived at the commodious depot, gondolas were waiting to take us to the Grand Hotel Victoria; and with two gondolas for our persons—four in each—and one for our baggage, we landed on the threshold of our hotel.

This city is said to have been built on seventy-two islands. Pedestrians can go into all parts of the city, but gondolas instead of horses and carriages are used, the people having no other means for riding. Yesterday afternoon our whole party took a gondola ride and visited a factory for the manufacture of glass, where they were making artificial eyes for men and animals, together with every fancy ornamental thing imaginable. The most beautiful looking-glass I ever saw, with a white glass frame most delicately wrought, was prized at three thousand five hundred francs. We were told that three of the kind were in America, purchased in Venice.

Our intelligence from Salt Lake has not been very profuse. The only paper received from there is the *Salt Lake Herald*, which comes occasionally and is a rich treat to us all. Arrangements are made with Brother Carrington to forward all trans-Atlantic mail matter from Liverpool to different points as President Smith designates to him from time to time. * * * By the *Herald* I learned the sad news of the death of your lovely, precious daughter. I can think of no one better prepared to go—although so young she was ripened for a higher state of existence. For her, there is no cause for mourning; but when I think of her father and mother, her young, bereaved husband, the loss to her brothers and sisters, and the loss to the community where her noble example has had a purifying influence, my heart overflows with sympathy and sorrow. How you will miss her! But trained as you have been in the gospel of Jesus, you know where to look for consolation. God alone can breathe comfort to the deeply stricken heart. When I think of the bereaved ones, I feel to mourn; but when I think of the pure, noble, lovely Julia, whose earthly mission is so soon accepted—she spared a longer period of toil, struggle and suffering, my feelings are buoyant and my imagination, if I may call it so, follows her triumphant spirit to the happy abodes of purity and eternal peace. May the daughters of Zion imitate her worthy example! God bless you my dear sister and fill your heart with his comforting Spirit.

ELIZA R. SNOW.

LETTER XXXIII.

Shores of the Mediterranean—At Venice—Genoa—Statue of Columbus—The Cathedral St. Lorenzo—The Chain that Bound John the Baptist—Desecration of the Sabbath—Start for Turin—Milan—The Arcade—Cathedral of Our Blessed Lady, the Grandest Religious Edifice in the World—Magnificent Marble Statuary—Statue of St. Bartholomew—Attend High Mass—Arrival in Venice, the City of Waters.

VENICE, Italy, January 4th, 1873.

EDITOR DESERET NEWS:

We left Marseilles by train, December 24th, continuing our route along the shores of the Mediterranean. Some portion of the country is rough and broken into hills and low mountains, generally covered with vineyards and olive orchards. The soil appears light, yet productive. Much labor has been required to bring this district to its present flourishing condition. A plan was adopted widely differing from that in Holland, which is a system of terracing, accomplished by removing the stones and rocks off the acclivities, and building them up into walls from three to eight feet in height, laterally, so as to form a level, varying in width from six feet and upward, according to the steepness of the hill to be terraced. Soil is gathered upon these levels, in which the vine, the olive, lemon and orange are planted. Mountains from base to summit adorned by these terraces, like rows of seats rising in systematic order one above another, form a pleasant picture, frequently lovely and fascinating.

We arrived at Nice in the evening. It is a beautiful

city, romantically located among the hills bordering the sea. It forms a fashionable resort for people of wealth in quest of pleasure, and invalids in search of health. The environs afford many attractions in promenades, extensive views, luxuriant vegetation, gardens and sloping hills covered with vines, olives, aloes, cypress, palm, together with lemon and orange trees loaded with golden fruit.

After spending two days pleasantly in Nice we left for Genoa, Italy, where we arrived on Friday, the 27th of December. I was not forcibly impressed in favor of Genoa, its streets narrow and crooked, some of them filthy. The dwellings built in blocks flanking these narrow, devious paths, in many instances nearly closed with each other at the top, appearing to form an archway over the streets. We felt to award a tribute of respect, however, to Genoa as the birthplace of Christopher Columbus. One of its squares is ornamented with a fine monumental structure erected to his memory.

Sunday morning we attended Catholic service in the Cathedral St. Lorenzo, the most celebrated church in the city. During worship an officer in uniform waited upon us through the building, pointing out and explaining various objects of interest. He conducted us to a small chapel enclosed by an ornamental paling and showed us the "identical" chain with which John the Baptist was bound while in prison previous to being beheaded, and also his ashes enclosed in a silver urn. Any doubts we entertained of the genuineness of these articles we refrained from expressing. No woman is allowed to enter this chapel of St. John, except one day in the year, because one of her sex instigated the death of this saint. My sister, who happened to be the only lady of the party present, bore this interdiction with her characteristic grace and fortitude.

On leaving the cathedral, we noticed immediately in front of it, a great variety of merchandise spread upon stands, and a lively business going on in the way of buying and selling. Shops and places of amusement are customarily open on Sundays.

Monday, 30th, we left for Turin. Some portions of this route were very attractive, in fact, I do not recollect ever having seen a landscape more lovely and enchanting. We arrived in Turin in the afternoon, and left the following morning for Milan, which we reached in the evening of the 31st of December.

Milan contains two hundred and seventy thousand inhabitants. It is situated on the river Alono, in the centre of the great plain of Lombardy, and is one of the richest and most beautiful cities of Italy; the streets regular, broad and well paved, the dwellings elegantly built, and commodious. The city embraces capacious squares, promenades and gardens, tastefully laid out and ornamented with fountains and statuary. The Arcade is a splendid structure; we visited it in the evening when lit up with its immense number of gas burners. An English company commenced this structure with speculative views, but after having sunk (so we were informed) nearly one million of dollars, relinquished the project, after which it became government property.

Milan is celebrated for its cathedral, built in honor of "Our Blessed Lady." Galeazo Visconti, Duke of Milan, owing to some cause which we failed to ascertain, made a solemn vow to build a rich and magnificent temple in honor of the Virgin Mary, and was joined in this undertaking by men of wealth and rank, with the intention of making it the most costly and beautiful ecclesiastical edifice in the world. For this purpose immense sums from time to time were contributed by distinguished individuals—single donations frequently reaching as high as from fifty to one hundred thousand dollars. Kings, popes, emperors and empresses bestowed their princely gifts; one Italian gentleman contributed thirty-five thousand gold ducats. The founder donated, together with other liberal gifts, marble at the quarry, sufficient to build the entire edifice.

This temple has been nearly five hundred years in course of construction, and will probably require another century for its completion. In gazing with astonishment upon the forest of pinnacles and thousands of marble statues, together with millions of rich ornaments and endless works of carved marble, and the great tower, with its lofty summit crowned with a colossal statue, one would fail to notice any deficiency or lack in its completion; yet millions are still required to carry out, in full, the magnificent design of the great artist who planned this astonishing specimen of Gothic architecture.

Up to the present about one hundred and ten millions of dollars have been expended, independent of the marble donated at the quarry. The walls are eight feet in thickness, built of fine white marble from Mount Gandoglia. The floors are paved with marble—the roof is formed with marble blocks united by cement. The length of the cathedral is four hundred and ninety feet, its breadth two hundred and ninety-eight, and its height to the summit of the tower is four hundred feet. It is built in the form of a Latin cross, divided into five naves, supported by fifty-two pillars, each about seventy-two feet high, and twenty-four feet in circumference. The interior of the building is decorated with fret-work, carvings, statuary and numerous paintings, the productions of the most skilful artists of Europe. The exterior is covered with marble statuary, representing some of the most remarkable events in biblical history—Moses rescued from the Nile by Pharaoh's daughter, Joseph's temptation in the house of Potiphar, the angel driving out Adam and Eve from Eden, Daniel in the den of lions, God appearing to Moses in a burning bush, David holding the head of Goliath, Sampson suffocating the lion, and carrying on his shoulder the gates of Gaza. Fifty-two representations of this character adorn the front of this temple

Writers differ in their statements of the number of the statues which ornament this building. In a work published by a Mr. Prioli at Milan, the present number is estimated at seven thousand, and additions are constantly being made. The most celebrated artists in Europe have been employed, and are still engaged in embellishing this edifice.

We ascended by a flight of five hundred and twelve steps to the platform of the great cupola, where we enjoyed a magnificent view of the city, and the immense plains of Lombardy, chequered with towns and villages, stretching far away till lost beneath the surrounding girdle of snow-capped mountains. From this lovely picture of nature, we turned to gaze on the countless objects of beauty and splendor, the productions of the highest efforts of human genius, which constitute the exterior decorations of this extraordinary temple. Before us stood a forest of towers—one hundred and thirty-six in number, each adorned with twenty-five marble figures, life size, and thousands of ornamental objects in white marble, imparting to the scene richness, beauty and grandeur. We descended to the interior of the building, where, among the numerous objects which attracted our attention, was a marble statue, life size, representing St. Bartholomew flayed alive and carrying his skin upon his shoulders. The artist was eight years engaged in this work, which is much admired as a specimen of the extraordinary skill and anatomical knowledge of the sculptor. In his right hand he holds a figure representing the knife with which his skin was taken off. The veins, arteries and muscles, together with the whole surface of the body and limbs in a flayed condition, are delineated by the hand of the sculptor with marvellous exactness.

We attended high mass in this church New Year's morning, the Archbishop of Milan presiding. But I must hasten to a close.

On the morning of the 3rd of January we left Milan and arrived here, in Venice, the city of waters, the following evening.

LORENZO SNOW.

LETTER XXXIV.

Venice—A Railroad on Piles—A City without Horses, Cabs or Omnibuses—Gondolas—Sailing Along the Streets—Method of Building—The Grand Canal—Three Hundred and Six Bridges—The Rialto—The Armenian Monastery—Former Residence of Lord Byron—A Mad-house—National Arsenal—Ancient Arms—Trophies of War—Flayed Alive—Terrible Method of Execution—The Republic—Last of the Doges—Mercantile Marine.

VENICE, Italy, January 6th, 1873.

EDITOR DESERET NEWS:

Having completed our explorations in this city, I will now send you a few items extracted from my journal.

The railroad over which we traveled, as it approaches Venice, is built on piles, extending about two miles from the main land before it reaches the suburbs of the city; the station was about one mile distant from our hotel, Grand Hotel Victoria. Our usual mode of conveyance was not at our command. We had passed the limits of cabs and omnibuses—they are known only in story by the Venetians. But three horses could be found in all Venice, and these were exhibited as objects of curiosity and as specimens of the singular quadruped employed for service and pleasure by people beyond the sea.

We took two gondolas, each propelled by two oarsmen,

and steered for the hotel. It was dark and we could discern objects around us only as they appeared in the light from lamps suspended, here and there, from buildings which lined the narrow passages through which we passed as we wended our way into narrow lanes turning this way and that, until we seemed lost in a labyrinth of turns and angles. At last we terminated our perambulations at the lower steps of a large stone stairway. Here we were received by the proprietor of the hotel, who conducted us up several flights of stairs, and into elegant, capacious apartments.

Venice contains a population of one hundred and thirty thousand. It is situated on a cluster of small islands, seventy or eighty in number, several miles from the main land, in the midst of a broad sheet of water, partially separated from the sea by a large sandbank several miles in length. These islands are made principally of mud thrown up by the currents of water, not sufficiently consolidated, however, to build upon, independent of artificial appliances. The following practice is commonly adopted in preparing the foundations: the spot selected for the edifice is enclosed by some substantial work, impervious to water, sunk into the mud. The water is then pumped out, and the mud or loose dirt excavated from six to eight feet in depth. The space is then filled with piles driven to a depth of fifteen or twenty feet. Cement is filled in between them and the tops covered with the same material. Thick planks are laid over this covering, upon which are built three or four feet of rock. The dirt or mud is replaced around this mass, so that the entire woodwork is perfectly covered. The walls of the buildings, consisting chiefly of small red brick, are laid upon this rockwork, which stands one foot or more above high-water mark. Except in one or two instances we saw no appearance of the walls giving way, although some of these edifices have been standing probably one thousand years. A vast amount of expense is incurred in constructing these foundations; it is said that half the cost of the buildings in Venice lies under water.

The Grand Canal runs tortuously through the city, and is the principal thoroughfare for traffic or amusement. The city is intersected by one hundred and forty-six small canals, which constitute the water streets of Venice, affording means for passengers to be conveyed to any quarter of the city. Three hundred and six bridges cross these canals. The Grand Canal, which varies in width from one hundred and fifty to three hundred feet, is crossed by the famous bridge Rialto, under which we passed on one of our excursions. There are passages alongside of some of these canals and in various other parts of the city leading over the bridges, but they are very narrow and crooked, frequently not over seven and generally not exceeding ten feet in width.

We visited the Armenian Monastery, on the Island of St. Lazarus, about two miles from our hotel. We reached it by the usual mode—the gondola, enjoyed a pleasant ride over a broad sheet of water dotted with ships, steamers and multitudes of gondolas. On arriving at the monastery, the presiding monk received us kindly, and conducted us through the establishment, and gave such statistical information as we required in relation to the affairs of the society and the institution. It embraces a college for young Armenians, a museum, a library of thirty thousand volumes, a printing press and office, and a beautiful chapel. Lord Byron lived here six months and studied the Armenian language. We saw his autograph, which was written in several languages. A singular custom prevails of hoisting the Turkish flag every Sunday morning upon the summit of the monastery. At the present time twenty monks, thirty students and some twenty assistants constitute the number in the establishment. The buildings were given by the Venetian government to a Benedictine monk, who had been expelled by persecution from his native country.

Some of their customs and regulations are rather peculiar. They arise in the morning at a given signal, breakfast at eight, dine at twelve, when portions of scripture are read, and retire at ten p. m. All are habited in black gowns. None are admitted as students but Armenians. They must possess a natural capacity for mental culture, and remain in the institution till they have acquired a highly finished education. Every department of this singular and interesting establishment bore a neat and orderly appearance, yet rather sombre and gloomy, owing no doubt to the fact that woman is excluded from the society.

President Smith described our pilgrimage to the great American Desert, what we had accomplished as a people, and explained some of the prominent features of our religion, all of which was listened to with marked attention, and enquiries were made on various subjects connected with our history.

On returning to our hotel we passed a mad-house. Some of the inmates were playing on musical instruments, others were silently gazing through their windows upon the sea, some fiercely gesticulating as though angry at our approach, while others again were rushing to and fro yelling and shrieking like so many demons. The scene was horrible. We had intended a visit inside the building, but what we witnessed answered our purpose.

We visited the National Arsenal, containing models of ships, galleys, &c., with specimens of various arms and armor used by the Venetians in their wars at different periods, also many trophies taken from the Turks and other enemies.

Two statues, standing together in a conspicuous position, appeared to attract considerable attention from visitors. They represented two Turkish generals chained together and suffering death by a singular method of torture. These officers, in a battle with the Venetians, had taken one of their generals prisoner, whom they caused to be flayed alive—his skin sewed together, stuffed with straw, the figure dressed in his own clothing, and then exhibited to the Turkish populace for their amusement. These officers were afterwards captured by the Venetians, stripped, chained together, placed in an exposed condition and covered from head to foot with honey or molasses, and left to be eaten by flies, gnats, mosquitoes and other insects.

Venice, which now forms a portion of the kingdom of Italy, for over thirteen hundred years maintained a republican form of government. It had a succession of one hundred and twenty-two Doges, the last of whom, Daniel Manin, abdicated in August 1849, and was driven into exile by the Austrians. He went to Paris, where he was obliged to give lessons in Italian to sustain himself and family. He died in September 1857.

In the brightest day of its prosperity, the republic possessed over three thousand mercantile ships and thirty-six thousand sailors, and considered itself mistress of the seas. Several interesting circumstances connected with the history of this government, strikingly illustrated by various objects we saw, I should like to notice, but must defer for the present.

LORENZO SNOW.

LETTER XXXV.

More about Venice—Historical Reminiscences—Administration of the Doges Destruction of the Republic—Vandalism of Napoleon—Curious Method of Burial—Popularity of Victor Emanuel—Old Palace of the Doges—Senate and Council Chambers—Bridge of Sighs—House of Shylock—Residence of Othello—Palace of Desdemona—Dwelling Place of Marco Polo—Remains of St. Marc the Evangelist—Columns of Solomon's Temple—Granite Slab from Mt. Tabor—Slab from the Prison of John the Baptist—Ancient Tombstones, &c.

HOTEL BRUN, Bologna, January 8th, 1873.

PRESIDENT BRIGHAM YOUNG:

With thanks to our heavenly Father for his mercies I can inform you that myself and company are in good health. Brother George Dunford, for business reasons, started for home yesterday. He was a pleasant companion to travel with and we regret much the necessity of his return.

We spent five days in Venice, which was peculiarly interesting to me for its historical associations and peculiar location. At the time that Attila invaded Italy, and destroyed Aquila, which was then the great mart of trade in northern Italy, the panic-stricken inhabitants of the neighboring towns, fearing a like fate from the barbarian, took shelter in some low mud islands or banks, formed by the wash of several rivers, north of the Po, in what is called the lagoon of the Adriatic, driving piles in the mud, using the various streams as canals, covering the piles with cement and mud, laying upon them foundations of rock, from which in an incredibly short time grew the great naval power of the republic of Venice, which retained its independence thirteen hundred years, and may probably during one thousand years have been considered a first-class power. Its government, though termed republican, was a consolidated aristocracy, and very tyrannical. But few of the people had the right to vote, and they elected from the aristocratic class the senate, and the senate selected forty of their number, who again selected ten, who again selected three of their number, in whose hands was centred a good deal of absolute power.

The Grand Doge or reigning duke was elected for life by the senators, and seemed to possess much greater powers than the sovereigns of England do at the present time. Some of these reigning presidents were men of extraordinary ability, and extended the dominion of Venice over many islands and countries. One of them captured and plundered Constantinople and brought from that place many trophies, which were shown us with pride and satisfaction.

The canals of Venice are streets, the carriages are boats called gondolas. They are all built of one pattern and painted black. There are but three horses in the city, which contains one hundred and thirty thousand inhabitants; every hotel, wealthy gentleman and business man have their boats tied to their doors. The republican government was extinguished by Napoleon I. in 1797, and although the place submitted to his authority without any resistance, he committed many acts of vandalism, such as carrying away to Paris many choice paintings, statues and souvenirs of Venetian greatness; plundering the churches of their gold and silver ornaments, and sending them to the mint; scattering the monks and nuns to the four winds, telling the nuns they should be raising boys to fill his armies; breaking in pieces the winged lion wherever it was to be found, it being the proud emblem of Venetian power; destroying the magnificent ship in which the Grand Doge of Venice had married the Adriatic seven hundred times, and cast into the sea as many gold rings. An immense amount of gold and silver used in ornamenting this vessel he sent to the mint. Venice had two hundred churches, many of them very costly edifices; sixty-seven of these he tore down, converting the land on which they stood and their materials to other purposes. A monastery which contained 1,200 monks was converted into a custom house. Up to this time all the dead had been buried in churches. This he prohibited, and since that time a cemetery has grown up in the lagoons, formed by the earth deposited there for the purpose of making an island, and is being enlarged from year to year by the mud which is taken from the canals, which are as numerous as the streets of other cities. This mud is a clay, and is secured by piles capped with cement, upon which walls are built next to the sea. The ground is raised six feet above high-water mark. The dead are buried four feet below the surface. The poor are buried in trenches, one coffin lying close against another, but only one tier deep. The last one buried is left uncovered ready for the next one to be laid against it, and then the trench is filled. Twenty-four of this class had been buried there this year when I was there, the sixth of January. Ground for single graves could be purchased by any persons for eighteen francs, and all who felt able buried their dead on their own ground thus obtained. These private graves are all marked with a cross, many of iron, some of wood and many of stone. These monuments were generally plain and tasteful. A small enclosure beautifully decorated is used for a Protestant burying place. Among the number buried there were many English and Germans, but only one American, William Sparks, aged 30, died August 19, 1849. Few Americans have had the opportunity to drop a tear over this lonely grave of their fellow countryman. He was U. S. Consul at Venice at the time of his death. A large addition to the Catholic cemetery has just been finished and brought into use. The hundreds of palaces along the Grand Canal, many of them fine specimens of architecture, are mostly going to decay. While Venice belonged to the Austrians, which was about fifty years, the Austrian government made Trieste the port of entry and few ships visited Venice. But now, under the Italian government, its trade has revived, and steamers and ships give sociability and character and commercial life to the almost dead city. We heard expressions of approbation and loyalty to Victor Emanuel and to Italian unity, though they seem to feel heavily the increased taxation which it has cost to bring it about—two wars with Austria, one with Naples and one with the States of the Church.

I am satisfied that Victor Emanuel is personally popular with the people. While in Venice we visited two glass factories, where many fine specimens of glass were produced. We visited the palace of Victor Emanuel, or about a hundred rooms of it, which he occupies during his annual visits to Venice, the old palace of the Doges, the Senate and Council Chambers, the ancient prison, crossing the Bridge of Sighs and returning. We ascended the monument in St. Marc's Square, the highest in Venice, visited the Academy of Arts, several galleries of antiquities, the arsenal, the Armenian convent, and many other places, particulars related concerning which may have been more imaginary than real, as the house of Shylock, the merchant of Venice, where the city now keeps a pawnbroker's office. Our guide showed us the first church built in Venice, in 421, the house of Othello, the palace of Desdemona, the house of Marco Polo the great Venetian traveller and explorer in Asia, the palace of the Queen of Cyprus, and many other places that history, art or poetry have rendered familiar with us. Our guide showed us many holy relics preserved in St. Marc's Cathedral: the coffin containing the body of St. Marc, which he assured us was genuine, it having been brought from Alexandria eight hundred years ago. The body had been smuggled on board a Venetian ship in a basket of vegetables, thus eluding the vigilance of the infidel guard, and bringing the remains of the Evangelist to Venice, to rest in a marble coffin and to become the patron saint of the city. Our guide showed us some columns of Solomon's temple, that were semi-transparent, a slab of granite, seven feet by seven, from Mount Tabor, upon which the Saviour stood when he was transfigured, a slab from the prison of John the Baptist, upon which his head fell when it was stricken off by the command of Herod. In pointing to the door he said, "There is preserved his head." The door is only opened on Fridays. The marble chair of St. Marc, and many other relics, he assured me, were genuine, as they had been brought to Venice eight hundred years ago.

I have to day been looking at some tombstones and remains of Etruscan nobles, which were buried nearly three thousand years ago. There are many good specimens of gold jewelry and ornaments of earth and glass and metal, showing that the inhabitants of Bologna three thousand years ago were acquainted with many of the arts.

GEORGE A. SMITH.

LETTER XXXVI.

Architectural Appearance of Venice—Ancient Customs—Fires—Plague and Pestilence—Council of Ten—Traitor Beheaded—Instruments of Torture—Bridge of Sighs—Bologna—An Arcade with 700 Arches—Leaning Towers—Florence, the Most Beautiful of Italian Cities—Paintings and Sculpture—A Wonderful Cabinet of Gems and Works of Art.

FLORENCE, Italy, January 13th, 1873.

EDITOR DESERET NEWS:

We left Venice on the morning of the 8th ult., stopped one day at Bologna, arriving in Florence on the evening of the 9th.

In the first place, allow me to copy a few more items from my journal in reference to Venice, and its celebrated republic. The physical appearance of the city—its private edifices, palaces, cathedrals and other public buildings, are in a state of decay, and portions of the city, which formerly were covered with fresco paintings and other decorations and shone in splendor, appear now as if clothed in habiliments of mourning. In passing along the Grand Canal, in our gondola, we were forcibly impressed with the gloomy and solitary aspect of the numerous mansions and palaces which line this great thoroughfare. The immense trade and traffic this city formerly commanded have been changed into other channels, leaving unfortunate Venice terribly crippled in her commerce and manufactures, and no longer able to use those strange methods formerly employed to preserve exclusively to herself men of skill and genius, whereby she compelled surrounding nations to pour their gold and silver into her treasuries; that day has forever passed. The following is a specimen illustrative of the style which Venice formerly adopted to secure the advantages of her manufactures—

"If any workman carry his art to a foreign country, to the prejudice of the Republic, he shall be ordered to return; if he do not obey, his nearest relatives shall be imprisoned that his regard for them may induce him to return, which, if he does, he shall be forgiven and employment again provided for him; if, in despite of the imprisonment of his relatives, he perseveres in his absence an emissary shall be employed to dispatch him; and after his death his relatives shall be set free."

One would hardly imagine that a city built in the sea would suffer heavy losses by fire; the history of Venice, however, proves the contrary—at various times fires have burst out, doing immense damage, in some instances consuming palaces, cathedrals and whole blocks of private dwellings. This city has also experienced heavy losses by inundations, which on one occasion threatened the destruction of the entire city. Neither has its favorable position, surrounded by sea breezes, protected it from the destructive hand of pestilence.

In the middle of the fourteenth century three fifths of the population were destroyed by contagious disease. In the latter part of the same century nineteen thousand people died by pestilence. In the beginning of the fifteenth century a pestilence swept away forty thousand inhabitants. From July 1630, to November 1631, the mortality of Venice amounted to forty-six thousand.

A long line of 122 Doges successively performed the executive functions of the Venetian government—many of them men of talent and great ability, administering the laws in wisdom and with unbiassed judgment. In the beginning of the fourteenth century the famous Council of Ten was organized and continued as a magistracy nearly five hundred years. Though this Council has been regarded as tyrannical and cruel, the object of its establishment was not objectionable, it being designed to prevent encroachments of the Doges and Senate upon the rights and liberties of the people; and it answered this purpose until demoralized by the innovations of luxury and extravagance, when it became an instrument of oppression and cruelty. Mementos of those deeds of darkness were pointed out to us, while others were shown us illustrative of the powerful manner in which this Council administered justice before it fell from its high moral position, as in the following examples: Fifty years after the organization of the Council of Ten, the Doge Manin Faliero had been guilty of conspiring to overthrow the Republic. This Council examined his case, found him guilty, and sentenced him to be beheaded. The sentence was executed on the same spot where he had been crowned with the ducal cap. He died begging pardon of the people and acknowledging the justice of his punishment. In a magnificent hall, splendidly decorated, we saw the portraits of the Doges placed in regular succession around the apartment; but Manin Faliero's place was covered with a painting of a black vail! One hundred and twenty years succeeding the appointment of the Council of Ten, they passed the following sentence on one of the Republic's most distinguished generals, who, having grown tired of patriotism, had organized a plot against the government:

"Francis Carmagnola, public traitor of our dominion, let him be led with a dovetail in his mouth and with his hands bound behind his back, as is the custom to-day, the fifth of May, afternoon, usual hour, between the two columns of St. Mark's Square, in the usual place of justice, and there let his head be severed from his shoulders, till he dies."

This sentence was directly executed.

We saw many objects of exciting interest associated with the history of the Doges, the Venetian Republic, the Inquisition, the Council of Ten, the instruments and modes of human torture, the loathsome dungeons, "Bridge of Sighs," the place of midnight executions, etc., which I will not at present attempt to describe.

Leaving this city of the sea, we came to Bologna, a town of about 110,000 inhabitants, arriving at 1 o'clock p. m., the 8th of January. Bologna is charmingly situated on an extensive plain, bordered by the lower slope of the Apennines. We visited several establishments containing many objects of curiosity and historical interest, and perambulated the city and its environs. It contains numerous churches and other public edifices, many of them very magnificent, among which is an arcade that has 700 arches. Two leaning towers attracted our attention, one of which, the Arsenelli, was built 764 years ago. Its height is 256 feet and it inclines three feet from the perpendicular. The other, the Garasandi, is 130 feet high, with an inclination of eight feet. Whether this leaning tendency was from design or accident, tradition differs.

We arrived in Florence on the 9th, with the intention of remaining four days. This city is situated on the river Arno, in a great plain enclosed by hills, clothed with fruitful vineyards and fine gardens, and checkered with lovely villas.

Florence numbers 150,000 inhabitants, and is the richest, the fairest and most beautiful city in Italy, and affords the most attractive residence for foreigners. The poet says of it, "Of all the fairest cities of the earth, none is so fair as Florence." The nobility and aristocracy of every nation, during this season of the year, rendezvous here for health and pleasure. A beautiful promenade and carriage drive extend several miles along the river Arno, bordered with rich shrubbery; adjacent is a fine park. In the afternoon the scene, in this vicinity, is lively and animating—multitudes of promenaders in fashionable attire, and gentlemen exhibiting their best horses, finest carriages and equipages, and the ladies their gayest plumage. One day, while amusing myself in noticing the fashionable and sparkling groups of ladies promenading the rock-paved side-walk along the Arno, I remarked to my sister that I thought we had found where the fashion of mis-shaping the naturally beautiful human figure, by back bustling, equals that of our ladies of Salt Lake. She differed in opinion—considering the style here less grotesque.

This city possesses many grand historical monuments and collections of art. In the gallery of paintings and sculpture we noticed the finest specimens we have seen since we came to Italy. A magnificent "Cabinet of Gems" attracted our attention, which is decorated with four columns of Oriental alabaster, and contains six large cases of upwards of four hundred articles of workmanship in precious stones, rock crystal, etc., enriched with pearls and diamonds. There are eight columns of sienite agate, eight of rock crystal, and eight statues of the Apostles. Three busts of women in hyacinth, a vase in agate, a cup in green emerald, also one of rock crystal with a gold enamelled cover, a statue of a warrior in gold, ornamented with diamonds, a jasper cup ornamented with gold, a head in torquoise, the eyes of which are diamonds, a bowl in form of a sea-shell in blood red jasper, a cup made out of a single garnet, etc., the whole constituting a wonderful exhibition of skill and art.

I close my description of this modern Athens. We leave here to-morrow for Pisa, celebrated for its leaning towers, where we remain one day; from there we go to Rome.

LORENZO SNOW.

LETTER XXXVII.

Visit to an Infant School—Singing—Exercises in Reading and Writing—Lunch Time—Excellent Order—Medicine and Beds for the Sick, &c.

DESCRIPTION OF A BABY SCHOOL.

FLORENCE, Italy, January 13th, 1873.

EDITOR JUVENILE INSTRUCTOR:

While in Paris, after having called on the "Prefecteur," President George A. Smith received a note from him, containing permission for all of our party to visit all, or any of, the schools in Paris.

We visited several with much interest, but were most amused with the one I am about to describe to the young readers of the *Juvenile Instructor.* It was composed of boys and girls from three to six years of age.

As we approached the door of the schoolroom, we were charmed with the sound of infantile voices, united in singing sweetly, as none but children can sing. We took them by surprise, for our visit had not been announced.

The room was large, and the seats, all facing the same way, were elevated one above another, with the largest children on the upper row, and all seated in gradation, down to the lowest, on which the little things looked like mere babies.

Our entrance did not seem to create the least excitement—no one moved out of place; and when called upon by their head teacher, a middle-aged, amiable appearing woman, to give specimens of exercises, they responded without hesitation. We heard several of the eldest, and some pretty small ones, read, and saw specimens of writing on the blackboard which were very creditable. They sang several pieces for our amusement, in which the whole school joined, even to the smallest baby.

I noticed three aisles—one through the centre of the rows of seats, and one at each end, so that the entire school could move out without confusion. Indeed, order seemed to be a very prominent feature in this school discipline, which we had a fine opportunity for witnessing.

It so happened that our visit in this department was at noon, the children's lunch time, and we saw them march in single file—the largest in front, and so along down to the smallest—each placing hands on the shoulders of the one fronting him or her, and all singing merrily as they went into a large adjoining room. This room had seats through the centre, and up and down the sides. Under the side seats, were deposited neat little baskets with the children's lunch; and, as they marched, under the direction of the teachers, around this room, in slow, regular order, each one took up his or her basket, swung it on an arm and marched on, until the last baby scholar had received hers. A few, who were too small to look after their baskets, were helped by larger ones, who took them up and hung them on the arms of their little owners.

A considerable length of time was required for this; and, as a matter of course, children in school from half past eight in the morning till twelve, as these had been, must be hungry; and it required a good deal of practice in self-denial to wait the proper time for eating. I watched them closely, but did not detect one child prying into a basket until the last one was seated. Then all at once stopped singing, and, raising the lids of their baskets, commenced to devour the contents, and with as much chit-chat and sociability as a group of philosophers, with the exception of a few who were out of health. Those, the matron called into a small adjoining room, which served as a drugshop, and dealt to each a dose of cod liver oil, before they lunched.

I took the liberty of examining their baskets, and found their lunch to consist, generally, of bread and butter and a bottle of wine, which, in this country, almost seems a necessity instead of being a luxury. Those mothers who wished their children to have warm lunches, could either bring or send it into the vestry, where the matron or teacher receives it; but neither parent nor servant is admitted in, so as to mingle with the children.

We saw little beds or mattresses on which the smallest ones are placed when they fall asleep, and they are permitted to sleep as long as they please. We were told that these children always sing when they move—singing seems to be their element. They looked happy in their schoolroom; and to see them at lunch—eating and drinking, and full of chat and fun, was a very amusing and interesting sight. I presume that as many as one hundred and fifty were present, perhaps more. This is the only school in Paris composed of boys and girls. This is called an "Object school."

I have not visited a "kindergarten," but hope to do so on my return, and report to the readers of the *Juvenile Instructor*.

ELIZA R. SNOW.

LETTER XXXVIII.

Bologna—House of Galvani, Inventor of the Galvanic Battery—University of Anatomy—Florence—Railroad through the Apennines—A Tunnel Two Miles Long—Damage by High Waters—Rome—The Forum—Triumphal Arch of Titus—Ruins of Heathen Temples—The Colosseum—Arch of Constantine—Famous Churches—Aqueduct of Nero—St. Anthony's Day, Blessing Horses and Asses—Pio Nono—Italian Unity—Victor Emanuel Denounced.

Hotel D'Allemagne, Rome, Italy,
January 17th, 1873.

President Brigham Young:

I wrote to you on the 1st, on the 3rd and on the 7th of the present month, at which time we were at Venice. Since then we have visited Bologna, a city of the Romagna, having about 100,000 inhabitants, somewhat remarkable for its walls and arcades. It was here that the galvanic battery got a start, and the house of Galvani was shown to us, and also the room in which the experiment was tried. Anatomy was first taught in the same room. The University has now 400 students, and claims to be one of the oldest in the world.

We spent several days at Florence, which is a very fine city, and has been for several years the capital of Italy, and there are less signs of rotting down and decay in this city than in any other we have seen. The railroad from Bologna to Florence, leading over and through the Apennines, passes through 45 tunnels, over many bridges, heavy fills and deep cuts, and finally comes down the mountains like a succession of mammoth W's. One of the tunnels is about two miles long, and several others are of considerable length.

Great damage has been sustained in many parts of Italy

by high water, and we have been several times delayed and had to change cars in consequence thereof.

To-day we have visited the ancient Roman Forum, with the ruins of the Triumphal Arch of Titus, the Temple of Augustus, of Castor and Pollux, of Vespasian, of the Basilica Julia, the Rostrum, etc., etc. Thence we went to the ruins of the Colosseum, to the Temple of Venus and Rome, the Arch of Constantine, the Cathedral of St. John Lateran, the Aqueduct of Nero, the Scala Sancta, the Church of Maria Maggiore, and the Church of St. Anthony, and as it was St. Anthony's day, we saw the blessing of horses, mules and jackasses. They were driven up in front of the church; the officiating priest in his robes, surrounded by a number of his assistants also in uniform, came out of the church, reading a solemn service in Latin, and when he got through he sprinkled a little water towards the horses, pocketed the money and retired. Though it may seem ridiculous, this service has been performed hundreds of times to-day, and there was a complaint of irreverent feeling, that all the people did not get their horses blessed.

Pio Nono keeps himself closeted in the Vatican, and does not intend to make a public appearance while the heretic Victor Emanuel controls the city.

The Italian Parliament is in session, and Italy is now enjoying the benefits of its united government in its postal arrangements, currency and custom dues. Instead of eight sets of officers there is but one, and the postal arrangements with America are better than those in France.

The high church party denounces Victor Emanuel in severe language, while the red republicans do the very same thing in nearly the same language.

Our party are in usual health. Since I left Bologna I have had enough of rheumatism to make me think of Dixie, for the climate is quite mild.

GEORGE A. SMITH.

LETTER XXXIX.

At Rome—Ruins of Ancient Temples—Excavating the Forum—The Holy Staircase—Arch of Titus—The Colosseum—St. Anthony's Day—Palaces of the Emperors—Ruins of Caligula.

Rome, Italy, January 18th, 1873.

My Dear Sister M. T. Smoot:

You in Provo, and I in Rome! Who would have anticipated this wide separation? Yesterday, Mr. Wood, Mr. Cook's agent, with whom arrangements were previously made to show us the most important points here, conducted us to some portions of the ruins of this ancient city. We were shown the remains of the Temple of Venus, Jupiter, etc., the ancient Forum, the Rostrum so famous for speechifying—portions of gigantic columns in a reclining position, several standing in their original places and in a good state of preservation, considering their great age. We were informed that the late Popes have exercised their influence in preserving these ruins, which are now attracting the attention of great numbers of people from other parts, particularly from England and America.

At the expense of the government, many hands are now employed in excavating a portion of the great Forum of the ancient emperors, the Cæsars, etc., which, by gradual changes and usages, has been at times occupied by shepherds, and has been buried to the depth of several feet by accumulations of debris. There is a paling around the ruins, and no one is allowed to enter without permission. As we stood on a portion that has been unburied, we saw the stalwart guard-officer hurry a man off from the premises, who, no doubt, had stealthily intruded. We were all right, for our guide, an Englishman, seemed to be of considerable consequence; he is agent and sub-editor of the Swiss *Times*, an archaeological lecturer, etc. When he conducted us to the "Holy Staircase," said to be the identical one that the Saviour ascended in the court of Pilate, I asked him if he would swear to it. He said, emphatically, "I will not swear to anything." But directly afterward he said, "I will swear to the aqueduct, and I will swear that the stairs were brought from Jerusalem, and I will swear to the Arch of Titus," which was before us. We saw a man and woman slowly ascending the stairs, which none are allowed to ascend except on their knees; our incredulity prompted us to accept the suggestion of our guide and ascend by a side flight, which was considered less sacred; we found a representation of Christ on the cross in front of the "Sacred Stairs." We visited the celebrated Colosseum, which must have been a most magnificent structure in earlier days, being capable of seating eighty-seven thousand, with standing room for twenty thousand more.

It was St. Anthony's day, and we witnessed the ceremony of blessing animals, which was the most amusing of all. On that day the priest blesses horses, mules, donkeys and all kinds of animals. A fine span of horses, richly caparisoned, was driven in front of the church; the priest, with several attendants, came out, dressed in black gowns with white tunics. Standing in front of the horses, with grave pomposity, he read a service in Latin, which probably the animals understood as well as himself; after which he took a long handled swab from a kettle, in the hand of a boy standing by his side, and spirted water (probably "Holy,") in the direction of the horses' faces, but not far enough to reach them; and then, after pocketing his fee, the priest returned into the church. The coachman, a young man, could hardly hold his countenance, looking as if he were witnessing a farce, and felt that the spectators all sympathized with him.

Monday, January 20th.

Yesterday afternoon Mr. Wood took us through, around and under many of the ruins of the palaces of the emperors—portions of the walls built by early Romans. Many of the specimens show vestiges of beauty and magnificence. In several instances, trees have grown in crevices of ponderous edifices which were constructed of rock, brick and cement, their growth having made large openings, forcing the structures apart and thus producing dilapidation. I will enclose you a leaf which I plucked from a shrub growing on the remains of the ruins of Caligula. In exhuming these ruins, inscriptions are found which identify many of them.

Last night Brother Carrington joined us, and brought what of our mail had arrived in Liverpool. * * * * We are all in good spirits; my health was never better, although "sight-seeing" is not the easiest work in the world. Clara and I get along just as well as two persons could do, and I feel no lack of companionship.

I get but little time to write, have done this by "piecemeal." With much love, I am as ever,

ELIZA R. SNOW.

LETTER XL.

Rome and its Population—The Seven Hills—Purchase of Real Estate by Napoleon III—Excavations by the Government—The Forum—Anthony and Julius Cæsar—Where Virginius Stabbed his Daughter—Famous Obelisks—Temple of Venus—The Tarpeian Rock—Dimensions of the Colosseum—Visits to Cathedrals—St. Peter's—A Call on the American Minister.

Rome, Italy, January 21st, 1873.

Editor Deseret News:

We arrived here on the 15th ult. This city is built on both sides of the Tiber, about fifteen miles from where it empties into the Mediterranean. In 1867, it contained 215,000 inhabitants, of whom 6,000 were clergymen, 5,000 nuns, 4,500 Jews, 450 Protestants, 7,300 soldiers, and, in the winter season, about 25,000 visitors. In the day of its greatest prosperity Rome exceeded two millions; in the middle of the fourteenth century it had been reduced by disease, poverty and war, to less than twenty thousand people. What is now understood as modern Rome, is surrounded by a wall twelve miles in length, about fifty feet high, and built of brick.

The famous "seven hills" on which Rome was principally erected are now measurably uninhabited. A few churches, monasteries, nunneries, old farm houses, gardens and vineyards occupy these hills which formerly astonished the world with marble edifices, palaces and magnificent temples; much of this glory and grandeur now lie from ten to twenty feet beneath the surface of the ground. Napoleon the Third purchased extensive grounds on which a portion of ancient Rome was built, and expended large sums in excavations to aid him in his "History of the Cæsars." He made many important discoveries, several of which we saw while exploring the ruins—portions of streets, temples, beautiful edifices, numerous statues, marble and granite columns, which were found buried twenty feet underground. The Italian government is now prosecuting the work commenced by Napoleon, constantly bringing to light Roman history and its antiquities. We saw sufficient of the remains of the ancient Roman Forum, the place of popular assemblies, where the orators addressed the people, to satisfy us of its former grandeur and magnificence. We stood where Anthony, in his artful speech over the murdered body of Julius Cæsar, aroused the indignation of the populace against the conspirators; and where Virginius procured his knife, and killed his daughter to preserve her from slavery. We also walked over the ground where the Sabine women rushed frantically between their husbands and fathers to prevent the impending battle.

In the Piazza di St. Pietro we saw a famous obelisk which was brought to Rome by the Emperor Caligula and placed in the Vatican Circus. It was removed in 1586 and erected on its present site under the superintendency of Dominica Fontana. This huge monument weighs nearly one million of pounds. It is said that Fontana in constructing his machines had neglected to make allowance for the tension of the ropes, produced by the immense weight, and that at the critical moment, though the spectators had been prohibited under penalty of death from speaking or shouting, one of the eight hundred workmen cried out "Aqua alle funi," i. e., water on the ropes, thus solving the difficulty. His descendants were granted important privileges for this hazardous interference. Another obelisk we noticed called the "Obelisk of the Lateran," of red granite covered with hieroglyphics, which was brought from Alexandria to the mouth of the Tiber in a vessel of three hundred oars. It is supposed to have been standing in Egypt anterior to the exodus of the Israelites, and probably is four thousand years old. It is 141 feet high, and weighs nearly 455 tons.

Some portions of the celebrated Temple of Venus and Rome still remain. It was built by the Emperor Hadrian after his own design; when it was finished, he asked Appolodorus what he thought of it. The architect replied that it was very good for an emperor, whereupon Hadrian ordered him to be beheaded.

We went to the "Tarpeian Rock," the precipice from which criminals were thrown down; there is considerable rubbish beneath, but it is still sufficiently lofty to insure unpleasant results of a fall from its summit.

There are very few monuments that exhibit more effectually the splendor of ancient Rome than the remains of the celebrated Colosseum. It was commenced by Vespasian and completed by Titus, after his conquest of the Jews. It is said that sixty thousand Jews were engaged ten years in this gigantic antique structure. After it had fallen into decay, it was used as a quarry from which were built churches and palaces until, by its consecration as holy ground, on account of the number of martyrs supposed to have suffered within its walls, this vandalism was discontinued. It seated 87,000 people, with standing room for 20,000. Its inauguration, anno domini 81, continued one hundred days, during which 5,000 wild beasts and 10,000 captives were slain. Its circumference is 1,641 feet, the height of the outer wall, 157, the length of the arena, 278, and its width, 177 feet, the whole superficial area, six acres. In the Museum of the Capitol, we saw a striking representation of the character of the former scenes enacted in the arena of this amphitheatre. A marble statue of a dying gladiator—a wonderful specimen of the perfection to which the art of sculpture had attained. The figure is in a reclining posture, a deep cut in the side, the blood trickling down, a broken sword lying beside it, the muscles gradually relaxing and strength failing, the lineaments of the face expressing intense anguish, yet determined resolution to conceal pain, as the poet says—

> I see before me the gladiator lie;
> He leans upon his hand—his manly brow
> Consents to death, but conquers agony,
> And his droop'd head sinks gradually low,
> And through his side, the last drops, ebbing slow,
> From the red gash fall heavy one by one,
> Like the first of a thundershower; and now
> The arena swims around him; he is gone
> Ere ceased the inhuman shout which hailed
> The wretch who won.

We visited several celebrated Roman cathedrals, St. Peter's first and foremost. The area of this church is 212,321 square feet, its exterior 651 feet in length, its height from the pavement to the cross on the summit is 448 feet. In contains 290 windows, 390 statues, 46 altars and 748 columns. The dome rises 318 feet above the roof, and has a circumference of 652 feet. In the seventeenth century the dome showed signs of giving way, and was strengthened by means of huge iron hoops.

We ascend to the lantern by an easy stairway, where we have a magnificent view of the surrounding country, extending to the blue waters of the Mediterranean. The ball on the summit affords room for sixteen persons, though from the ground it appears little larger than a man's hat.

Previous to the Papal states being incorporated into the Italian kingdom, it was customary, on certain days in the year, to present from this church a grand spectacle—a vast illumination of the dome, facade and colonnades by 4,400 lamps. It is thought that this great display will never be repeated. The Pope has remained singularly quiet, refusing to officiate at public festivals since "Victor" took possession of Rome. Some attribute this inaction to a design to awaken sympathy and create a stirring interest in his favor with Catholic communities throughout the world. We were informed to-day that the Pope had just received a delegation of distinguished gentlemen from England, representing a large body of men who had solemnly engaged to render whatever assistance he might require.

We called at the American Minister's to-day; not finding him at home, we left our cards with his secretary. We shall probably have an interview with him before leaving Rome. Our tour under Mr. Cook's management thus far has proved perfectly satisfactory. Our railroad transits have invariably been first-class, and' our hotels generally. We remain here three days longer, then go to Naples.

LORENZO SNOW.

LETTER XLI.

Leave Venice—A City with One Hundred and Thirty Churches—A Famous University—Villa of King Victor Emanuel—Leaning Towers—Road over the Apennines—"The Garden of Italy"—At Florence—Pisa—The Campanile—The Basilica—Rome—Ancient Ruins—Beggars—Santa Scala, or Holy Staircase—Aqueduct of Nero—The Apollo Theatre—Palaces of the Cæsars—The Pantheon—Capitoline Hill—Prison where St. Peter and St. Paul were Confined—House of Rienzi—Column of Pius Antoninus—The Chamber of Deputies—The Sixtine Chapel—Cemetery of the Capuchins—Visits to Famous Localities and Places—The Quirinal—The Appian Way—Tombs of Celebrated Romans—Tumuli of the Horatii and of the Curatii—Circus of Romulus—The Vatican—Baths of Caracalla—Golden House of Nero—Statue of Moses.

Hotel D'Allemagne, Rome, Italy,
January 23d, 1873.

Editors Salt Lake Herald:

After I had mailed my last letter to you from Venice, on the 5th inst., Mr. George Dunford, of our party, received letters from home that required his immediate return on account of business matters, and he left us on the morning of the 7th inst., very much regretting that circumstances did not permit him to go with us any further. We left Venice on the 8th at 7.40 a. m., *via* Padua and Ferrara, for Bologna, where we arrived at 12.16 p. m. This is one of the most ancient and important towns of Italy, the capital of the Romagna, situated in a fertile plain at the base of the Apennines, between the Reno, and the Aposa and the Savena rivers; population about 90,000. It possesses 120 churches, twenty monasteries and a venerable and celebrated university. The town was founded by the Etruscans. Irnerius introduced the study of the Roman law in 1262, whilst his successors, the Glossators, devoted their energies in its interpretation. The studies of medicine and philosophy were introduced at a later period, and a theological faculty was established by Pope Innocent VI. The anatomy of the human frame was first taught here, in the 14th century, and here galvanism was discovered by Joseph Galvani in 1789. It is a remarkable fact, that this university has numbered members of the fair sex among its professors, among them Vovella d'Andrea, a lady of great personal attractions, who is said to have been concealed by a curtain during her lectures. The antiquated aspect of the town, its picturesque mediæval architecture, lofty arcades and venerable churches, all bear testimony to the peculiar character of the place. We visited the Gallery of Fine Arts, the Anatomical Museum, said to be one of the finest in the world, and took a drive through the town and to the villa of King Victor Emanuel, situated on a hill, from which a very fine view is obtained of the city and its environs. Bologna also boasts of two leaning towers. One of them, the Torre Asinelli, was erected by Gherardo degli Asinelli in 1,109, is 272 feet high and three feet four inches out of the perpendicular; the other, the Torre Garisenda, was erected in 1,110 by Filippo and Ottone Garisenda, is only 138 feet high, but eight feet out of the perpendicular. On the 9th we left Bologna at 1.25 p. m. for Florence. The road over the Tuscan Apennines is one of the most imposing structures of the kind in existence. Bridges, forty-five tunnels, and heavy fills are traversed in uninterrupted succession. Beautiful views are obtained of the valleys and gorges of the Apennines, and toward Florence we descended on a very steep grade in a regular zig-zag, and going three times over the same ground, to the luxuriant plains of Tuscany, called the "Garden of Italy." We arrived at Florence at 5.46 p. m., and put up at the Hotel Victoria. During our stay we called upon the American vice-Consul, Mr. J. C. Matteini, No. 7 Via Maggio, and registered our names. Of the principal churches we visited the cathedral, a very fine edifice, on the outside 555 feet long, 340 feet wide, 354 feet high; the Battistero, Carmine, San Croce, San Lorenzo and San Michael, the palaces of Vecchio and Pitti, and a fine gallery of pictures and statues. Florence has now about 140,000 inhabitants, and is beautifully situated on both banks of the Arno. The principal drives and the park are every afternoon crowded with the finest turnouts of the fashionable world, and we have never before seen so much display since we left home. On the 4th inst., we took train for Pisa at 9.20 a. m., and reached there about 11.30 a. m. In the afternoon we visited the Campanile, or clock tower, remarkable for its oblique position. It was commenced in 1174 and finished in 1350; it rises in eight different stories, is 151 feet high and 12 feet out of the perpendicular, and is usually known as the "leaning tower." The Basilica or cathedral close by is a fine edifice, constructed entirely of white marble, with black and colored ornamentations, 292 feet in length. These being the principal attractions of Pisa, we left next morning at 9.50 a. m. for Rome, where we arrived in beautiful moonlight at 10 p. m. We put up at the Hotel d'Allemagne and commenced our arrangements for sight-seeing with the agent of Messrs. Thomas Cook & Son, Mr. Shakespere Wood, on Friday morning the 17th inst., and I will give you the names of all the places of interest which we visited every day, as it would be impossible for me to go into details. If you can form any idea of the distances of this city, once the mistress of the world, situated on seven hills, you will see that we have been doing hard work to see all that could be seen in so short a time as was allotted to us. Friday 7th, we visited the old Roman farm, between the Capitoline and Palatine hills, saw the ruins of the Basilica Augustus and that of Julia, the Temple of Castor and Pollux and that of Vespasian, the ruins of the

L

Public Treasury, the Arch of Titus, the Rostrum of the celebrated Roman orators, the Via Sacra, the old water drain and marks on the pavement of different games played at that early period by the "boys" of those Roman citizens. Thence we drove to the Colosseum, the Temple of Venus and Rome, the Arch of Constantine, the Church of St. John Lateran, the Baptisterie close by, where there is a font in which Constantine is said to have been baptized, thence to the Church of St. Maria Maggiore and the Church of St. Anthony, where we witnessed the blessing of horses, mules, etc., as it was St. Anthony's Day. Some of the horses driven up to the door of the church, and even our own team that we had that day, really seemed to be in need of a first-class blessing. The place around the door of the church was lousy with beggars. After looking at the Santa Scala, or holy staircase, which is said to have been brought here from the Palace of Pilate, and on which the Saviour came down from the Hall of Judgment, and the Aqueduct of Nero, which was thirty-five miles long, we returned to the hotel, being satisfied that we had done a good day's work. The following day it rained very hard and we spent our time in writing up our journals. In the evening some of our party visited the Apollo Theatre, and witnessed the performance of the Opera of Ballo il Mashere, which, as the name indicates, includes a regular Italian masquerade ball, and finished with the ballet of Gilileo Galileo. Sunday the 19th we had a sacramental meeting in the morning and in the afternoon we drove to the extensive ruins of the palaces of the Cæsars.

At 7 p.m. President Albert Carrington arrived, to join our party, and he brought us our letters from home up to December 25th, and our semi-weeklies of December 21st and 25th. Monday the 20th, we visited the Pantheon, the Capitoline Hill and Museum of Sculpture, the equestrian bronze statue of Marcus Aurelius, the Marmertine Prison, where Peter and Paul are said to have been imprisoned, the gate Janus Quadrifons, the Goldsmiths' Arch, ruins of the Temple of Vesta, of the Temple of Fortuna Virilis, the house of Rienzi, the Theatre of Marcellus, the Column of Pius Antoninus, the Basilica of St. Paul, which is one of the finest churches of Rome, the Chamber of Deputies, which was in session, and the Church of Santa Maria Sopra Minerva. Sunday, the 21st, we went to the Sixtine Chapel in the Vatican, containing Michael Angelo's celebrated painting of "The Last Judgment" and the "Loggie and Stanze" of Raphael. We then went through the greatest part of the Vatican picture gallery and the lower portion of St. Peter's Church. In the afternoon we visited the cemetery of the Capuchins, where the skulls and skeletons of about 5,400 members of that order, who had died, were piled up in columns, pilasters and wall and ceiling ornaments of every conceivable shape, in a subterranean vault. It was a very peculiar sight indeed. Then we visited the Church of St. Maria degli Angeli, the Baths of Diocletian, the Basilica of St. Clement of the 12th century, below that the Basilica of St. Clement of the 4th century, with well preserved frescos, which were only discovered several years ago; and below that the house of St. Clement and the Temple of Methras. We also called the same day on the American Minister, Mr. George P. Marsh; but, as we did not find him in, we left our cards with the secretary of legation. Wednesday, the 23rd, we visited the Church St. Augustine, the piazza (square) Navona, which is the site of the circus Agonalis, the statue of Pasquin, the Varnisi palace, a very large building, erected of stones taken from the Colosseum, the guard house of the 7th cohort of the Vigiles, the Church of Chrysogono, Monte Cavallo, with two large bronze statues of horses, and on the same square, in the Quirinal Palace, a number of very elegantly furnished rooms, now occupied by king Victor Emanuel. In the afternoon we drove five miles out of the city on the once celebrated Appian Way, which leads from Rome to Brindisi. The road is lined on both sides with tombs of celebrated ancient Romans, some of them very large, and among the rest the tumuli of the Horatii and Curiatii; also the ruins of the large villa of the Quintilli; the Ustrinum, a place surrounded with walls, where the dead bodies were burned in former times and the ashes were put in vases for burial; thence we drove to the world-renowned catacombs of Calixtus, the old circus of Romulus, the Arch of Drusus, the Columbaria, where the vases, containing the ashes of burnt bodies were preserved in the walls of the building in niches, similar to pigeon holes on a large scale. This finished another day's work. On Thursday, the 23d, we drove to St. Peter's, and ascended the dome, visited the Vatican sculpture gallery, the ruins of the Baths of Caracalla, covering 40 acres of ground, the Church St. Stefano Rotonda, containing on its walls paintings of all imaginable kinds of martyrdom to which the early Christians had been subjected. From there we went to the ruins of the golden house of Nero, which contains some very well preserved frescos; to the Baths of Titus on the Esculine Hill, and finished our programme with the Church of St. Pietro, in Vinculi, which contains a beautiful white marble statue of Moses, by the celebrated Michael Angelo. Saturday, the 25th, we intend to leave for Naples, where we stay till the 30th, thence we go to Brindisi, where we take steamer for Corfu, and thence, on the 1st of February, we go aboard the Lloyd steamer for Alexandria. All of the party are in usual health.

Very truly yours,

PAUL A. SCHETTLER.

LETTER XLII.

Go to Turin and Venice—A Hotel in Water—A City Without Carriages—Famous and Curious Glass Manufactures—Bridge of Sighs—Bologna, Florence and Pisa—At Rome—Cemetery of the Capuchins—Burial Place of Five Thousand Monks—Arches, Chandeliers and Candlesticks of Human Bones—Palace of Victor Emanuel.

Rome, Italy, January 24th, 1873.

Editor Woman's Exponent:

From Genoa, where I wrote you last, we went to Turin, from Turin to Venice. The time has been when Venice exercised a powerful influence at home and abroad, and claimed to be "mistress of the seas." That day has gone by. The hotel at which we put up appeared to be completely imbedded in water; but we found, on the opposite side from where we entered, stepping from our gondolas on to stone steps, it claimed a narrow strip of *terra firma*. There is not a carriage in the place—in the public garden three horses are kept on exhibition—all travel and business, except that of pedestrian capacity, is done on the water by the means of oars propelled by human muscles.

The once boasted silk manufactures of Venice have dwindled into a solitary one, and that, I was informed, is worked by hand. In the manufacture of glass I think they are nowhere excelled, especially in that of the ornamental kind. We visited one establishment. It is a curiosity to see into how many forms and textures glass can be worked. We saw women spinning and reeling it into fine threads, while others wove it into fancy plates, necklaces, etc., which seemed elastic and strong.

The Grand Hotel Victoria, our stopping place, is a fine establishment, and affords good accommodations for travelers.

But I must hasten on, and leave Venice with its palaces, palazzas, prisons, Bridge of Sighs, gondolas and canals, for another consideration; and from thence to Bologna, thence to Florence, where for the first time since leaving home we are located on the ground floor of the hotel

FLORENCE.

Beneath high, villa-dotted hills,
  That in succession rise
Like rich gemm'd parapets around,
  The lovely Florence lies.

The Arno, broad and gentle stream,
  That flows meand'ring through,
Divides, but in unequal parts,
  The city plat in two.

I've seen its princely palaces
  Where wealth and ease reside,
Where independence fills her sales
  With luxury and pride.

I see you, Florence, all the while,
  So beautiful and gay;
I ask, Is this your common dress,
  Or, this your holiday?

Bo wise, and, while their golden show'rs
  The bounteous heav'ns distil;
Avoid debasing luxury,
  Prolific source of ill.

The crown of peace is on your head,
  Its wreath around your brow;
The royal carpet, newly spread,
  Adorns your threshold now.

From Florence we went to Pisa, from thence to Rome.

Of the much I have seen here, I can say but little in one letter. We are traveling under the direction of Mr. Cook, the London tourist. He furnished a guide to take us out five days, and show us the most interesting portions of the city. Our programme concluded last evening; and feeling that I have "done" Rome, I am doing up matters to-day, preparatory to leaving for Naples to-morrow—writing you is one of the items.

Among the many curiosities witnessed, I will mention one remarkably singular, although not the most pleasing. It is the Cemetery of the Capuchins, in the Franciscan Monastery. Our guide took us to the door, where we were met by a monk who conducted us through four apartments in which five thousand and four hundred monks had been buried, and nearly all of the bones of these persons were in plain view. A narrow path on one side of the room afforded a passage, parallel with which was a railing over a very low wall to prevent intrusion into the main portion of the room which the bones occupied. It is impossible to describe the sensation produced by the sight of millions of human bones assorted and arranged—some on arches from four to five feet high, under which a body, apparently in a similar state to that of an Egyptian mummy, was standing dressed in a black gown, others were symmetrically formed into niches where other bodies were placed in a reclining position; others were arranged in fanciful forms and figures on the ceilings above. The long bones were packed by themselves—the arches being mostly formed by them, and some of them crowned with several rows of sculls—the small ones being used in making ornaments. Everything—the chandeliers, candlesticks, etc., were made of bones! The arrangement of them required much care and study, and no very slight artistic skill.

The manner of these monks is, when they bring a body, to take up the bones of the one that had been longest buried, and place the fresh one in the vacancy, and in this way the bones are accumulating from time to time.

Those bodies which do not decompose are placed in the arches and niches of these bony structures, and preserved in this state. We saw a number of them, one, who died as late as 1867, with whom our guide had been well acquainted.

With all the seemingly ludicrous arrangements, these bones are sacredly prized by the living monks. On being asked if they would sell a skull, the answer was decidedly "no." The strange curiosity of this exhibition interested me much, but I was glad to turn my face in the direction of fresh air as soon as the novelty of the scene was explained.

We visited the palace of Victor Emanuel—passed through halls, reception rooms, ante-chambers, state rooms, dining rooms, etc., very beautiful—the furniture rich, and altogether magnificent. We should have been better satisfied had we interviewed the occupant, but that was not included in the programme.

ELIZA R. SNOW.

LETTER XLIII.

Description of the Vatican—Decorations of Michael Angelo—"The Last Judgment"—Anecdote of Paul III and Michael Angelo—The Appian Way—Remains of Seneca—Baths of Caracalla—A Much Venerated Chapel—Footprint of the Saviour—Obelisks—Forum of Trajan—Statue of St. Peter—Constantine Embracing Christianity—Naples—Herculaneum—Pompeii—Mount Vesuvius.

NAPLES, Italy, January 28th, 1873.

EDITOR DESERET NEWS:

I will now mention a few more items which came under our observation while in Rome. We were much interested in the Vatican Palace, the residence of the Pope. It embraces an immense area, 1,151 feet in length, 767 in breadth, eight grand staircases, 200 smaller ones, twenty courts and 4,422 apartments. It contains a vast collection of the most celebrated marble statuary and paintings in the world.

The ingenuity and wealth of the Roman pontiffs during many centuries have been employed to make this palace suitable for the accommodation of the representatives of St. Peter in regard to splendor and magnificence.

The distinguished artist, Michael Angelo, was engaged a number of years in decorating some of these apartments with his best paintings. One of these we noticed in particular was a large picture in fresco, covering one end of a lofty room, fifty feet wide; it is called "The Last Judgment." Michael Angelo labored nearly eight years upon this work. Pope Paul III manifested much interest in this painting, and, to encourage the artist, went to his studio accompanied by ten of his cardinals, which was considered an extraordinary condescension on the part of "His Holiness." He wished the picture painted in oil, but the artist would not consent, declaring that "oil painting was an occupation fit only for women and idlers and such as had plenty of time to throw away." In the upper part of the picture is the Saviour seated in the act of pronouncing judgment. On one side are a multitude of saints and patriarchs, on the other the martyrs with the symbols of their sufferings—St. Catherine with the wheel on which she was broken, St. Sebastian, with the arrows by which he was killed, St. Bartholomew, carrying his skin, &c. Below is a group of angels sounding the last trumpet, and carrying the books of judgment. On the left is represented the condition of the damned—the demons are seen coming out of the pit to seize them as they struggle to escape, their features expressing the utmost despair, at the same time exhibiting passions of rage, anguish and defiance. On the opposite side the saints are rising slowly from their graves, aided by angels to ascend into the regions of the blest.

Paul III was displeased with the nudity of the figures and intended to destroy the whole. On hearing this objection of the Pope, Michael Angelo said, "Tell the Pope that this is but a small affair, and easy to be remedied—let him reform the world, and pictures will reform themselves." The Pope engaged Volterra to cover the most conspicuous figures with drapery, which caused the Italians to nick-name him Braghettone, that is the breeches maker. Michael Angelo was obliged to submit to the Pope's will, but revenged himself in the following style upon Biagio, master of ceremonies, who suggested the indelicacy of the figures. He represented him in one of the angels of the picture standing in hell as Midas, with asses' ears, his body encircled by a serpent. Biagio requested the Pope to compel the artist to expunge this figure, but he declared he could only release from purgatory.

We made an excursion of several miles in the country,

traveling on the celebrated Appian Way, a road built in ancient times by the Romans. They were accustomed to bury their dead beyond the city along the sides of this thoroughfare, for which purpose thousands of monuments were built, thickly studding both sides of the way, the distance of about thirteen miles—many of them massive and lofty, built of brick, stone and concrete, with an external covering of polished marble, ornamented with beautiful statuary, and otherwise magnificently decorated. Among the monumental ruins is one said to contain the remains of Seneca, the great moralist, one of my favorite authors, who unjustly suffered death by the order of Nero. His statue in marble, like a protecting angel, still remains over the crumbling ruins of his monument, and even should this statue also disappear, the elevating moral sentiments he inculcated cannot perish, but will ever perpetuate his memory.

We saw a spacious enclosure where the Romans practised burning the bodies of the dead, in order to place their ashes in urns or vases to be deposited in tombs. We were shown the remains of the bathing establishment of Caracalla, constructed somewhat on the principle of the Turkish bath. It embraced an area of about forty acres, most of which had been covered with arched mason work, now fallen down. A large portion of the wall still remains; some fifteen feet depth of earth has been excavated to show its original plan and grandeur.

We were conducted into a small chapel held in high esteem by the Catholics through a tradition that Peter, when imprisoned in Rome, escaped in the night, and upon reaching this point the Saviour met him and told him he was going to Rome to be crucified the second time, whereupon Peter, taking the hint, returned to the city and suffered crucifixion. On the floor of this church is a marble slab with a fac-simile of the footmark of the Saviour, which is pretended to have been made upon the road pavement on which he stood.

Rome possesses many obelisks and monumental columns, one, erected by Bernini, formed of red granite covered with hieroglyphics, stands in the Piazza Navona, in the midst of a fountain, on rock-work forty feet high ; the height of the obelisk is fifty-one feet. I was amused with an anecdote connected with this monument related by our guide. Bernini had bitter enemies who insisted that the foundation was inadequate to the support of the column. With the greatest difficulty, overcoming the immense influence against him, he succeeded in erecting the obelisk. One day his enemies raised a tremendous excitement by reporting that the foundation was giving way. The square was soon filled with an enthusiastic populace, every moment expecting the superstructure to go down. Bernini, on hearing this state of things, proceeded to the square in his carriage—arriving in front of his work, disregarding the hisses and groans of the people, he ordered ladders, connected them together, and ascending to the top of the obelisk, drew from his pocket a ball of twine, unwound until he had four strings, each of sufficient length to reach across the square, and fastened one end of each to the top of the column. He then descended—gathered the opposite ends, walked around the square, fastening each end at opposite points to the buildings, by means of small nails driven into the plaster of the walls. He then coolly stepped into his carriage and drove home. Before he left the square, however, the people comprehending the joke, honored him with thundering applause, to the great discomfiture of his enemies.

The Forum of Trajan has been partially uncovered, revealing statues, broken columns and many other relics in great numbers. One obelisk one hundred and twenty-four feet high still stands in this Forum, formerly surmounted by a colossal statue of the Emperor Trajan, now by that of St. Peter. It is covered with upwards of 2,500 human figures, averaging two feet in length. In this Forum it is said that

Constantine, in the presence of the dignitaries of the Empire, and a vast assemblage of the people, renounced Paganism and declared for Christianity; that upon this announcement the Christians present raised a loud and prolonged shout of five minutes continuation. Some Pagan officers, who were present, looked glum and sullen. The Christians, noticing this, and firing up under the excitement, motioned that every Pagan should be compelled to follow the example of their illustrious Emperor.

We arrived at Naples from Rome on the 25th ult.; have visited Herculaneum and Pompeii, and to-morrow expect to climb Mount Vesuvius, notwithstanding the following, which appeared in the Naples papers of yesterday:

"There has been a slight eruption of Vesuvius in the last twenty-four hours; flames and red-hot stones were projected to a great height all day yesterday, and windows at Castellamare were shaken out by the earth's vibratory motion. There is an unusual volume of smoke issuing from the mouth of the crater, and the instruments at the observatory indicate the presence of strong electrical currents."

Should the aspect of the mountain appear to be threatening in the morning, we may change our present intentions, and gratify our curiosity in contemplating it in the distance.

LORENZO SNOW.

LETTER XLIV.

Cathedral of St. Januarius—Beggars and Peddlers—Excavations of Pompeii—Villa of Diomede—Villa of Cicero—Inn of Albinus—Vestals of Narcissus—House of Sallust—Bread Baked 1800 Years Ago—Ancient Baths—Temple of Fortune—Temples of Jupiter and Mercury—National Museum—Relics of Pompeii—Herculaneum—Ascent of Vesuvius.

HOTEL DES ETRANGERES, Naples, Italy,
January 29th, 1873.

EDITORS SALT LAKE HERALD:

On the 25th inst., we left Rome at 1.5 p. m., for Naples, where we arrived at 8.16 p.m. Next day, Sunday, the 26th, we had a meeting in the morning, and in the afternoon we drove through the city and the principal promenades, to get a general idea of this place. This city is beautifully situated in the form of an amphitheatre, on the bay of Naples, and has 600,000 inhabitants. The principal church is the Cathedral of St. Januarius, with many fine statues and tombs. The streets are full of beggars and peddlers, who use all imaginable tricks to get some pennies out of your pocket.

On the morning of the 27th we drove through the villages of Portici and Resina to the excavations of Pompeii, which city has been buried nearly eighteen centuries. Among the principal places visited we saw the villa of Diomede, in which the skeletons of seventeen persons were found, and the villa of Cicero in the Street of Tombs, outside of the gate of Herculaneum; then inside the gate we visited the inn of Albinus, the house of the Vestals of Narcissus, the house of

Sallust, one of the most elegant in the city, and near by a bakery where several loaves of bread with the baker's name stamped on the top were found in the oven, several wine shops, and the house of Polybius. In the street of Thermæ or Baths, are the houses of Apollo, Meleager, &c. In the street of the Forum is the Temple of Fortune, the Public Baths and the School of the Gladiators. In the Forum are three triumphal arches, built with brick and lava, encased in marble, the Civil Forum, paved with marble, the Temple of Jupiter, the Temple of Venus, the Basilica, the tribunals, the prisons, and the Temple of Mercury. Then we visited the ruins of the great theatre, 223 feet internal diameter, and the amphitheatre, with thirty-five rows of steps, divided into three stages.

The following day we paid a visit to the National Museum, where we found a large and interesting collection of statues in bronze and marble; agricultural, mechanical and surgical implements, articles of glass, etc., which had been found in Pompeii, showing that the people living there at that early period, were highly advanced in many of the arts and sciences. On our way home from Pompeii we had paid a short visit to the excavations of Herculaneum twenty-six feet below the modern town of Resina.

To-day we visited Vesuvius, and had very favorable weather, and a fine view over the city, and bay of Naples, the island of Capri, the villages of Portici, Resina, Torro del Greca, Castellamare and Sorrento. We drove to the Hermitage, where we arrived at 11.30 a. m. At noon we started on ponies, and President Smith in an arm-chair, carried by four men, for the foot of the cone. Arrived there at 12.45 p.m., and after a very steep and fatiguing ascent through loose gravel, we reached the crater at 2 p.m. We could at times see almost down to the bottom, and then again heavy masses of smoke hid up the view entirely. The smell of sulphur in some places was almost unbearable, and the guides made it a business to cook eggs over the hot cracks around the crater.

To-morrow we leave for Egypt, *via* Brindisi and Corfu, all of us enjoying good health.

Yours truly,

PAUL A. SCHETTLER.

LETTER XLV.

City of Naples—Dwellings of the Poor—Beggars—Pompeii—The Earthquakes of Anno Domini 63 and 79—Excavations and Relics—Herculaneum—The Museum of Naples—The "Secret Cabinet"—Ascent of Vesuvius—Pliny the Elder—Thirty-four Volcanic Eruptions—The "Hermitage"—From Naples to Brindisi—Hardworking Women—Turkish Towns and Villas—Corfu—Olive and Grape Culture—Religious Service in a Greek Cathedral—No "Grecian Bend"—Take Steamer for Alexandria.

ALEXANDRIA, Egypt, February 6th, 1873.

EDITOR DESERET NEWS:

I will commence where I closed my last letter, at Naples. The city of Naples contains a population of over half a million. It is beautifully situated on the slope of a range of hills bordering the Mediterranean. Including its suburbs, it is nearly eighteen miles in circumference. The streets, like those of most other cities of Europe, are generally narrow, though some are wide, handsomely paved and bordered with elegant buildings, five, six, and seven stories high. We noticed in many parts of the city, that the lower stories are built without windows; air and light being admitted through the door in front, which is generally large, always standing open except at night, when the occupants retire to rest. These apartments were swarming with laboring people, many of whom appeared in great poverty. We have visited no city where so much begging is practised as in Naples. In many places beggars thronged us by multitudes.

We visited Pompeii, distant a few miles from Naples, and spent several hours in walking through the streets and examining its interesting and mournful ruins. In the year A. D. 63, the city was partially destroyed by an earthquake. The inhabitants abandoned the town but returned directly afterwards, and it had regained nearly all its splendor, when, at mid-day, on November 23d, A. D. 79, the eruption destined to destroy it commenced. The wooden roofs of the houses were either set on fire or broken in by the weight of the matter deposited on them. It is thought that, inasmuch as but few skeletons have been found, nearly all of the inhabitants were enabled to escape. They returned soon afterwards to dig the soil in which the town was buried, and carried away the valuables left in their houses, and some precious objects from the public edifices. The villa of Diomede is one of the largest establishments. The remains of seventeen persons were found there during the excavations. Some of them were shown us at Pompeii, others we saw in the National Museum in Naples. Close by the garden gate of this villa were discovered the skeletons of the proprietor and his attendant—one holding in his hand the keys of the villa; the other, a purse which contained one hundred gold and silver coins.

Quite a large portion of the city is now excavated, exhibiting streets, private buildings, temples, theatres, fountains, wine cellars, public squares, etc., etc., in a wonderful state of preservation. The whole resembles a large, magnificent town, the inhabitants of which had suddenly fled, or gone out on a general excursion.

In returning to Naples we stopped a short time in Hercu-

M

laneum, which contains some objects of interest. The ancient theatre has been excavated, which appears to have consisted of nineteen tiers of seats, sufficient to accommodate ten thousand persons—its orchestra is twenty-six feet below the surface of the present town, Resina.

The next day we spent a few hours very agreeably in the celebrated Museum of Naples, which contains a vast number of apartments richly stored with relics of ancient art and science, and constitutes a general depot of the two ancient cities, Pompeii and Herculaneum, and other localities of Naples and Sicily. The "Secret Cabinet," which was formerly closed to all visitors, is now open to gentlemen, but is still closed to ladies and the Catholic clergy. Its contents exhibit, in a striking manner, the dissipated public taste, and the licentious and beastly practices of the inhabitants of those doomed cities, Pompeii and Herculaneum, showing that they well merited the terrible judgment meted out to them so suddenly.

We concluded to pay our respects to Mount Vesuvius. It is nearly four thousand feet above the level of the sea. In the eruption of A. D. 79, the elder Pliny lost his life. In 1631 several currents of lava burst forth at once and overwhelmed a number of cities at the foot of the mountain. Resina, partly built upon the site of Herculaneum, was consumed by the burning torrent, and it is said that four thousand persons perished in the catastrophe. Thirty-four eruptions have taken place since 1750, extending to April, 1872. In this last, thirty persons perished upon the mountain, simply through venturing incautiously. We left our hotel in a carriage at 9 a m. and reached the "Hermitage" at 11.30, situated upon the slope of the mountain, about one mile below the foot of the cone. The road to this point has been built at great expense, is very good, but extremely serpentine, passing over fields and hills of lava, which have been thrown out from the crater at different periods. We could proceed no further by carriage. President Smith, according to previous arrangement, was carried in an armchair, upon the shoulders of four Italians, to the foot of the cone, while others rode on ponies to the same point, over a tortuous path, in places very narrow and rocky. Here we left our ponies. President Smith, borne upon the shoulders of his stalwart bearers, took the lead, while we followed, assisted by our strong walking-sticks. The ascent was difficult and fatiguing, in places very steep, with ashes and sand nearly one foot and a half deep. We enjoyed a magnificent view of the surrounding country, the long range of the Apennines in the distance, covered with its snowy mantle, the ruins of Pompeii, the beautiful city of Naples and its great bay, dotted with many ships and steamers. We were one hour and a quarter in making the summit after leaving the foot of the cone. The crater was partially clear of smoke, affording a fine opportunity for examining the wonderful abyss. We tumbled a few rocks over the rim, which were more than thirty seconds reaching the bottom. Some of the party tried their strength of nerve by standing upon a craggy point, which appeared to hang over the burning chasm, and thrusting sticks into the smoking apertures, which inflamed in a moment. One of the party also sought to acquire fame in boiling and eating an egg in the midst of the burning heat and sulphurous smoke. It was judged that the mouth of the crater would equal in dimensions a ten acre block. The mountain, all around, appeared only a thin shell in a heated state, and for a long distance below the summit, here and there, volumes of smoke are issuing. We descended the mountain at nearly a running pace, which occupied only about fifteen minutes, arrived at our hotel at nearly six o'clock p. m., and indulged in a remarkably late breakfast the next morning.

We left Naples by train on the 30th, for Brindisi. A great portion of the country through which we passed, is cultivated by the spade; and we saw here, and also in many other parts of Italy, the women engaged in this laborious employment—in one instance we noticed a company of women repairing a break in the railroad, by carrying gravel upon their heads in baskets.

At Brindisi we took steamer for Corfu. We had a pleasant passage—the sea smooth, the weather fine, like Spring, and the air pure and bracing. We passed close to the coast of Albania, and had a fine view of Turkish towns and villas, which appeared here and there on the slopes of the moutains.

The city of Corfu contains about twenty-four thousand people, the island some fifteen villages with seventy thousand inhabitants, and forms a portion of the Grecian Government. The olive and grape are cultivated upon the island very extensively.

Sunday morning we attended Greek service in a magnificent cathedral. The psalms, prayers and portions of Scripture were read in modern Greek, and in a very amusing operatic style.

In the afternoon, the capacious square in front of our hotel was enlivened with thousands of promenaders gaily and richly dressed. The fashionable Grecian ladies, however, made no display of the "Grecian Bend." A company of politicians passed us—directly a row ensued, and one was stabbed to the heart a few steps from where we stood.

We took steamer for Alexandria and arrived here early this morning. We had fine weather, a smooth sea the whole distance, and no sickness, a very remarkable circumstance. We remain here four days, and then proceed by rail to Cairo, one hundred and thirty miles distant.

LORENZO SNOW.

LETTER XLVI.

Railroad Ride Across Italy—At Foggia—A Filthy Hotel—A Night in a Railway Station—Brindisi—Arrival at Corfu—Mementos of Venetian Rule—Services in a Greek Church—Holy Water—Kissing Pictures of Saints—A Political Meeting—A Man Killed—Take Steamer for Egypt—Alexandria—Pompey's Pillar—Cleopatra's Needles—A Mahommedan Cemetery—Wailing for the Dead—A Mussulman Gala Day.

ALEXANDRIA, Egypt, February 8th, 1873.

PRESIDENT BRIGHAM YOUNG:

Our railroad ride across the ankle of Italy was interesting, passing through many tunnels and much heavy work, and giving us a hurried view of the agricultural aspects of this portion of southern Italy, some of which is very fertile and well cultivated, though in the hands of an indolent and degenerate race. At about 9 p.m. the train stopped at Foggia, and we were told we must remain there all night. This information annoyed us, as we were apprehensive it would cause us to miss connection with the steamer. We went to the principal hotel in the small town, and found it so filled with lazzaroni, vermin and filth that we returned to the station and spent the night on the benches in the waiting room.

At the appointed hour in the morning a telegram arrived announcing the train two hours behind time. We then telegraphed to the steamboat office at Brindisi, but soon learned from a Greek trader, who spoke English, that the boat would not leave until after our arrival. Brindisi has a beautiful small harbor, completely land-locked. In the days of the Roman emperors it was a place of much importance, being the terminus of the great road known as the Appian Way from Rome. It was a great depot of supplies for Roman military operations to the eastward.

We arrived at Corfu at 2.30 p. m. of Feb. 1, and took our quarters at the St. George Hotel. These islands were under British protection from 1818 until ceded to the Greek Government by the request of the inhabitants a few years ago. They send nine members to the Grecian Parliament. They had been for hundreds of years under the Venetian Government, as many monuments of Venetian celebrities and the frequent sight of the two-winged lion still testify. The fall of Venice left them under the control of the French. Great Britain, being unwilling they should fall into the hands of the Austrians under the reconstruction of the European map in 1815, caused them to be constructed into a republic under the name of the Republic of the Ionian Isles, under the protection of Great Britain, then sent a commissioner and an army to govern the islands until the recent cession, blowing up, in the mean time, the immense fortifications that had been erected there by the Venetians, fearing, as they said, that they might fall into the hands of the Austrians.

The Island of Corfu is about thirty miles long, and in one place fifteen miles wide; is mountainous and rocky; produces grapes in great abundance and many choice fruits; the grass, grain and many of the trees were green, while several varieties of trees were without leaves. Twenty-five hundred years ago these islands contained " the most learned and highly civilized nation of antiquity;" but now their appearance does not justify the rule of progress, only in the backward way. The Greek church has been the religion here for 1,400 years. We went to the principal one on Sunday, Feb. 2. The service consisted in reading, in an operatic way, from the New Testament, to which the large audience was very attentive, the reading being in modern Greek, certainly an improvement on the Latin service in the Roman churches, which nobody understands; it was, however, all Greek to us. The church was decorated with crosses, paintings and holy water vases, and lighted with numerous wax tapers; hundreds of people were dipping their fingers in holy water and crossing and sprinkling themselves, and with great gravity kissing the pictures of the Saints in the same manner as the Romans kissed the toe of the image of St. Peter, in St. Peter's Church in Rome.

Sunday p. m. a political meeting occurred, and many thousands of people assembled in the Grand Square, the next Saturday, being the day of election for members of the Greek Parliament, they were selecting candidates. We could not understand the nature of the questions, but they became so exciting that one man saw proper to kill another, and during the evening the government kept soldiers on patrol through the city.

About one a. m. of the 3d we went on board the Austrian Lloyd's steamer *Saturno*, and found our state rooms had been secured by an agent of Mr. Cook. We had a very pleasant steam over a smooth sea, and arrived in this port at 7.30 a. m. of the 6th. There were a great number of passengers, including clergymen, doctors, lawyers, and others from England and America, mostly *en route* for Upper Egypt. They were much surprised to find live specimens from "Mormondom;" and, as they would keep talking to us, we preached to them nearly the whole voyage. They were a class of people that would not go to our meetings, but by this means heard something of the gospel.

The Turks are the rulers here. The Egyptians are descendants of the Arabs, who conquered the country in the 7th century, and the numerous crosses with other nations cause the streets to display a fine mixture of Europeans, Nubians, Abyssinians, Bedouins, Jews, Copts, and degenerate Greeks, and the greatest variety of costumes of any place

I ever visited. In the days of the Roman emperors this place is said to have been fifteen miles in circuit, and to have contained 600,000 inhabitants, and some of the finest temples and palaces in existence. But little remains to mark even the site of this ancient city. Pompey's Pillar is a fine column, 98 feet 9 inches high. Cleopatra's Needles, one of which, 77 feet high, is standing, and the other fallen and covered with debris, point out the spot where the Temple of Cæsar stood.

We visited the Mahommedan cemetery; the monuments are plain and without statues. Thousands of Mussulmen were to-day engaged in wailing over their dead; many had pitched tents for that purpose to keep off the sun, and others were in the open air. Most of the women wear vails, which hide the face except the eyes. We also visited the Christian burying grounds, which contain many fine monuments, mostly to Europeans, among which we saw two American graves. The fig trees are at present leafless; the bananas are covered with foliage and have fruit two-thirds grown. The date is a beautiful tree and in full foliage. Many fruit and flowering shrubs are in bloom.

We expect to leave on Monday morning, 10th, for Cairo. We have met Mr. Alexander Howard, the principal dragoman for Mr. Cook's trains in Palestine, and according to programme shall arrive in Jaffa on the 23rd. Alexandria is situated so near the sea that it has rains at certain seasons, and is now well stocked with mosquitoes. Irrigation is necessary and is managed much as we do it in Utah. They are now irrigating portions of their gardens.

Our party are all well and in good spirits. The water was so smooth that none of them was sick while on the Adriatic and Mediterranean seas. To-day is a Mussulman gala day, and while some are wailing for the dead, others are firing cannons, and thousands in the market places are engaged in sports and pastimes.

Bro. Schettler has had a ride on a donkey, and has

bought Turkish caps for several of us, which give us quite a Turkish appearance.

I learn that the firing and celebration to-day are in commemoration of the day that Mahomet ascended the mountain from Mecca, and that the pilgrims to Mecca have ascended the mountain to-day, and all the faithful rejoice.

GEORGE A. SMITH.

LETTER XLVII.

Leave Naples—Arrival at Foggia—On Board the "Trebisonda"—Cross the Adriatic—Corfu—Visit a Greek Church—Embark on the "Saturno"—Correcting False Impressions—The Ionian Islands—Reach Alexandria—Crowds of Arabs, Turks, Greeks, Copts, Armenians, Syrians, &c.—Mahommedan Passover—Summer Gardens and Palace of the Viceroy—Cleopatra's Needles.

HOTEL DE L'EUROPE, Alexandria, Egypt,
February 9th, 1873.

EDITORS SALT LAKE HERALD:

According to our programme, we left Naples on the 20th of January, at 4 p. m., for Brindisi, but on our arrival at Foggia, at 10.40 p.m., we were told that no train was going to Brindisi before 6.25 the next morning. We took a couple of hacks to drive to the finest hotel of the place, but on arriving there we found it such a filthy place that we could not make up our minds to stay there over night, and preferred to pass the night at the waiting room of the station. The train, next morning, was one hour and a half behind time, and we feared we might be too late for the steamer. We telegraphed to the office of the Austrian Lloyd Steamship Company, and found out soon after that the steamer was not leaving Brindisi before midnight. We reached there at 3.35 p. m., and went immediately on board the *Trebisonda*, 400 horse power, and 2,303 tons capacity. She is a fine boat, almost new, and we had good accommodations and a pleasant passage. When we awoke in the morning, we had crossed the Adriatic, and were sailing along the bare mountainous coast of Turkey. At 2 p. m. we reached the harbor of Corfu, were taken ashore in boats, and put up at the St. George Hotel, which was so crowded that three of us had to sleep in one room. Several of the party took a carriage and drove about seven miles over the island, which contains 74,000 inhabitants. Sunday morning we visited a Greek church and witnessed the ceremonies, which in some respects much resembled those of the Catholic Church. Parts of the Evangelists and some prayers were read by the priests in modern Greek, so that the people could understand, which is not the case in the Catholic churches, where the ceremonies are performed in Latin. About midnight we went aboard the steamer *Saturno*, Captain Leva, 400 horse power, and 3,308 tons capacity, which touched here on her way from Trieste to Alexandria. We had good berths reserved for us on the deck, and found a large party of Mr. Cook's on board, mostly English and some Americans. Among the English were several clergymen and doctors, with whom we had a good deal of conversation during the passage, and corrected them in many foolish ideas which they had picked up about us in sensational newspaper reports. We had a beautiful passage, the sea being remarkably smooth, and weather fine and warm all the time. The table was well supplied, and fruit of this country was abundant. We passed the Ionian islands of Santa Maura, Zante and Argostoli the first day, and the following morning the island of Candia.

On awakening on Thursday morning, the 6th, we were

in sight of the Egyptian coast, and dropped anchor at 7 a. m. in the harbor of Alexandria.

Crowds of Arabs soon came aboard our steamer to get hold of our luggage and take us ashore, but Mr. Alexander Howard, Mr. Cook's chief dragoman, soon made his appearance and brought us safely ashore with our baggage, which had to undergo a very superficial examination at the custom house, and we had to leave our passports with one of the officials, with instructions from him to call for them at the American Consulate, which we did yesterday and got them vised. Alexandria has at present about 220,000 inhabitants, composed of people of almost every nation, and in seeing the streets filled with Turks, Greeks, Arabs, Syrians, Copts, Armenians, the genuine Negro from Nubia, Bedouins, etc., in their very different and sometimes romantic costumes, we very soon realized that we had reached another continent. Our hotel is situated on the Grand Square, and from our windows we can look down upon this mixed crowd, and take our notes. We visited the Mahommedan burial place, where the people gathered in large crowds, yesterday and to-day, to weep and wail over the graves of their dead friends, as this is the passover feast of the Mahommedans, called "Biram." Close by, on an eminence, which was probably the highest ground of the ancient city, is the "most striking monumental relic of Alexandria, called Pompey's Pillar, of beautiful red granite, ninety-eight feet and nine inches in height. Thence we drove to the summer palace and gardens of the Viceroy of Egypt, and to the public gardens, through groves of date palms, and saw many wild and tame fig trees, bananas and other tropical plants and flowers. On our way home we looked at Cleopatra's Needles, two large obelisks, one erect and one fallen, which were set up in front of the Temple of Cæsar, which the Alexandrians had erected in honor of the Emperor. Another account assigns the erection of this temple to Cleopatra, to commemorate the birth of her son by

Julius Cæsar. The standing one is seventy-one feet high, and the fallen one sixty-six feet. To-morrow we leave for Cairo, where we intend to stay about one week, thence we go to Suez, Ismaila, and Port Said, where we take steamer on the 22nd inst. for Jaffa.

Yours truly,

PAUL A. SCHETTLER.

LETTER XLVIII.

Rome—Excavations by Napoleon III—Naples—Pomp and Beggary—Thousands of Homeless People—Ascending Vesuvius—Brindisi—Corfu—Women "Beasts of Burden"—Embark on the "Saturno"—"Sunrise on the Mediterranean"—Alexandria.

ALEXANDRIA, Egypt, February 9th, 1873.

EDITOR WOMAN'S EXPONENT:

I wrote you last in Rome. We found very much in that ancient capital of the world strikingly interesting. The unremitting work of time is nowhere more apparent than in the ruins of that once magnificent city. The excavations commenced at the expense of Napoleon Third, and which are continued by the present government of Italy, have brought to light most astonishing specimens of former grandeur and architectural skill. Although much has been unburied, much more remains, not only many feet beneath the surface of the earth, but also below spacious palaces and temples of comparatively modern structure, which have been erected upon the ground formed by accumulations through the lapse of ages, that constituted a sepulchral arch over the Rome of the Cæsars. While there we were informed of a design to remove these modern buildings in favor of perfecting the work of excavation, and since leaving have read a published article announcing that the work of demolishing had commenced.

But I must leave Rome for the present and hasten on to Naples, where we arrived in the evening of the 25th of January. That is a city of pomp and beggary; in fact, there, begging appeared to be more a necessity than in Rome, where children well clad, fat and apparently well fed, seemed to beg for mere amusement, no doubt being trained to the business. But in Naples we saw poverty strikingly apparent, and beggars clustered in droves. Thousands of men, women and children were on the side-walks and in the streets, lounging about as though they had no abiding place; most of the men smoking pipes and cigars, some of the women knitting, others spinning flax in the most simple manner, with a distaff, from which they drew the thread, and a bobbin or spool which they twirled to give a twist to the thread and then wound upon it.

Many of these people have no resort for the night only as they huddle into the porches of the churches, on the steps, or in niches in the corners of the streets. Returning rather late from Pompeii one evening, we saw groups of these houseless people on steps leading into churches. They are accustomed to this manner of existence, it can hardly be called living. Warm climates, in which people easily exist, foster indolence; and it is doubtful whether any inducements could prompt these people to industry.

President Smith and most of his party ascended to the crater of Vesuvius; my ambition was satisfied with excellent views of this natural wonder at a lower point. Continually throwing out volumes of smoke, and frequently ashes and stones, it is a marvel that people residing near, and at the base of, this fiery mountain, can feel the serenity they manifest.

From Naples we went by rail to Brindisi, from there by steamer to Corfu, one of the Grecian isles, thirty miles in length, and from one to fifteen in breadth. It seems like a cluster of high hills and low dells, mostly covered with olives and grape-vines, with here and there a cypress. Varieties of vegetables are growing in some parts, also flax, which we saw nearly in bloom. The Grecian women, living in the country, are, many of them at least, "beasts of burden." I never saw such gigantic bundles carried by human beings as these poor women carry on their heads. In the city of Corfu, as in most of the cities we have visited, America and England are represented in the circles of fashion. The grand promenade and public gardens were very gay, especially in the afternoon of the Sunday we spent there.

At 12 (midnight) of the 2nd of February we embarked on the *Saturno,* an Austrian steamer, and arrived in Alexandria on the morning of the 6th. We had a delightful voyage, no one of our party was sea-sick; the sea was calm, although the day before and the day after our voyage were very boisterous.

SUNRISE ON THE MEDITERRANEAN.

We mounted "Saturno's" deck to see
   A grand, magnificent scene—
The rising Sun in its majesty,
   Diffusing its golden sheen.

A charming precursor first appear'd
   In volumes of golden rays,
Increasing their splendor till all around
   The horizon seemed to blaze.

Anon, the disk of the "king of day,"
  O'er the wat'ry main arose;
Now upward and onward he makes his way,
  Till the canopy gaily glows.

The morning is fine, the air serene,
  And the sky above is clear,
Except where a beautiful cloud
  Like a floating nymph appears.

The sparkling waves of the sea below,
  The blazonry over head,
The horizon wrapp'd in a burning glow,
  A thrilling enchantment spread.

No place that we have visited makes one feel so thoroughly from home as Alexandria; and in no place have we had more comfortable quarters and better fare than here. Yet the medley of nations, religions, costumes, colors, dialects, etc., etc., and the dilapidated appearance of the city, constitute a scenery at once interesting, ludicrous and extremely amusing. But my sheet is full, and I will leave Alexandria, with this introduction, for a future opportunity. We go to Cairo to-morrow.

                        ELIZA R. SNOW.

LETTER XLIX.

In Cairo—Description of Alexandria—People of Various Nationalities—Riding on Asses—Arab Runners—Turkish Dresses—Veiled Ladies—Cleanliness of the Mussulmen—Washing and Prayer—The Mahommedan Hegira—Mourning for the Dead—A Famous Greek Church—Joseph's Well—The Pyramids—The Sphinx—Gardens and Palace of Gizeh—Marriage Festivities.

CAIRO, Egypt, February 14th, 1873.

EDITOR WOMAN'S EXPONENT:

We are now in the flourishing city of Cairo, but I will take you back to Alexandria, to which I introduced you in my last.

Although the buildings generally, in that once celebrated, antiquated city, are specimens of age and decay, it contains some respectable appearing ones, recently built and owned by foreigners. Most of the streets are unpaved, narrow and filthy. Our hotel in Alexandria occupied a pleasant position; our rooms, on the third floor, fronting a public square, eight or ten rods in width, affording us full views of two streets and four sidewalks, which were, most of the time, thronged with people and animals. From our balcony and windows, which opened at full length, we had an excellent opportunity for studying national peculiarities. The sight was at once intensely amusing and interesting. It would be impossible to give more than a faint idea of the strange varieties to be seen at a glance: men, women and children of every shade of complexion, from the fairest blonde to the most glossy jet, with every variety of feature, and in every imaginable costume. In five minutes I counted twenty different styles of covering on the heads of that number of male bipeds, saying nothing of those of the feminines. Mixed up with pedestrians may be seen men, women and children on donkeys, men on horses and mules, camels laden with enormous masses of straw, grass, lumber, rock, and frequently with a man on the top of the load; people of all classes, in carriages and buggies, rudely constructed vehicles containing twenty persons—men, women and children; and, to complete the medley, dogs and monkeys.

The most comically amusing practice, and one of constant exhibition, is a person, either Turk or Christian, on a donkey, with a man or boy in gown or turban, running in the rear, and with a stick punching or striking the animal to quicken its speed. Our highly respected cashier and interpreter, Brother P. A. Schettler, adopted this fashionable style, but much to the regret of Miss Little and myself, he disappointed us of the gratification we anticipated in witnessing the interesting and undignified exhibition, by performing it clandestinely. These Arab runners outstrip donkeys, and equal horses at pretty good speed. It is quite customary for people of consequence to have one of these runners in front of their carriage-horses, clearing the street before them. President Smith and party rode out this forenoon in two carriages, with a runner in white gown and turban, in advance of each. They felt themselves to be men of authority—stick in hand, ordering people, donkeys, etc., aside to clear a passage.

On the streets, Americans, English, French, Germans, Italians, Greeks, Turks, Abyssinian Jews, etc., etc., mix, and it is impossible to discover from appearance who feel most at home. Several of an English party who crossed the Mediterranean with us, have already adopted the neat little Turkish cap, which, with turban and gown, is the predominant style in Egypt. In Alexandria, most of the hotel servants appeared in no other. I had tried to persuade some of the gentlemen of our party that this costume might become them, but, up to date, they have only donned the cap, the gown is only yet in prospect.

The custom of veiling the face, which is much practised here by Egyptian women, appears to be very inconvenient. I have already seen thousands with only the eyes, and sometimes the forehead exposed; some with white veils and dressed in white; others with black and dressed in black, and also in various colors; some very richly clad. Most of the veils are short, made of thick lace, and fastened across the face just below the eyes. The outside garb or covering, nearly square in form, is laid over the head, fastened under the chin, falling loosely over the shoulders, reaches to the instep, and frequently parting in front, exposes to advantage a beautiful, rich underdress. Walking in the public garden, seated in an arbor, on the sidewalk, riding on a donkey or in a carriage, every Turkish or Egyptian woman you see, looks as though she had a large shawl over her head. Considering the outside appearance of the den-like houses of the Arab Mahommedans, it is very surprising to see how neat they look. Many, both men and women, dress in white, and *really* white; their religion enjoins cleanliness. They have fountains in front of their mosques, where the people wash before prayer. We frequently see them washing themselves beside the street, probably preparatory to praying, for wherever a true Mahometan is, when the hour of prayer arrives, he bows to service. We have seen several, where we were passing, bowing their heads to the ground while their lips moved as in silent devotion.

But to Alexandria. The first morning after our arrival, the early and frequent discharge of cannon, reminded us of our "Fourth" and "Twenty-fourth." On enquiring the cause, we were informed that the pilgrims were then ascending the mountain in commemoration of the Hegira, or flight of Mahomet to Mecca. It was also the time for the "Wailing for the dead" in the Mahommedan cemetery. Our curiosity prompted us to walk a tiresome distance through dust, filth and crowded streets, to the place designated, where we found thousands of people of all ages, and, with very few exceptions, all in Mahommedan costumes.

The graves are covered with clay moulded into a compact oval form, raised from one to two feet above the surface, and many of them surrounded with one, two and three steps. Beside many of the graves were those, apparently, who were relatives of those interred, weeping, mourning or praying, while another class, with no mourning sympathies whatever, was exhibiting the greatest mirth—playing on rude instruments, dancing-monkeys, buying, selling, eating, drinking, smoking and having a gala time. Not comprehending their words and doings, the entire scene seemed to us a masterpiece of confusion. The throng was so dense it was difficult to wend our way into the midst sufficiently to gratify our curiosity, which we did as soon as possible, lest we might be thought intrusive; and in coming out, we were beset with importunities to purchase all kinds of trinkets, bread, cakes, figs, oranges, dates, and many other things altogether anonymous to us; but it being Sunday, we were out without any "backsheesh" in our pockets, and of course were not prepared to trade.

In Cairo we have visited a Turkish mosque, a Jewish synagogue, a Greek church, in which we were shown "where Joseph, Mary and the Saviour resided when they fled from the wrath of Herod;" a church of the Copts, "Joseph's Well," which is two hundred and fifty feet deep, the Pyramids and "Sphinx," the Museum of Antiquities, the gardens and palace of Gizeh, which belong to the Khedive, of whom we had a good view as he passed us in his carriage while promenading on his premises. He has four wives and quite a number of children, four of whom were married during the past month, which has been a continued holiday festival. Many thousands of lamps have gorgeously illuminated, it is judged, more than fifty acres in extent—hung in arches, over gateways, in arbors, and most tastefully arranged in every direction. Yesterday the festival closed and many were engaged in removing the lamps and other costly ornaments. During the festivities, firing of cannon was frequent, and the exhibitions of fireworks in the centre of the illuminations were exceedingly grand. Three of the recently wedded are sons; the daughter's nuptials were since our arrival. It is said that her intended had seen her photograph previous to marriage, but not her face. If that is so, it is to be hoped that he has met with no unfavorable disappointment. She has the reputation of being very pretty and amiable.

On the 17th we leave Cairo for Suez.

ELIZA R. SNOW.

LETTER L.

Leave Alexandria—Cross the Nile—Irrigation—Method of Cultivation—Arab Mounds—Primitive Mode of Dressing—A Famous Mosque—Joseph's Well—Cairo—Church where Joseph, Mary and Jesus Tarried—The Oldest Mosque Known—Visit to the Khedive's Gardens—A Drive to the Pyramids—Backsheesh—The Sphinx—Religious Services by the Dervishes—Marriage of the Khedive's Children—City of Heliopolis—Temple of On—Fountain of the Sun—A Famous Sycamore Tree.

Hotel Shepheard, Cairo, Egypt,
February 16th, 1873.

Editors Salt Lake Herald:

We left Alexandria at 9.40 a. m. on the 10th instant, by rail, for this city, and crossed the Rosetta branch of the Nile near the station Kafr-ez-Zyat, over a fine iron bridge of twelve spans, which had cost £400,000, and also the Damietta branch of the Nile, near the station Birket-es-Sab. Part of the country we passed through was highly cultivated, and a most perfect system of irrigation is used, without which the inhabitants can raise nothing. They divide the fields and gardens by dams, in small squares of from twelve to fifteen or twenty feet, and flood them one after another, and the sand being impregnated with the rich alluvial deposits, gets exceedingly productive. We also passed many Arab mounds, like mud villages, and many of the inhabitants approached pretty near in their clothing to the fashion prevalent in the Garden of Eden. We reached our hotel at 4 p. m., and were comfortably quartered, though we had to take double-bedded rooms, as the house was full. The party has visited the

Mosque Mahomed Ali, which is one of the principal ones, built of white oriental alabaster on an eminence called the "Citadel," from which a very fine view of the city, with its 400 mosques, minarets, churches and palaces, and the pyramids, can be obtained. On the east side of the Citadel Hill is Joseph's Well, 290 feet deep, and immediately below the Citadel the fine mosques of Sultan Hassan.

On the 12th we drove to the old city of Cairo, about three miles out, and entered through one of the arches of the old aqueduct. We went into a very old Coptic church, where, it is said, Joseph and Mary tarried with the child Jesus, then to an old Jewish church and a Greek church of very early date, dedicated to the patron St. George; but the first monument of interest is the Mosque of Amer, to the east of the village, which is said to be the oldest mosque known. In the afternoon we called upon the vice consul of the United States, who promised us tickets of admission to two of the finest gardens of the Khedive, which we have since visited, and through the politeness of one of the French guards in charge of one of the summer palaces in these gardens, we were conducted through the principal rooms, which were fitted up in a most magnificent Oriental style. The name of this palace and garden is Ghezireh, and that of the other Choubra.

On Thursday we drove to the Pyramids of Gizeh, and arrived there in about two hours. There are three large ones, called the Great Pyramid, or Pyramid of Cheops, the Chephren Pyramid, and the Mycerinus Pyramid. The great one is 756 feet long, 480 feet high, and has an area of 571,536 square feet. The weather being warm and the ascent fatiguing, only Mr. Thomas W. Jennings and myself made up our minds to climb to the top platform, with a number of the other travellers who were continually arriving. With the assistance of four strong Arabs, two of whom took me by the hands, and two of them pushing and lifting me from behind, where the steps were four feet high, and after resting several times, I reached the top in seventeen minutes, when my Arabs gave me three cheers and a tiger in regular Yankee style, and tolerably good Arab English, asking me of course for the unavoidable "backsheesh," or fee, which you hear from early morning till late in the evening sounded in your ears for real or imaginary services rendered. I stopped about fifteen minutes and enjoyed a beautiful view over the Nile valley, the city of Cairo, the sandy desert of Saharah, with Memphis and other pyramids in the distance. This pyramid is over 4,000 years old, and it took 366,000 men about twenty years to build it. My Arabs took me safely down again, and accompanied me with candles to the inside to see the sarcophagus of the builder. The narrow passage was floored with finely polished marble, in some places only three feet high, and as the way was first downwards, and then rising at an angle of twenty-six degrees, and the air rather close, it was almost more difficult to see the inside than to climb to the outside platform. Near to this great pyramid is the worldwide celebrated Sphinx, of fine red polished granite, of which the head and neck are only visible, the rest being buried in sand. The head measures from the forehead down to the chin thirty feet. It is the work of Chephren, the builder of the second pyramid, and was situated to the south of the Temple of Isis, and north of the Temple of Osiris.

The following day we visited a mosque of the Dervishes, and saw them perform their religious exercises, which consisted in their forming a semi-circle, in the centre of which stood an old Dervish, who directed the services. The persons in the circle had their long dark hair hanging down over their shoulders, and to a kind of drum music stooped down forward, touching the ground with their hands, and then throwing their heads with flowing hair backward as far as they could, groaning and howling fearfully and working so fast that the perspiration was running down their faces, and once in a while one fell down exhausted, when they put something in his mouth and he was foaming like a madman. Some others were whirling around inside the circle, and it was altogether the most singular and horrible-looking religious exercise to witness.

The Khedive has married off several of his children lately, and great festivities have been going on here for the last thirty days at his expense, as balls, suppers for foreigners, who only required a card from their consuls, fireworks, illuminations, etc. We were in time to see some of the latter, which were very fine indeed, and far surpassed anything Europeans had seen before in their own great cities. The illuminations of the palace, the gardens, and surrounding grounds, covered about fifty acres of ground.

Most of the party being occupied with letter-writing for this mail, yesterday President George A. Smith and myself took a drive to the ruins of the old city of Heliopolis. We passed the ruins of the Mosque and Tomb of Melek Adel, and drove through vineyards, olive groves, and highly cultivated gardens and fields to the oldest obelisk in Egypt, which, with another, stood in front of the great Temple of On, in which Joseph's father-in-law officiated as a priest, and where Moses studied. (See Genesis xli, 45). Close by in the village Matareeah is the Fountain of the Sun, which, as tradition says, was salt until the holy family arrived there, and "Our Lady bathed in it, when it turned soft and sweet." A few steps from it is an old sycamore tree, under which the holy family is said to have camped. This city contains 400,000 inhabitants, and the Khedive is making wonderful improvements in the new part of it. As in Alexandria, a great many donkeys are used to get about, and numbers of camels for riding and for carrying burdens are seen in the streets.

PAUL A. SCHETTLER.

LETTER LI.

Cairo—Mosque of Mahomet Ali—Joseph's Well—The Khedive's Festivities—Visit a Coptic Church—A Sheik Hanged—Hieropolis and City of On—The Place where Moses was Educated—Virgin Mary's Sycamore Tree—A Salt Well Miraculously Sweetened—Plain of Heliopolis—Defeat of the Mamelukes—Egyptian Hotel Accommodation—Land of Goshen—Suez—Where the Israelites Crossed the Red Sea—An Arab Village.

Ismalia, Egypt, February 19th, 1873.

President Brigham Young:

I wrote to you from Alexandria, from which place we went to Cairo, the capital of Egypt, understood to be the largest city in Africa, said to contain more than 400,000 inhabitants. It presents the strange mixture of a European, African and Asiatic town all under one. The Frank quarter contains many fine European buildings, and some newly made and very pleasant public gardens, but the whole city is unpaved. A few streets that are newly made are wide and convenient and have flagged sidewalks; all the others, embracing an area of some three miles by two, are very narrow, many of them too much so for one loaded camel to pass another. Most of the houses are built of concrete, and many of them are out of repair. The Mosque of Mahomet Ali, commenced by that prince, and finished after his death, is the finest public building that we saw in Cairo. A great portion is very neatly finished inside with Oriental alabaster, and is better suited to the purposes designed than any Catholic church I have visited. It is erected in the old citadel, rendered famous by the destruction of the Mamelukes by Mahomet Ali, and on the site of the old Palace of Saladin. The view of Cairo from the south side of the mosque is the finest I saw. Near this building is a well they call Joseph's, and many travellers have rejoiced in seeing what they believed was the well of the son of the old patriarch Jacob; it would seem, however, that Saladin, the Fatimite Calif, so renowned in the history of the Crusades, located the citadel here, not because it was the most commanding point in the then new city of Cairo, but because he learned by experiment that fresh meat would keep much longer here than in any other place in the city. In clearing off the spot of ground for the foundation an old well was discovered, which had been dug and walled by the ancients. Saladin ordered the sand to be cleared out with which it had been filled, and his other name being Yoosef, the well has taken that name. Its depth is 290 feet, and is descended by a gently sloping staircase. The water is raised by mule power, and is only fit for irrigating and for animals to drink.

We called on the Consul General, Mr. Beardsley, who treated us very courteously. His health is delicate. He complained of having had to attend the Khedive's festivities twice a week for four weeks, given on account of the marriages of three of his sons and one daughter; his delicate health and apparent fatigue caused us to make our call brief.

The United States Consul for Cairo treated us courteously; he is a native Egyptian; he procured us passes into two of the gardens of the Khedive, and told us if we had arrived one week sooner he could have procured us admission to the rooms of the harem, but the close of the festivities made it impossible.

We visited a Coptic church, and employed one of its members, Solomon Monsoor, for our dragoman while in Cairo. The Copts are bigoted and ignorant. The Greek Church also has its organizations here, one of which we visited, but Christianity here is of a low type, though the present government protects all religions in a 'manner entirely disliked by the more zealous Mahommedans. Mr. Beardsley told us that the Khedive had recently hung a Dervish sheik for interfering improperly with his neighbors' religious rights. He thinks that while the present Khedive lives any one is free to follow his religious convictions, but remarked that he has much prejudice and bigotry to combat.

We visited several palaces and their surrounding grounds belonging to the Khedive, constructed and laid out with the spirit of modern improvement, and which are highly creditable. We paid a visit to the obelisk at Heliopolis, which is all that remains of the renowned city of On. The obelisk is supposed to be one third of its length in the ground; there are sixty-two feet above ground, and it is surrounded by a luxuriant sugarcane field. The surrounding ground is a vast accumulation of the ruins of the old city, and is exceedingly fertile, a considerable portion having been recently brought under cultivation by the Khedive, who brought to it the waters of the Nile. The obelisk is six feet square, tapering to the summit, and is covered with hieroglyphics.

Joseph's wife Asenath was the daughter of Potiphar, priest of On, our grandmother, of course. Moses was educated here, as this was the seat of the great college where the Egyptian notables received their schooling. Its name, On, is said to have been determined from the interpretation of an inscription on the obelisk.

Near this place we visited a sycamore tree which bears the name of the Virgin Mary; it is said that Joseph and Mary camped by this tree when on their flight to Egypt with the young child Jesus in the days of Herod. Near this tree is a well which was salt at that time, but Mary washed in it, and it made it sweet. A donkey was at work raising the water by a rude wheel to which were attached several earthen jars. We drank, and found the water pure, but warm, the taste much resembling that of the big spring at St. George in Utah. The tree is very old, and has suffered severely by devout people carrying off pieces of it and carving their names on it, to prevent which the owner has surrounded it with a substantial picket fence, and that has been disfigured, although neatly painted, with awkwardly cut Roman initials.

The large plain of Heliopolis has recently been brought into cultivation, by bringing the Nile waters over it, and is very productive. It is memorable in Egyptian history as the battle field upon which Selim the Second, Sultan of Turkey, defeated the Mameluke Caliph in 1517, reducing Egypt to a Turkish province for 356 years, except the three years it was occupied by the French. The Sultan put the Caliph to death, but retained the Mameluke aristocracy, on condition that they paid tribute, renounced their religion and adopted his, and inserted his name in their prayers, which they continued to do until they were destroyed by Mahomet Ali, the grandfather of the present Khedive, in 1811.

Our hotel accommodations at Shepheard's were much better than I had expected to find in Egypt, though so crowded that two had to occupy a room. The floors were stone, but carpeted. They furnished meat, potatoes and wines; the hotel fare was sixteen shillings a day. When driving out we took with us a dragoman to interpret and keep from us a numerous lot of beggars and bummers, clamorous for backsheesh, and only equalled, as far as we had traveled, by the beggars in Naples.

We left Cairo on the 17th by rail for the Red Sea. Several hours of our journey lay through one of the finest cultivated regions I have seen, all irrigated by water from the Nile. We lunched at Zagazig, supposed to be in what was the Land of Goshen. Zagazig is near some extensive ruins of an ancient city, Bubastis, said to have been the capital of Egypt in the days of Shishak, and to have contained a magnificent Temple of Mercury; the ruins indicate the site of an extensive city. A fresh water canal has been constructed from the Nile on or near the line of an ancient canal, which existed in the days of the Pharaohs, to Ismalia, whence it is forced in a pipe 50 miles to Port Said on the Mediterranean, and the canal continues in an opposite direction to Suez on the Red Sea, the railroad lines following near this canal.

A portion of the way from Zagazig a strip is cultivated on one side, while the other is naked sand, and this line leads through what was, probably, once a choice portion of Egypt, but now it is so desolate that our Utah deserts are but semi-deserts compared with it.

Suez was considerable of a native town, though the fresh water had to be brought from a distance on pack animals. The story so widely circulated, that an artesian well had been sunk here, is a canard. A railroad by a more direct route was constructed between Cairo and Suez, but having to carry water in cars, it was discontinued when the fresh water canal was completed, notwithstanding the present line is one-third or more longer. For some time Suez and the canal laborers were furnished with water by the short road. The presumption is that the children of Israel crossed the arm of the Red Sea, named the Gulf of Suez, near this place. A band of English clergymen were about starting on camels this morning to visit Sinai, said to be a 60 hours' journey. The gardens at Suez and Ismalia show that the most desert sand will produce vegetation wherever water can be applied. There is but little to encourage the growth of these towns, as the shipping trade goes directly through. No great expense is required to keep the Suez canal in order, as we are told the current keeps it clear of sediment. Among the most unthrifty and cheerless of all human habitations is an Arab village, located above irrigation, treeless, a mere collection of miserable mud and concrete huts.

Our party are all in our usual health, and the prospect is that we shall not think any the less of our mountain home and friends after our return.

GEORGE A. SMITH.

LETTER LII.

Tour of Egypt—Love of Children among the Egyptians—Divorce and Marital Infidelity Rare—Turkish Mosques—The Turkish Sabbath—The Copts—Lack of Education—Mahommedan Schools—Sobriety and Honesty among Mahommedans—Male and Female Attire—Religious Sects—Modes of Worship—The Dervishes—Visit to a Dervish Place of Worship—Hotel Accommodations in Alexandria—Agriculture and Irrigation—A Steam Plow in Egypt—Suez and the Red Sea—Leave for Jaffa.

Port Said, Egypt, February 22nd, 1873.

Editor Deseret News:

We have now completed our tour in Egypt, which in many respects has proved the most agreeable and interesting of any country we have visited in regard to its physical appearance, and the character, religion, customs and manners of its inhabitants. It occupies the north-eastern part of Africa and embraces nearly six millions of people—Egyptians, Turks, Arabs, Greeks, Armenians, Jews, Syrians and Mamelukes. The great majority are husbandmen, and their social condition of a low grade, generally ignorant and uneducated and fond of frivolous amusements. The climate being warm, and their style of living cheap and simple, their habitations consisting chiefly of low mud huts, very little labor or expense is required for the maintenance of families. I noticed, in passing through many of their mud villages, that they appeared to be swarming with children. We were told, and from personal observation believed it to be true, that in Egypt the practice of raising offspring is the general rule and is fashionable and popular, and that the estimation in which the wife is held by her husband, and even by her acquaintances, depends in a great measure upon her fruitfulness and the preservation of her children. By men and women, whether rich or poor, barrenness is considered a curse and a reproach, and it is regarded, also, as disgraceful in a man to divorce, without some substantial reason, a wife who has borne him a child, especially while her child is living. If a woman desires a husband's love, or the respect of others, her giving birth to a child is a source of great joy to her and him, making her own interest a sufficient motive for maternal tenderness. Children here appear to have great respect for their parents. We are informed that an undutiful child is scarcely known among the Egyptians or Arabs, and whenever such an instance does occur, being considered one of the greatest crimes, its punishment is very severe. It is said that cases are very rare in Egypt of wives being unfaithful to their husbands.

In visiting the Turkish mosques, we observed that there were no pictures, images, statues or altars, which universally decorate the cathedrals in Catholic countries. Friday is their day for worship. The public service commences about noon by reading portions of the Koran, and delivering sermons or addresses by the "Imens." They hold Moses in profound reverence, and also Jesus Christ, but Mahomet as God's last and greatest prophet. Their creed is "There is no Deity but God, and Mahomet is God's Apostle." Adam, Noah, Abraham, Moses and Jesus Christ were all God's servants in their various ages, but the greatest and best is Mahomet.

The Copts are avowed Christians, the descendants of the ancient Egyptians, and are very numerous. They have regular convents, nunneries, monasteries and about two hundred churches. The other religions are the Greek Church and the Latin or Roman Catholic.

But little attention is paid to education. Parents generally content themselves with instilling into the minds of their children a few principles of religion. The child, as early as possible, is taught to say, "I testify that there is no Deity but God, and I testify that Mahomet is God's apostle." The boys are placed under a schoolmaster to be instructed in a few simple rudiments of education. The common manner of instruction is to sit upon the ground or floor, pupils and schoolmaster, each boy with his tablet in hand or a portion of the Koran or a kind of desk of palm sticks. All the boys recite or chant this lesson aloud, at the same time rocking their heads and bodies incessantly backward and forward, this practice being thought to assist the memory.

While in this country I have not witnessed a single case of intoxication, though I have been in many places of large gatherings for general amusement. On every occasion the people were remarkably orderly—no boisterous speeches, loud talking or laughter. In these large crowds, and at hotels where only Egyptian servants and Arabs were employed, I considered my little effects more secure than at American or European establishments.

The dress of the men of the middle and higher classes, consists generally of the following articles—first, a pair of drawers of linen or cotton tied around the body by a drawstring or band, the ends of which are embroidered with fancy colored silk. The drawers descend a little below the knees or to the ankles. Next is worn a shirt with full sleeves reaching to the wrists, which is made of linen or cotton, muslin or silk; over this is worn a garment of silk or cotton descending to the ankles, having long sleeves. The costume of men of the lower classes is very simple. These, if not of the very poorest class, wear drawers, or shirt or gown with wide sleeves and a woollen girdle or broad red belt. Their turban is generally composed of a white, red or yellow woollen shawl, but we saw many different forms of turbans—the common style among the servants consists of several spiral twists, one above another like the threads of a screw. Those worn by the upper class are of a better style. The dress of the Egyptian ladies is much after the fashion of that of the men, but more handsome and elegant.

The Mahommedans, like the Christians, are divided into various religious societies, each having its peculiar tenets and practices. The Dervishes constitute an important sect—are very numerous and in many parts of Egypt are highly respected. Their customs and modes of worship are singular and curious. Sometimes they enter a solitary cell, remain forty days and nights, fasting from daybreak till sunset, employing their time in imploring forgiveness, praising God, &c. Their religious exercises consist chiefly in the performance of what is called "zikers." Sometimes standing in the form of a circular or an oblong ring, or in two rows facing each other, sometimes sitting, they exclaim or chant " Lailah, Ella-llah" (there is no Deity but God); "Allah! Allah! Allah!" (God! God! God!); or repeat other invocations until their strength is nearly exhausted, accompanying their ejaculations or chants with a motion of the head, or of the whole body.

I felt a great curiosity to witness their manner of worship—fortunately an opportunity presented. We took carriages, accompanied by a Dervish guide of some distinction, and proceeded to one of their mosques in Cairo. We were requested to take off our boots before entering the building—their places of worship being considered sacred and holy. About fifty Dervishes were standing in the form of a semi-circle—their head priest in the centre. They were bowing their heads and bodies nearly to the floor simultaneously and very rapidly, keeping time to miserably wretched music, their long, flowing hair, and wild, fanatical expressions, together with their horrible ejaculations and howls, made them appear more like lunatics or demons than rational beings. They continued their exercises about fifteen minutes, until, becoming exhausted, they rested a few moments, then commenced repeating the ceremonies. One of them, either through a high state of religious enthusiasm or vehemence of exertion, with a terrible groan fell prostrate, foaming at the mouth, his eyes closed, his limbs convulsed and his fingers clenched. The Dervishes were pleased with this occurrence, considering it a divine manifestation, which increased their enthusiasm. At length the presiding Dervish raised the fallen man and placed him in the circle in charge of two of his companions. Another occurrence of similar character happened previously to our leaving the mosque. While these exercises were going on, two Dervishes stepped inside the circle and commenced whirling around, using both feet to produce the motion, extending their arms, and spinning around like tops, with great velocity. I expected every moment to see them precipitated headlong upon the floor, but having continued nearly ten minutes they joined the circle, apparently but little exhausted.

We were pleased with our visit in Alexandria, and with our Hotel de l'Europe, which nearly equals the first-class hotels in America. Pompey's Pillar, Cleopatra's Needle, the Catacombs, Museum of Antiquities, &c., received a due share of our attention. But little improvement is at present being made in Alexandria, compared with that of Cairo—it seems merely of importance as a maritime city.

In traveling in Egypt along the delta of the Nile, whereever its waters can reach by overflow or irrigation, the soil is remarkably rich, fertile and productive. Heavy growths of wheat, barley, clover, cane, cotton, with now and then a field of flax, also fields of beans, orange, lemon and fine vegetable gardens, with peach trees now in full bloom.

In passing from Cairo to Ismalia, we saw one steam plow in operation, but generally the ground is cultivated by rudely constructed plows drawn by oxen or an ox and camel yoked together—sometimes by two camels.

We have visited Suez and looked upon the beautiful

waters of the famous Red Sea, and enjoyed a delightful sail over a portion of the great Suez Canal.

This afternoon, we leave by steamer for Jaffa, where we arrange for our Palestine tour, which will occupy about four weeks, and be performed on horseback.

LORENZO SNOW.

LETTER LIII.

Leaving the Land of Egypt—Going to Jaffa—Land of Goshen—City of Bubastis—Suez—Mount Sinai—At Kantarah—Lake of Menzaleh—The Suez Canal—Port Said.

HOTEL DE FRANCE, Port Said, Egypt,
February 22nd, 1873.

EDITORS SALT LAKE HERALD:

This afternoon at 5 o'clock we intend to leave the land of Egypt by the Austrian Lloyd steamer, for Jaffa, where we expect to arrive to-morrow about 9 a. m., and step our feet for the first time on the soil of the Holy Land, where so great events in sacred history have transpired. On the 17th we left Cairo, per train, for Suez, *via* Zagazig and Ismalia, passing through what was formerly called the land of Goshen, and reached Suez at 7 p. m., where we stopped at the Suez hotel. About forty-five miles from Cairo and near the station of Zagazig, we saw the extensive ruins of the old city of Bubastis, which was one of the most ancient cities of Egypt, where a magnificent temple of the goddess of Bubastis was erected. It measured 500 feet in length, and was built of the finest red granite. At Zagazig we stopped half an hour for lunch, and at the next station, Aboo Hamed, we met the train from Suez with Mr. Cook and party, who passed through Salt Lake City in October, 1872, on their trip around the world; but as we were leaving the station when they came in, we could not speak to them. In Suez, but little of interest is to be seen. It is situated near the northern extremity of the western branch of the Red Sea, or Gulf of Suez, and it is supposed that near this place the Israelites passed through this sea. In clear weather you can discern in the far distance some peaks of the Mt. Sinai range of mountains. On the morning of the 19th we rode back over the same road we had come to Ismalia, which was a very lively place during the building of the Suez canal. It is very regularly laid out, has good and wide streets, planted with shade trees, and some fine vegetable and flower gardens; and we were told that the sandy soil, when well watered, would produce almost anything. There is a nice Swiss chalet of Mr. M. De Lesseps, the principal designer of the Suez canal, which was the first building erected here; then there is a palace of the Khedive, and the water works, by which fresh Nile water is pumped from the Cairo Canal in a double row of cast iron pipes, a distance of fifty miles to Port Said.

We left Ismalia yesterday morning on a small steamboat of the Egyptian line, only forty-eight feet long, and passed through the Suez Canal. We stopped an hour and a quarter at Kantarah, which is a half-way station, and reached here at 3.30 p. m. We passed five large ocean steamers, and in approaching Port Said we saw thousands of scarlet flamingoes, rosy pelicans, herons and ducks on the Lake of Menzaleh, through which the canal continues thirty-seven miles. The width of the surface of the canal is 328 feet, where the banks are low, and 190 feet through the deep cuttings; at the base it is 72 feet wide, and the depth is 26 feet. The slope of the bank is one in five near the water line, and one in two at the base; the total length is 100 miles, and the cost was about seventeen million pounds sterling. Port Said has at present about 8,000 inhabitants; and it being a port of the Mediterranean, there is a good deal more life in the streets and more business transacted here than at either Suez or Ismalia.

We have not heard from home for four weeks, but hope to find a large batch of mail matter at Jaffa on our arrival there to-morrow morning. We are all in usual health.

PAUL A. SCHETTLER.

LETTER LIV.

Near Jaffa—The Martyrs' Tower—Plains of Sharon—Battle Ground of David and Goliath—Church of the Holy Sepulchre—St. Stephen's Gate—Valley of Jehoshaphat—Sacred Relics—Centre of the Earth.

CAMP NEAR JAFFA GATE, Jerusalem,
February 26th, 1873.

ELDER ROBERT L. CAMPBELL:

Your favor No. 7, of December 28, and January 7, was received in our noon halt in a ruin containing the Martyrs' Tower, near Ramleh, February 24. I thank you for your correspondence, and hope you will continue it. Others of the party got letters fourteen days later than mine. I stand riding an Arab horse better than I had anticipated. Our arrival in Jaffa was on Sunday morning, 23rd, the sea smooth, and the day very fine. I presume all the party were disappointed in the fertile character of the Plains of

Sharon, and the extent to which they are cultivated. The mountains of Judea are rocky and barren, but flocks of fat sheep were grazing on the brook Elah, where King David and Goliath had their encounter. We were tired by our horseback ride when we arrived here last evening.

We have three large circular wall tents, lined, carpeted, and furnished with iron bedsteads, tables and camp stools. We have a Syrian dragoman, who is a Roman Catholic, named Antonio Macloof. Our cook supplies us with three excellent meals each day. To-day we have visited the Church of the Holy Sepulchre, or more properly, the Church of the Holy Places, for the mother of Constantine was so exceedingly fortunate in grouping the localities of several mammoth events as to enclose them all in one building, which contains chapels and churches for Greeks, Roman Catholics, Armenians and Copts. These are enriched with many very costly presents, of various descriptions, from nations and individuals.

We met Mr. Cook near Zagazig and passed him by rail without being able to speak to him, his train having been detained by drifting sand, or we should have met him at Zagazig, Egypt. Two of his "round the world" party are now with us; they joined him at Chicago, and speak highly of their tour; they left him at Cairo to do Palestine, etc.

Sister Eliza R. Snow proves to be a first-class horsewoman, and endures the labors of the journey very well. Brother Carrington found it severe on his rheumatic ankles in riding down hill. My grey Tartar has not stumbled with me; the worst thing I dread is the sun on my head, to mitigate which I wear a cork hat, with an inside rim, the whole wrapped with a white and then a straw-colored scarf, and also have a light colored umbrella, lined with green. I think I shall be able to stand it, though the sun is pretty sharp here.

Standing just outside of St. Stephen's gate, and looking into the Valley of Jehoshaphat, where the Brook Kedron once ran, I read Zachariah 14, 4, and my impressions of the spot and situation were far more pleasing than any I have had since coming to Jerusalem. I do not wonder at Mark Twain burlesquing the ancient sites, when our guide, Isaac, told us gravely that there was the rock cleft at the crucifixion, from which was taken the skull of Adam, and took us into an adjoining room, called the Greek Church, and there showed us a small pedestal which he said was the centre of the world, and under it was buried the skull of our father Adam, which they had moved some thirty feet from where it was claimed to be found, for the sake of laying it in the exact centre; it even made me smile, and when Sister Snow gravely enquired how they identified the skull to be Adam's, he honestly replied he did not know.

God bless you.

Yours, &c.,

GEORGE A. SMITH.

LETTER LV.

View of Jerusalem—Solomon's City Wall—Hole "Made by the Saviour's Elbow"—Crowds of Beggars—Mourning Women.

CAMP NEAR JAFFA GATE, Jerusalem,
February 26th, 1873,

MY DEAR SON:

My first view of Jerusalem was from the northwest, the worst view from which to form an impression, being mostly the wall which must have been chiefly built by the Mahommedans since the days of the Crusaders. Some English archæologists, led by Captain Warren, sank a shaft 140 feet, near St. Stephen's Gate, and found the city wall of Solomon, showing that a big levelling had been done by ruins, and there is plenty of room for more. The Turkish government stopped the explorations, and they are closed up. This explodes most of the identical spots that are shown, though in some cases the original rock appears at the present surface.

The mountains that we passed over are as thoroughly rocky, and the rocks broken in shivers, as could well be imagined. I think they must at some time have been covered with a coat of soil which has been either blown or washed away.

I could but be amused to-day when the guide showed us a rock with a hole said to have been made by the elbow of the Saviour when he sank under the cross. The rock is built into a wall claimed to be near or at the spot where he sank; the hole is large enough for Christians to have dug out quite a number of relics. Beggars are almost innumerable, and they beg, and follow, and whine, and cry, until one almost has to strike them to get rid of them. One old man, nearly naked, squats by the roadside near the Jaffa gate, trembling all over. Mr. Bergheim tells us he is a professional beggar, and owns 600 olive trees and four orchards, and spends a couple of months, while foreigners are visiting Jerusalem, in begging. We saw bands of professional mourning women, dressed in white, going to the graveyards to mourn for the dead; they do it better than amateurs.

Love to all the folks. It is raining States' fashion, and is quite chilly, and our tent leaks a little, though we have a very good one.

GEORGE A. SMITH.

LETTER LVI

Leave Port Said—Jaffa—Mussulman Customs Officials—Travelling Arrangement—The Oldest Seaport in the World—Place where the Ark was Built—Jonah's Place of Embarkation—House of Simon the Tanner—Mahommedan Funeral Ceremony—Plains of Sharon—The Martyrs' Tower—A Night in the Desert—Start for the Holy City—Battle Field of David and Goliath—Resting Place of the Ark of the Covenant—Rose of Sharon—St. George's Church—Mount Zion—Mount of Olives—In Camp before Jerusalem.

JERUSALEM, February 26th, 1873.

EDITOR DESERET NEWS:

Saturday evening, the 22nd inst., we steamed out from Port Said, and the following morning anchored within a half mile of Jaffa, the first seaport of Palestine. In boisterous weather and rough seas, landing is difficult and dangerous—frequently impossible, occasioning much annoyance and great expense to tourists. As we arose at early dawn, our anxiety was relieved by finding we were favored with a smooth sea and fine weather, and we were enabled by means of small boats to disembark with comparative safety. On approaching Jaffa from the sea, it presents a charming and picturesque appearance, being situated upon a high eminence, its streets rising one above another like seats in an amphitheater, surrounded by beautiful lemon and orange groves and tall waving cypresses. On entering the custom house with our baggage, some francs bestowed upon the smiling, obsequious Mussulman official saved the trouble of looking up our passports and occupying time which otherwise would have been employed by officious Turks in ransacking our satchels and trunks. We proceeded on foot to our encampment, carriages being out of the question, through the suburbs of the town, till we came to a Turkish cemetery near the shore of the Mediterranean. We found the arrangements completed for our travelling expedition—two sleeping tents, a separate one for the ladies, a kitchen tent with cook stove, a saloon or dining tent, iron bedsteads, mattrasses, clean white sheets, abundance of bedding, carpets and camp stools. We were provided with good horses, saddles, an efficient dragoman, plenty of servants and preparations to serve three meals per day under the supervision of an experienced cook.

Jaffa is considered the oldest seaport in the world; it has a population of about five thousand, principally Arabs, Greeks, and Mahommedans.

The interior of the city does not compare favorably in its appearance with its exterior. The streets are narrow, crooked, and filthy in the extreme—the houses uncomfortable, dark and gloomy, and the occupants are certainly unprepossessing in manners and general appearance. This is the ancient Joppa of Bible history, and is supposed to be the place where Noah's Ark was built, the port where the prophet Jonah embarked when fleeing from the presence of the Lord, and where Hiram, King of Tyre, brought the cedars of Lebanon for the building of the Temple at Jerusalem.

Among other places of sacred interest, we visited the "House of Simon the tanner, by the sea side," where Peter had the remarkable vision in which the will of God was revealed concerning the Gentiles, by letting down a sheet containing all manner of beasts, &c., and heard the voice commanding him to "rise, kill and eat."

During our encampment we witnessed a ceremony of Mahommedan burial. The corpse o fa child, wrapped in white, was borne to the grave, without a coffin, in the arms of a Mussulman, attended by the parents and a few friends. The body was placed in a small enclosure formed at the bottom of the grave by stones placed around, after which several small paper packages were emptied into the grave; the enclosure containing the corpse was overlaid with flat rocks, the grave filled with earth, then a half bushel of beautiful little sea shells scattered over. Several women, clothed in white, knelt around the grave and commenced weeping and wailing in the most affecting manner, which they continued for several hours.

The next morning our tents were struck and we mounted our horses, following our dragoman in single file along the winding streets of Jaffa, lined with crowds of gazing Arabs and Mussulmen. After leaving the town we passed through extensive and lovely orange and lemon groves loaded with golden fruit, and presently reached the flowery Plains of Sharon. The atmosphere was sweet and balmy, the gorgeous sun spreading its enlivening rays upon the beautiful country around, the morning lovely as ever dawned upon the holy land of Palestine. We felt that we were passing over the land once occupied by the children of Abraham, the plains once trod by the kings of Israel with their marshalled hosts, the land of the apostles and prophets. We were in Palestine! The Holy Land! The consciousness of the fact was inspiring. Hour after hour we rode onward in silent and solemn meditation; at length we reached the city of Ramleh, four hours distant from Jaffa, where we stopped to rest our animals, and partake of refreshments. Here is " The Martyrs' Tower." We ascended a flight of stairs to its lofty summit, which commands a magnificent view of the surrounding country—the Plains of Sharon, Arab villages here and there upon rising mounds, gigantic prickly pear hedges, olive orchards, and now and then a palm tree rising majestically above the whole, and the mountains of Judea appearing in the distance.

We resumed our journey, passed trains of loaded camels

mounted by half naked Arabs, smoking their long pipes, looking down smilingly from their "ships of the desert," doubtless sympathizing with us in our humbler mode of travelling.

The soil is generally rich and fertile, growing fields of wheat and vegetables. The dews fall profusely, and we were informed that latterly rain is more frequent in Palestine than in former years.

About 4 p. m. we arrived at our encampment, a beautiful basin enclosed by romantic hills at the entrance of the Valley of Ajalon. Through the night we were serenaded by bands of musical frogs accompanied by howls of jackals in the adjacent hills, relieved by the low plaintive chants of our Turkish guards, and charming songs of cuckoos perched in the branches of olive trees around our camp.

On the following morning, after an early breakfast, with our faces toward the "Holy City" we moved forward, passing through the Valley of Ajalon, and soon commenced ascending into a more elevated region of country, generally rocky and mountainous, producing but little more than required for the flocks of sheep and goats ranging upon it.

About 12 we stopped to lunch under the shade of olive trees in the Valley of Elah, where it is said David selected his stones with which to combat Goliath, while the two contending armies were encamped on the slopes of the adjacent mountains. At a short distance from this locality we were shown the Kirjath-jearim of sacred history, where the "Ark of the Covenant" is said to have rested twenty years.

The Valley of Elah is richly ornamented in the midst of its rocky surface and sparse vegetation, with what is called the "Rose of Sharon," a flower of a deep red, velvety appearance, three inches in circumference or thereabout, growing from six inches to one foot in height. We saw but few on the Plains of Sharon, more in the Valley of Ajalon and in some other parts of the hilly country. They were blooming on the top of the crumbling ruins of St. George's Church, built by the Crusaders on the identical spot where the Ark is said to have rested.

One hour's ride from our lunching place will bring us to Jerusalem. We move on and at length ascend an eminence, and gaze on the "Holy City," Jerusalem. Away to the right is Mount Zion, the city of David. Off to our left, that lofty eminence, with an aspect so barren, is the Mount of Olives, once the favorite resort of our Saviour, and the spot last pressed by his sacred feet before He ascended into the presence of His Father. These interesting historic scenes, with all their sacred associations, inspire thoughts and reflections impressive and solemn. Yes, there is Jerusalem! Where Jesus lived and taught, and was crucified, where he cried "It is finished," and bowed his head and died! We slowly and thoughtfully wind our way down the hill, passing the Russian buildings and other prominent establishments, until we reach the city and enter our encampment.

LORENZO SNOW.

LETTER LVII.

On the Mediterranean—At Jaffa—Cheap Oranges—Visit a German Colony—Arimathea—Hills of Judea—Valley of Ajalon—Lydda of the Acts—Kirjath-jearim—Mount of Olives—The Holy City—Camp by the Jaffa Gate—Church of the Holy Sepulchre—Where the Saviour was Scourged—Judgment Hall—Place of the Crucifixion—Valley of Jehoshaphat—Garden of Gethsemane—Tomb of Zacharias—Jacob's Well—Solomon's Pools—Bethlehem—Church of the Nativity—Dead Sea—Ruins of Jericho—Elisha's Fountain—Gilgal—Christ's Hotel—Mosque of Omar—Judgment Seat of Solomon—Tomb of Aaron's Sons—Pool of Bethesda.

IN CAMP BEFORE THE JAFFA GATE OF JERUSALEM,
February 25th, 1873.

EDITORS SALT LAKE HERALD:

We went on board the steamer *Vesta*, at 5 p. m. on Saturday the 22nd, at Port Said, and had a very fine and smooth passage over the Mediterranean to Jaffa. When we awoke on Sunday morning, we were in sight of the coast of Judea, and dropped anchor in the harbor of Jaffa, the ancient Joppa, at 7.30 a. m. In stormy weather landing is very difficult here, and in rough weather it is quite impossible, so that the steamers have to go on to Beyroute; but we were favored with a smooth sea, though the breakers on the coast run pretty high. Our boats passed safely through the huge rocks, and we stepped ashore at 8.15 a. m.

By the aid of a backsheesh, which was openly asked of us from a custom-house official, our luggage was allowed to pass without any examination, and we went immediately through narrow, filthy, crooked and ill-paved streets to our camp outside of one of the gates, where we found our tents pitched and ready to receive us. Mr. Alexander Howard, the chief dragoman, had come here a few days ahead of us, and all the necessary preparations for our party, and for others, who are travelling with Mr. Cook, were made.

Jaffa is a very old seaport, and makes a fine appearance from the sea as it rises in the form of an amphitheatre. It also looks well from the surrounding hills in the distance, as it is surrounded by beautiful orchards of oranges, lemons and almonds. Some of our party bought one franc's worth of oranges (about 20 cents), and got thirty. A few of those we bought measured thirteen inches in circumference, and we were informed that extra specimens sometimes measure from eighteen to twenty inches. They are also of very good quality. We were quite astonished at the richness of the soil around Jaffa and through the Plains of Sharon, as we expected to see nothing but a barren waste.

Sunday afternoon we had to select our horses and saddles, as we were to leave early in the morning. We visited the German colony close by our camp, about half a mile outside the gate, and were introduced to its superintendent, Mr. Christoph Hoffman, by the American vice consul, Mr. Ernest Hardegg, also a German, who lives there and keeps a hotel. We had quite a pleasant interview with Mr. Hoffman and some of his associates, and got from him some information in regard to their colony, and how they obtained a clear title from the Turkish government for their lands. In the course of the afternoon Mr. Hardegg called upon us in our tents and kindly offered his services.

The principal point of interest here is the "house of one Simon, a tanner," beautifully situated by the seaside, (see Acts X), which we visited, and went on the roof, where it is said Peter had that remarkable vision recorded in Acts X—11. It was also here that the cedars of Lebanon were brought from Tyre, and then transported to Jerusalem. Here Peter restored Tabitha to life, (see Acts IX—36) and tradition says that this is the place where the Ark was built.

Shortly before we struck our tents on Monday morning, the 24th, the prince of Saxe-Weimar, whose tents were close by ours, arrived with a small suite and was received with military honors. At 8.30 a. m., we were all in the saddle and commenced our thirty days' trip, on horseback, through Palestine. We rode for some time through beautiful orange groves, fenced in with gigantic prickly pear hedges, and then came upon the fertile Plains of Sharon. At 11.30 a. m., we reached the ruins of the old Mosque of Ramleh, supposed to be the ancient Arimathea; ascended the Martyrs' Tower, from which a beautiful view of the surrounding country and the Mediterranean is obtained; and took our lunch in the shade of the old walls. We had been sadly disappointed on our arrival at Jaffa in not finding any letters from home, and had been without any news for four weeks. It was, therefore, a matter of great rejoicing among us, when a special messenger reached us here with our long expected letters, dated up to January 21st; especially as the contents were generally satisfactory.

At 1.30 we broke camp, and rode over the hills of Judea to the mouth of the Valley of Ajalon, which we reached after a three hours' ride, and found our tents pitched, as the pack animals, with all the baggage, had gone through without stopping. We have two large round wall tents, about sixteen feet in diameter, one of which is our dining tent, which President Smith and myself occupy as our bedroom during the night, and on the top of which the stars and stripes are flying to the breeze. The other one, of the same size, is occupied by Messrs. Lorenzo Snow, Albert Carrington, Feramorz Little and Thomas W. Jennings; and a smaller one, of about twelve feet in diameter, is for the ladies, Miss Eliza R. Snow and Miss Clara S. Little. We have iron bed-frames, and a mattrass and sufficient blankets to keep us pretty comfortable.

We have three meals a day, and pronounce the table as one of the best we have had since we left home. Then there is a tent for our dragoman, Mr. Antonio, a Syrian, for the chief cook, and for his two assistants. Besides, we have ten muleteers, and fifteen pack animals in our outfit.

At 7.30 next morning we were all in the saddle, and traveled for some time through the Valley of Ajalon and then over the rough and barren mountains of Judea, passing within sight of Ludd, which is the ancient Lydda of the Acts IX—32, and stopped a short time at Kirjath-jearim (I Sam. VII —12), at the ruin of the Church of St. George, which was built by the Crusaders in 1200 on the spot where the Ark of the Covenant rested for twenty years. A few miles further on we stopped for lunch at 11 a. m., in the Valley of Elah, where there is the brook from which David is said to have taken the smooth stones with which he slew Goliath. We continued our journey towards the "City of David," at 1.30 p. m., and our road led us over very steep and barren hills, from which at some points we had a fine view over the Plains of Sharon and the Mediterranean in the distance. About 2. 15 p. m., we came in sight of the Mount of Olives and a portion of the "Holy City," when various meditations passed through my mind. We rode along by the Greek, the Russian and the Prussian convents, also some fine private buildings of Europeans, outside the walls of this city, till we reached our camping ground on the northwest side of the city, within a few minutes walk of the Jaffa gate, at 2.30 p. m.

To-day we engaged a guide to show us through the city, the streets of which are very narrow and badly paved. The principal street, called "Christian Street," is only from twelve to fifteen feet wide, and the population is variously estimated from 20,000 to 30,000 inhabitants. Jerusalem has a number of gates, which are closed during the night. On the north is the Damascus gate, on the south the Zion gate, on the east

St. Stephen's gate, and on the west the Jaffa gate. Several others, as those of Herod, the Golden gate, etc., are always closed.

After visiting a few shops we went to the Church of the Holy Sepulchre, in which we were shown a good many sights. At the entrance we saw the slab on which the body of the Saviour was anointed for his burial; the place where Mary stood at the crucifixion; the sepulchre itself, with most gorgeous decorations, and covered with a large number of golden and silver lamps, which are always kept burning; the stone where the angel sat when Mary came to the grave; the spots where the Saviour and Martha stood, when she met him after his resurrection and thought he was the gardener; the sword and spurs of Godfrey of Bouillon, who was King of Jerusalem in 1100; the pillar of flagellation, on which the Saviour was scourged; the stone which was rolled from the mouth of the sepulchre; the tombs of Joseph of Arimathea and of Nicodemus: the place where the Saviour stood before they took him to Mount Calvary, and where he left his footprints in the rock upon which he stood; the place where Mary sat after the crucifixion, and was comforted by the other women; a rock which was rent during the earthquake; the place where they divided his clothes, and cast the lots over his coat; the place where St. Helena, mother of the Emperor Constantine, sat to pay off the workmen; the place where she found the three crosses; a very fine altar erected and presented to the church by Ferdinand Maximilian, Archduke of Austria, in 1857; a reddish column on which the Saviour sat when they crowned him with a crown of thorns, also an imitation of the original crown. Then we went into the Greek chapel, in the centre of which is a kind of platform, which they point out as the centre of the world. Below this is the Chapel of Adam, where they told us that the skull of Adam was buried. Then we were shown the place where the cross of the Saviour stood and the crosses of the two thieves; close to it a large rock, rent during the earthquake; the tomb of Melchizedek; the places where the Saviour was nailed to the cross, and where he was taken off. Our guide was honest enough to tell us that he did not believe all these places to be the identical spots, and when it came to the story about Adam's skull and some other legends, we could not help smiling. From the Church of the Holy Sepulchre we proceeded to the ruins of the Church and Hospice of the Knights of St. John, which were destroyed by the Saracens in 1178. The Superintendent, a German, told us that the Sultan had made a present of these grounds to the present Emperor of Germany about three years ago, but it was a very expensive present, as they had already removed 500,000 donkey loads of dirt to make the excavations, and it would take from two to three hundred thousand loads more to finish the job. From there we passed the Pillar gate, through which condemned criminals were led out to Mount Calvary, to be executed; thence we turned into the "Via Dolorosa," or way of sorrows, where Veronica wiped the perspiration from the Saviour's face, and where an impression of his features was left on her handkerchief. Close to this spot is the place where her father burnt her in a small oven because she believed in Christ. A little beyond was the spot where the Saviour fell a second time with the cross, and left a large mark of his elbow in a rock. Then we came to the rich man's house at whose door Lazarus lay, and to the place where the Saviour fell with his cross the first time, and where Mary met him and wept. We passed the Catholic church, "Ecce Homo," the site of Pilate's palace, of which one arch is left; and the pool of Bethesda, which is now dry and being filled up—it measures 360 feet in length, 130 feet in breadth and is 75 feet deep. From there we went through the St. Stephen's gate outside the walls, and had a fine view of the Mount of Olives; the road on which David ran from Absalom; the Valley of Jehoshaphat; the Garden of Gethsemane, and the place where Stephen was stoned. In returning outside the city walls to our camp, we passed the Tomb of Zacharias, which has an elevation of thirty feet, and is cut out of solid rock, (see Matthew XXIII—29 to 35) and the quarries of Solomon under the walls of the city.

March 3, 1873.—The night of the 26th to the 27th of February was cold, and it was raining quite hard, but as it looked like clearing up in the morning, we struck our tents and left for the Dead Sea.

At 7.30 a. m. we passed Jacob's Well, where he met Rachel with her father's sheep; at 9 a. m. stopped at Rachel's Tomb a little beyond, a few minutes, and rode over an exceedingly rough and stony road to Solomon's pools. There are three of them, the upper one 380 feet long, one end 250 feet wide, the other 160 feet, and 25 feet deep; the middle one is 423 feet long, west end 148 feet wide, east end 250 feet wide, and 39 feet deep; the lower one is 582 feet long, 207 feet wide, and 50 feet deep. They are filled from a spring in the neighborhood. The walls are partly formed of massive hewn stone, and partly by excavations in the solid rock. We rode along the aqueduct to Bethlehem, where we arrived at 11.15 a. m. The streets are very narrow, steep and crooked and we stopped only long enough to visit the Church of the Nativity, with its many stories and legends. On the alleged spot where the child Jesus was born is a silver star, laid in the floor with the inscription, in Latin, " Hic de Virgine Maria Jesus Christus natus est." We rode about one mile down the hill-side, and lunched under an almond tree. At 2.30 p. m. we again mounted our steeds, and rode over the mountains of Judea in an easterly direction. We soon came in sight of the Dead Sea in the distance, and the high mountains of Moab on the eastern shore. We visited the Greek convent of Mar Saba, where John the Baptist is said to have commenced his ministry; and camped two miles beyond, near the dry bed of the Brook Kedron. The following morning we had to get up at 5 o'clock, because we had a long day's ride before us. The road was partly very rough, but the weather was fine. We had a Bedouin sheik, or chief, and three armed Bedouin guardsmen along. When we neared the shore of the Dead Sea, nine Bedouins came out of the canes and wanted to stop us; but as soon as they saw that we were guarded, five of them fled and our men took the guns of the four others. We stopped about forty-five minutes, filled several bottles with water, and three or four gentlemen of our party and of another one that was traveling with us, indulged in a bath. About an hour's ride brought us to the banks of the Jordan, where we lunched under the shade of the olive trees, and about 4 p. m. we reached the ruins of Jericho, which consist of an old tower and parts of an aqueduct. (See Joshua II—1; VI—1; XXIV—11; also Matth. XX—29; Luke XIX—1.) Here is also Elisha's Fountain, the water of which is very good. Near to this place is Riha, the ancient Gilgal. (See Joshua IV, 19,20, Judges II-1, and I. Samuel X-8.) After supper some fifteen Bedouins came to our camp from the neighboring village to dance for us; they also performed a sham fight, and finished the programme of their evening's entertainment with the song, "May the ladies' eyes be like the moon," in Arabic.

The following morning, the 1st of March, we started back for Jerusalem; stopped for lunch at a fountain near some ruins called "Christ's Hotel;" passed through Bethany, where are the houses of Mary, Martha and Lazarus, and the tomb of the latter, and two miles further we crossed the Valley of Jehoshaphat, passed through the Jewish graveyard, and reached our old camp ground outside the Jaffa gate about 3 p. m.

On Sunday, March 2nd, we visited the Mount of Olives, in the forenoon, and, in the afternoon, held a sacramental meeting in one of our tents, and strolled through the narrow, dirty streets of the city. To-day we visited the Mosque of Omar, the grounds of which cover an area of 1,500 feet long by 1,000 feet wide, and are said to be the site of Solomon's Temple. The mosque stands about in the centre of these grounds, and is a fine piece of Saracenic architecture. It is considered the second holy place in the Mahommedan world, and is built on Mount Moriah. It was begun in A. D. 680, and finished in seven years. In front of the east gate, or gate of David, is the throne or judgment seat of Solomon, under a beautifully ornamented dome in the open air, supported by pillars. We entered by this gate, were shown the inside of the roof, finished in carved cedar wood, the beautifully colored windows, and the rock Es-Sukrah in the centre of the mosque, said to be the top of Mount Moriah, on which Abraham offered his son Isaac. Under this huge rock is a cave, in which it is said that Jesus, Abraham, David, Solomon, Moses and Elijah have prayed; and in the centre of the floor of this cave is a marble slab, beneath which the Mahommedans say is the "Well of Souls," sometimes called the "Gate of Hell," and by others the "Gate of Paradise."

In passing through the yard to the Mosque El-aksa, in the same enclosure, we saw an old, dry fountain, of Solomon's time, where the people made their ablutions before going to prayer. In this last named mosque we saw the tomb of the two sons of Aaron; the pulpit of Omar, finely carved in cedar wood and ornamented with ivory, said to be the only part preserved from the inside of Solomon's Temple; the studio of Omar, with ancient marble columns; and a marble cradle, in which, tradition says, Jesus slept during the three days he was lost from his parents, when twelve years old. Under another building, our guide showed us about twenty-six feet of the original wall of the "Horse gate," and some pillars of Solomon's time; and below another building, the extensive "Stables of Solomon." We then ascended one of the towers of the city wall, which forms one side of the enclosure of the grounds, near the pool of Bethesda, and had a very fine view of the city and environs; saw the Golden gate, the "Place of Wailing," close to the outside of the wall of the mosque, where, against a wall of huge blocks of stone, the devout Jews go to mourn over their calamities every Friday evening.

Before returning to camp, I called with President Smith on Mr. Abraham Askenasi, the Rabbi of the Portuguese congregation in Jerusalem, to whom he had a letter of introduction from a Rabbi in San Francisco. We were kindly received, treated to some refreshments, and the Rabbi said he would return the call at our tents to-morrow.

I forgot to give you the dimensions of the Dead Sea. It is a beautiful smooth lake, of extremely saline and bituminous water, about forty miles long by ten miles wide, and covers the destroyed Cities of the Plain. There is a remarkable stillness brooding over the whole region. The surface of the water is upwards of 1,300 feet below the level of the sea. Among the party traveling with us, part of the way, are two pleasant gentlemen by the name of N. C. and E. O. Hills, from Illinois, who are of Cook's around the world party, and who passed through Salt Lake last fall.

Wednesday morning, the 5th inst., we intend to leave Jerusalem for the division of Samaria, *en route* for Damascus and Beyrout, which we expect to reach on the 22nd, if all is well.

Yours truly,

PAUL A. SCHETTLER.

THE DEAD SEA—A MONUMENT.

Though "dead," it is a living monument.
'Tis peerless, archless, towerless, and, though
Devoid of every architectural
Embellishment, it justly claims to be
The prince of monuments in Palestine.

It is a monument of justice, and
Of righteous doom, of crime and wickedness,
A speechless, speaking monument of wrath
Divine, poured out on guiltiness
Of dark abominations—monitor
Of warning to the generations past,
The present, and to all that are to come.
It stands where stood the "Cities of the Plain"—
Where Sodom and Gomorrah, steeped in sin,
Were first devoured by fire, then swallowed up!

Its dense, saline, preserving properties
Are morally significant of the
Great purposes of God concerning sin—
Whene'er iniquity attains its full,
To sweep it with destruction's besom, and
To ultimately purify the earth.

O'er cliffs precipitous—thro' winding trails—
Rocky acclivities and frightful steeps—
At times, in zig-zag course, to cut the heights
That otherwise were inaccessible,
O'erlooking dark abysses, gaping chasms,
And, sometimes, beautiful sequester'd dells,
Where Nature, most successfully, has made
Attempts at wildly grand sublimity.
We went in search of this strange monument,
And found it nestled quietly beneath
Judea's mountains—on a sterile plain,
Where solitude in death-like stillness reigns.

This Sea, when seen as we beheld it—'neath
The cloudless noon-day sun, is beautiful.
The lucid rays appeared on crystalline
To fall, creating myriads of gems,

Which sparkling, glowed with dazzling brilliancy,
As if the Sea's smooth crest were overspread
With little, shining pearls most bounteously
To crown with gaiety the briny deep.

We gazed upon the Sea: 'Twas motionless,
As if in reverence for the Almighty power
Of Deity, whose awful mandate called
It into being. In deep silence wrapped—
Without a sound of moving waters, or
The gentle murmur of a stirring wave,
All, all is silence, and this silence speaks
Far more impressively than uttered tones.
'Tis God's own monument, and proof against
The wreck of ages and the waste of time.

JERUSALEM, March 3d, 1873. ELIZA R. SNOW.

LETTER LVIII.

Land at Jaffa—Orange and Lemon Orchards—German Settlements in Palestine—Valley of Ajalon—Ancient Battle Field—Church of the Holy Sepulchre—Start for the Dead Sea—Famous Localities Mentioned in the Scriptures—Novel Water Vessels—Bethlehem—Monastery of Mar Saba—Brook Kedron—The River Jordan—Ruins of Jericho—Mountain on which the Saviour was Tempted—A Bedouin War Dance—Bethany—Church of the Ascension—Backsheesh—Mosque of Omar—Saddle of Mahomet—Mount Moriah—Garden of Eden—Sacred Cradle—Foundations of Solomon's Temple—Visit to the Chief Rabbi—Ancient Parchments.

CAMP NEAR JAFFA GATE, Jerusalem,
March 4th, 1873,
PRESIDENT BRIGHAM YOUNG:

DEAR BROTHER:—We landed at Jaffa at about 8 a. m. of the 23rd ult., after a pleasant twelve hours' ride by screw steamer, the *Vesta*, over a smooth sea from Port Said, none being sea-sick; the sea, being smooth, was very favorable for landing. We went directly from our landing to camp, where our tents were ready pitched, just outside the walls of the small town of Jaffa, and near a Mahommedan cemetery. The Turkish officials only took time to look at our passports, and the custom house officers examined but one trunk, which did not happen to be ours. Mr. Alexander Howard, Mr. Cook's dragoman, met us on board the ship. The orange and lemon orchards at Jaffa are the finest I have yet seen. The town is a disgusting, dirty little jumble of narrow, crooked streets and small buildings.

Mr. Hardegg, the American vice consul, treated us with courtesy and introduced us to Dr. Hoffman, the President of the Temple of Jaffa, as they term an association of about 600 Germans, who believe God is rebuilding the temple spiritually through them. They have purchased some land from the Sultan, and showed us an Arabic deed of the purchase, and a plot of it. Although they have been there but a short time, they have proved to be successful farmers, as it has rained sufficiently to enable them to raise wheat and barley, but fruit and vegetables require irrigation. Several had recently died of liver and bowel complaints, but they were now healthy. The German settlements in Palestine are being increased by some Germans who have lived in Russia, and are leaving the country in consequence of the Russian Government's requiring them to ignore their own and learn the Russian language; this will likely strengthen the German interests in Palestine.

We moved out of camp about 9 a. m. on Monday, the 24th ult., and passed over the beautiful Plains of Sharon, much of which is in cultivation, and very productive. After lunching at the Martyrs' Tower, near Ramleh, we camped for the night near the entrance to the Valley of Ajalon, where there was good water, and which reminded us of Joshua's commanding the sun to stand still in the Valley of Ajalon. From this camp, on the 25th, we at once entered the mountain region, and nooned in the Valley of Elah, near the place where King

Saul encountered the armies of the Philistines, and where David selected the five smooth stones for his contest with Goliath. This valley is very narrow. From the Plains of Sharon to Jerusalem the country is very rocky; if ever there was any soil in this country, it seems to have disappeared from some cause. We camped near the Jaffa gate, on the west side of Jerusalem, pretty well tired and lame from our two days on horseback.

On the 26th we visited the Church of the Holy Sepulchre, and came to the conclusion that the mother of Constantine was very successful in grouping into so small a space so many of the notable places connected with the death and resurrection of the Saviour as to get them within the walls of one building; it is certainly immaterial as to where the identical square yard is, but the old monks have carried the matter of identity farther than we feel to endorse.

Our mail from Liverpool reached us at our noon halt at Ramleh, and some of the party received letters to January 21; I received one to January 12.

It rained all the night following our visit to the Holy Sepulchre, but our tents protected us very well; three of them are circular wall tents, with fly and lining, provided with iron bedsteads, camp stools, carpets, tables, wash-bowls, excellent bedding, &c.; Sisters Snow and Little occupy one, Brothers Snow, Carrington, Little and Jennings another, and myself and Schettler the one in which our meals are served, and over which flies the United States flag. They furnish us three substantial meals a day, very well cooked and served. There is also a circular tent in which the cooking is done on a range heated with charcoal burned from the trimmings of the olive trees.

February 27th, we struck tents about 8 a. m., and started in the direction of the Dead Sea, by rather a zigzag route, to enable us to visit certain points. We passed Joseph's Well, Rachel's Tomb, and over rough and stony hills to the Pools of Solomon, and followed the aqueduct to Bethlehem, where we visited the Church of the Nativity, saw the star indicating the spot where the Saviour was born, the manger in which he was cradled, the spot where Joseph was warned to flee into Egypt, and several other notable points, which are said to be of mathematical accuracy, all grouped within the walls of a Greek church, which contains many rich gifts and fine ornaments. On nearing Bethlehem we met large numbers of young women carrying pig skins full of water; the aqueduct is out of repair, and would require a little work to fix it, but failing that little, the water has to be carried some half a mile. The town is on a side hill, and may contain 2,000 or 3,000 inhabitants. The passages through it are narrow, crooked, steep, and in many places difficult for horsemen to pass. Great numbers of traders surrounded us at the church to sell us trinkets manufactured from pearl, olive wood, and stones from the Dead Sea. We lunched in what is called "The Shepherds' Field," and thought it might be the place where the shepherds were informed of the birth of the Saviour. We saw sheep on the mountains, and thought of King David, barley growing, and of Ruth and Boaz. The buildings around the place of nativity are divided into three portions, by Greek, Latin and Armenian Christians. We visited the Monastery of Mar Saba, and the men of our party were admitted, our dragoman having procured a permit from the Greek Bishop of Jerusalem. An ignorant monk established this place about 1,400 years ago, and since then, they say, no woman has ever been permitted to enter its precincts. the monks are civil. Mar Saba, the founder, died A. D. 532, aged 94. The present convent is so massive as to appear almost impregnable, and would perhaps be so to any arms but artillery. They have an immense number of skulls, which they say belonged to their brethren who were killed by the Saracens, and it is said there were 12,000 monks at one time connected with this establishment. The Brook Kedron, when it has water, runs by this convent. We passed some tents of Bedouins, and camped near them, about two miles from Mar Saba.

On the 28th we ascended some hills, and descended many, some of which were steep, rocky and sideling, visited the Dead Sea, rode to the ford of Jordan, and lunched where it is said Joshua and Israel crossed dry-shod, by a great miracle, although the river was overflowing its banks, as was usual in those days at harvest time; where Elijah and Elisha crossed in the same miraculous manner, and where John baptized the Saviour and repentant Israel. It is asserted that John began his preaching at Mar Saba, said to be the reason why the convent is placed there. We rode across the Valley of the Jordan, and came to the conclusion that a farm of several thousand acres might be irrigated from the river. The ruins of Jericho consist of a tower, foundations of an old wall, a broken arch, and several large mounds. The site is covered with a species of thorn resembling that which grew on the site of St. George. We camped at Elisha's Spring, so named from his having healed the waters, which are now excellent. Our dragoman showed us a mountain, the highest in sight, which he said was the one upon which Satan took the Saviour and showed him all the kingdoms of the world; Antonio said he was so informed, but he was not sure of it. About fifteen Bedouins came to our camp and performed a war dance, and a sham fight, which would have done credit to Utah Indians in Walker's palmy days, and sang, no doubt in elegant Arabic, accompanied by instruments, "May the ladies' eyes be like the moon." We paid the sheik eleven francs for the performance.

On the 1st inst. we lunched at the ruins called Christ's Hotel, and, passing Bethany, reached our former camp ground about 2 p. m., our whole journey with slight exceptions being over high hills, rough rocks, and interesting rocky desolation.

March 2nd, Mr. Antonio, our dragoman, packed one of our tents, &c. to the Mount of Olives, and pitched it a little north of east from the Church of the Ascension, in which is shown a print of the Saviour's foot in a solid rock, said to have been made by him when he ascended. From this mount one has the finest view of Jerusalem, and can also see the site of Jericho, a portion of the course of the river Jordan, the point where it enters the Dead Sea, and several reaches of the sea. We returned to camp about noon, going and returning by the Damascus and St. Stephen's gate, and the Garden of Gethsemane.

Backsheesh! Everywhere we hear this word, from little and great, sick and well, young and old; the almost naked man, who lies trembling in the Jaffa road, imploringly reaches out his hands for backsheesh; he is a professional, and has 600 olive trees, and four or five orange orchards, and spends two months in begging during the season of travelers passing through. All the holy places are thronged with beggars.

Our dragoman hired a Bedouin sheik to accompany us to the Dead Sea, to keep the Bedouins from robbing and plundering us, and notwithstanding he paid him, he called on us to-day for more, and we deemed it best to give him an additional 10 francs.

After getting the mail matter off in the afternoon of the 28th ult., Brother Carrington walked around Jerusalem outside the walls, and on the 1st inst. he walked through many of its streets, and again examined it from different points outside, and after all he says he cannot imagine why King David selected it for a site for his capital.

March 3rd, I, with the rest of the party, visited the Mosque of Omar. They had no slippers large enough for me, so I tied two pocket handkerchiefs over my boots. We employed a very efficient guide, and I subjoin from my journal the chief items of his comments. The Mosque of Omar and the Mosque of El-aksa are within an enclosure of about 1,500 feet. The guide first showed us the north, or Paradise, gate, then the east gate, in front of which he pointed out the site of the judgment seat of Solomon, under a small dome called the dome of chains; then through the east or David's gate into the mosque, where he pointed out a green marble slab in the floor, in which 19 nails from the cross had been inserted, of which all but three and a half had disappeared, and when they disappear the world will come to an end; he then pointed out the saddle in which Mahomet rode before he went to heaven; then a number of korans; then a large rock in the centre of the mosque on which tradition says Abraham offered up Isaac, and which is said to be the summit of Mount Moriah; on one side of this rock he pointed to a place from which Mahomet ascended to heaven, leaving the impression of his feet in the rock, and to the finger prints in the rock made by the angel Gabriel when he stayed the rock from following the prophet; the Mahommedans had kissed the footprint so much, that, to preserve it, they cut the piece out and locked it up with seven hairs of his beard, which are shown but once a year. He then took us into a cave under the rock, and pointed us to a tongue of rock, on the right hand side, which said to Mahomet: " Peace be with you, you prophet of God," to which Mahomet replied: " Peace be with you, you rock of God;" he then pointed to an altar in the cave where Solomon prayed, to one where Elijah prayed, and to places where Abraham and David prayed; then to a cavity in the top caused by Mahomet's bumping his head against it when rising from prayer; then to a hole in the centre of the top through which they threw down the ashes of the sacrifices; then to a round slab, in the centre of the cave, over the mouth of a deep well, called the Well of Souls. We then went outside the mosque and were shown a pulpit in the open air; near by is a fountain, now dry, used for ablutions previous to praying. We then passed under another building, and were shown a portion of the old wall and several columns of the horse gate; from that to the Mosque of El-aksa, in the same enclosure, and were shown a small black marble slab in the wall, brought from Mecca by Mahomet; those who can walk some fifteen feet, blindfolded, and touch the slab, are pure, the others not. We then went into the mosque, built about A. D. 607, and were shown the tomb of the two sons of Aaron, the footprints of Jesus in a rock, a marble altar where Moses offered prayer, the pulpit of Omar, made of cedar and ivory, said to be from Solomon's Temple, then two sets of two pillars, each set near together—those who can pass through are pure, the rest not; then the studio of Omar, surrounded with columns; then a well down which is the Garden of Eden, then a marble cradle in which Jesus slept when twelve years old, at the time he was lost from his parents. From that mosque, still in the same enclosure, we went to the stables of Solomon, now underground; then along the east wall, this wall being also the east wall of the city, to a point where a stone pillar projects horizontally some three feet beyond the outer face, and on which Mahomet is to sit in judgment on the world. From there we went to the site of the Golden gate, and had a fine view from one of the towers of the wall. We then went outside the enclosure to a Jewish wailing place, the only spot where the foundations of the Temple of Solomon are visible, outside the enclosure. Brother Schettler and I then called on the Rabbi of the Portuguese congregation, to whom I presented a letter of introduction from the Rabbi of San Francisco. He said the letter was a good one, and that he liked the looks of my face. I talked to Brother Schettler, he to a German Jew, and the Jew to the Rabbi, as the latter could only speak in Hebrew, Portuguese and Turkish. He offered me a cigar; I told him I did not smoke. He said he was glad I had called on him, and brought a glass of water and some preserves, also cups of coffee for each of us. He remarked that the Jerusalem

Jews were very poor, but if they had control, they would make great improvements. He said the Mosque of Omar was on the site of Solomon's Temple, but not in the centre: also that no Jew goes inside the mosque inclosure. He believed the God of Hosts would some day redeem the land. He introduced me to two of his friends, who showed us some ground they had bought from the Turks, and were erecting upon it a hospital and some dwellings for the poor Jews, with funds from abroad. We then went to their synagogue, and found it a plain, well-furnished building; and from there passed through the grain market, and through a jumble of narrow lanes, arched over in places, and returned to our camp. The Rabbi very courteously said he would call upon me in camp.

March 4th, at 10 a. m., we received a visit from Abraham Askenasi, chief Rabbi in Jerusalem; we understand he is selected by the Turkish Sultan, and has received some titular orders from him. They express a firm faith in the redemption of Israel and the return of the ten tribes. They say there are no springs here now, but used to be in the days of Israel's prosperity, and there will be again. Rain water is now their only supply, and later in the season it sells at a farthing a bottle. Europeans have been boring for water, but unsuccessfully, it not being time for it. The interview was very pleasant and interesting, and the Rabbi and three of their principal men who accompanied him appeared to be men of intelligence.

We visited Mr. Shapira's collection of ancient parchments, some of them very old, dug from beneath the ruins of synagogues both in Palestine and Arabia; they possess much interest. These writings are on various kinds and qualities of parchment, one of which, found in the mountains of Moab, discloses the idea that the Gods were male and female, and religion older than the law of Moses.

Your brother in the ministry of the priesthood,

GEORGE A. SMITH.

LETTER LIX.

Suez—Red Sea—Port Said—On Board the "Vesta"—Anchor off Jaffa—Passports Demanded—Commencement of Tent Life—House of Simon, the Tanner—Traveling to Jerusalem—Plains of Sharon—Valley of Ajalon—Valley of Elah—Mount of Olives—Church of the Holy Sepulchre—Tomb of Rachel—Bethlehem—Dead Sea—Jordan—Jericho—Gilgal—Bethany—Mosque of Omar.

JERUSALEM, March 4th, 1873.

EDITOR WOMAN'S EXPONENT:

I wrote you last in Cairo, Egypt, from whence we went to Suez, where we paid our respects to the Red Sea, of antique celebrity. I walked up and down its low bank, admired its beautiful, calm surface, as it lay in sweet repose with wave unstirred, and reflected deeply on the past of its interesting history.

From Suez we went by rail back to Ismalia, which we passed on our way from Cairo to Suez. From Ismalia we went by steamer on the great Suez Canal, one of the modern "wonders of the world," to Port Said, a town built on artificial ground, made of material taken from the bed of the canal. On the evening of the 22nd of February, by the aid of boats, we went on board the *Vesta*, of the Austrian Lloyd line of steamers, and early the next morning anchored off the coast of Jaffa, which we safely reached in boats, although this is considered the most dangerous of seaports. The Mediterranean washes the foundations of the buildings. We ascended a few steps, and entering a narrow, muddy street, were met by a host of natives, clamoring for our satchels in anticipation of a fee of backsheesh for relieving us from carrying them. Presently a smiling, corpulent biped, in turban and gown, demanded our passports, at the same time giving us a hint that he would compromise his demand for a fee, to which our cashier readily assented, and thereby, also protected our baggage from being overhauled at the Custom House.

We walked directly to our encampment, found our tents in readiness to receive us, and were delighted with the many conveniences provided by Mr. Howard, agent of Mr. Cook of London, under whose arrangements we are traveling.

Thus, under as clear sunshine as had ever shone on the ancient Joppa, and on as bright a morning as ever dawned on the land of Palestine, we commenced tent life, and, to render it more impressive, it was Sunday morning.

There is nothing attractive in the appearance of the interior of this ancient town. It is said to contain about five thousand inhabitants. As we saw them in crowds in the narrow, crooked streets, they are the representatives of low life and degradation. We walked a long, roundabout distance to visit the "house of one Simon, a tanner," situated "by the sea side," and were glad to return to our tents in the suburbs, where we breathed the pure fresh air. The surroundings of the city are pleasant and richly decorated with groves of the lemon and orange, which are watered from wells dug in their vicinity. With me, the reflection that we really were in Palestine, the land rendered dear to the Saints of God by some of the most interesting associations of mortal life—the history of the past in connection with the anticipations of the future, which no other people than Latter-day Saints can so fully appreciate—was the all-absorbing thought.

Early on Monday morning our camp equipage, which consists of everything necessary for genteel boarding houses, was packed, and, in monstrous bundles, lashed to the sides of donkeys, mules and horses; our tents struck and packed; the laden animals and their drivers started off; when we mounted our horses, and, following our dragoman, went in the same direction, leading to Jerusalem.

For a considerable distance after leaving the city, the street, on both sides, is lined with the most luxuriant orange groves we have seen, the limbs bending with the weight of large clusters of the golden fruit, and protected by hedges of cactus of an enormous size. We traveled till noon over the beautiful Plains of Sharon, and stopped to lunch in the vicinity of Ramleh, where the attendants who had our mid-day refreshments in charge, consisting of light bread, cold boiled mutton, chicken, a boiled egg for each, an orange each, and bottles of water, had preceded us, and opened our lunch on mattrasses provided for the purpose. The majority of the attendants proceeded ahead in time to pitch tents, put up for each an iron bedstead, (which, by the way, is rather a small pattern for President Smith, but very comfortable for the rest) tables, seats, etc., and get the camp stove and cooking apparatus all into working order preparatory to evening dinner, served with soups, meats, vegetables and pastries.

The country through which our afternoon ride led is very uneven, some portions rocky and barren. We encamped for the night on a lovely green, called the entrance to the Valley of Ajalon, conspicuous in the history of Joshua. Next day we rode through the Valley of Ajalon, up mountain ridges, where we had delightful views of the Plains of Sharon and the Mediterranean. The country is very picturesque, the road zigzag, winding around and on the sides of mountains — pass Kirjath-jearim, famous in the history of David, lunch in the Valley of Elah, and, in the afternoon in view of the Mount of Olives, which we leave at our left, and arriving at the memorable city of the ancient Jewish nation, the once favored of the Most High, the site of the Jerusalem from which the "Word of the Lord" shall yet go forth, we found our tents in readiness and entered them with hearts of thankfulness to God for His protecting care and blessings in bringing us to this destination in safety.

But I must hasten to a close. The next day, the 26th, we spent in and about Jerusalem, visited the Church of the Holy Sepulchre; had a fine view of the Garden of Gethsemane; and the next morning struck tents, and spent three days in visiting the Pools of Solomon, the Tomb of Rachel, Bethlehem, the Dead Sea, Jordan river, Gilgal, Jericho, Bethany, etc.,—have not time for description. On the evening of the 1st of March returned to this city, visited the Mount of Olives and the Mosque of Omar. To-morrow we leave for Syria.

ELIZA R. SNOW.

LETTER LX.

One Day in Jerusalem—Rachel's Tomb—Description of the Pools of Solomon—Birthplace of the Saviour—Church of the Nativity—Grotto of the Nativity—Altar of the Innocents—Studio of St. Jerome—Bedouin Arabs—The Shepherds' Field—Convent of Mar Saba—Skulls of the Dead—An Ancient Palm Tree—River Jordan—Rencontre with Bedouins—Description of the Dead Sea.

JERUSALEM, March 5th, 1873.

EDITOR DESERET NEWS:

After remaining one day at Jerusalem, according to programme, Feb. 22 we struck our tents, resumed our saddles, and started on an excursion of three days to Solomon's Pools, Bethlehem, Convent of Mar Saba, the Dead Sea, the Jordan, returning by the way of Bethany to Jerusalem.

About six miles' ride over a rocky, sterile country,

brought us to Rachel's Tomb. It is a small, stone building, forty feet long and twenty wide, and is respected by Christians, Jews and Mahommedans. Here we made a detour over a miserable, rocky, tortuous path of some three miles, to the Pools of Solomon. These pools consist of three immense reservoirs, situated in a broad valley about three miles from Bethlehem. They are partly excavated in a rocky bed, and partly built of large hewn stones, and so arranged that the bottom of the upper pool is higher than the top of the next, and the same with the second and the third. The first pool is three hundred and eighty feet in length, twenty-five feet deep, and about two hundred and forty feet broad. The second is about one hundred and sixty feet from the upper pool, four hundred and twenty-three feet in length, about two hundred and forty in breadth, and thirty-nine in depth. The lower one, nearly two hundred and fifty feet from the middle pool, is five hundred and eighty feet in length, about two hundred feet wide and fifty deep.

These pools receive their supplies from a subterraneous fountain, some distance up the valley. The water from these pools was formerly conveyed in an aqueduct by Bethlehem, in a winding course, to Jerusalem; but at present it only goes to Bethlehem. These pools are supposed to have been built by Solomon. From this point we continued our course over rocky ridges, following a narrow, winding trail, till we reached Bethlehem, the birthplace of our Saviour.

This city is pleasantly situated upon a mountain ridge, the slopes of which are terraced with rows of fig and olive trees, rising one above another in regular gradation. The population of Bethlehem is about three thousand, principally Christians. The Church of the Nativity is about the only attraction. We entered it and followed a winding staircase to the Grotto of the Nativity, which is brilliantly lighted with about thirty silver lamps, kept continually burning. The floor is laid with precious marbles. A white marble slab, placed in the pavement, set around with jasper, in the centre of which is a silver sun, is encircled with the following words: *Hic de Virgine Maria Jesus Christus Natus Est.*, i. e. Here Jesus Christ was born of the Virgin Mary. Though we had scruples respecting this being the identical spot it represented, still these words, in connection with the peculiar circumstances around, produced impressions never to be forgotten. Near by was pointed out the place where the wise men stood while presenting the Royal Infant myrrh and frankincense. A little distant from this we were shown an altar which is said to indicate the place where twenty thousand children, murdered by Herod's order, were buried; now called, on this account, "The Altar of the Innocents." A painting directly over it represents the massacre.

We were conducted into a retired, solitary niche of this church, almost devoid of light, the identical Studio of St. Jerome, where he spent most of his life in deep study, and produced those works which gave celebrity to his name.

Before leaving Bethlehem it was considered policy to employ a Bedouin sheik, as security against these barbarians who inhabit the mountains through which we were to pass. These Bedouins chiefly live in tents, their flocks and herds constituting their principal means of support. Their dress is plain and rather primitive—a flowing skirt or gown and a scanty undergarment of coarse calico fastened around the waist by a leather belt, ornamented with rows of cartridges in brass tubes; to these are added a long-barrelled shotgun, with flint-lock, slung over the shoulder, and knife stuck in the belt. This wandering people cultivate the soil to some extent. In passing over the mountains of Judea we sometimes saw enclosed patches of cultivated ground near their camps, and many flocks of sheep and goats feeding in the glens and upon the adjacent mountains. Tourists are not safe in traveling through their country unless accompanied by some of their own people.

We stopped to lunch in an olive orchard a short distance from Bethlehem, an enclosure called "The Shepherds' Field," where the shepherds watched their flocks by night, when the angels appeared to them announcing the grand and glorious event.

From here our route was over a rocky, tortuous path through the wilderness of Judea, scarcely a tree, shrub or brush to be seen in any direction. The whole country is barren and rocky, herbage here and there sufficient only for the sustenance of sheep and goats. The mountain scenery was beautiful and sublime ; occasionally I stopped my horse upon a lofty summit to gaze upon the surrounding scenery, a vast wilderness of mountains in an endless variety of form and size. Towards evening we arrived at the Convent of Mar Saba, about ten miles from Bethlehem. We descended a broad, paved staircase to a small platform in front of the massive walls, in which was a small iron door. We were closely watched by a singular looking friar, peeping through a loophole overhead. Presenting our letter of introduction from the Greek authorities at Jerusalem, which was scrupulously examined, we were admitted and conducted through the building, by the presiding friar, a tolerably good looking and intelligent gentleman.

This convent, in some respects, is the most singular and extraordinary building in Palestine. It is situated in the midst of the wilderness where John the Baptist commenced his ministry. It is built upon the side of a terrific ravine, and consists of irregular massive walls, towers, chambers and chapels, built upon narrow rock terraces and precipices, advantage being taken of natural caves and grottos in the rocks and sides of the cliffs, insomuch that we could scarcely tell, as we passed along the narrow galleries and flights of stairs, what was natural and what artificial; the ravine is several hundred feet deep, the side of it covered from top to bottom with these natural and artificial works, woven imperceptibly one into another, forming a fortress of immense strength. It is considered one of the richest convents in Palestine; and the strictest precaution and watching are observed to prevent the wild Bedouins, who are constantly hovering in the vicinity, from entering and carrying off its treasures. St. Saba, the founder of this convent, was born in the year 439. He was a man of remarkable sanctity, and held in such high veneration that he drew thousands of followers to this desolate region. He had around him, at one time, fourteen thousand people in this glen and its neighborhood. He died in this solitary retreat at the age of ninety-four years. We were shown his tomb in a small, neat chapel, also an apartment containing a pile of skulls of monks who had been martyred by the Persians, and a grotto where St. Saba spent many years of his life, which, according to tradition, was originally a lion's den. We saw a palm tree still flourishing, said to have been planted nearly fourteen hundred years ago, by St. Saba.

This convent belongs to the Greek Church. The monks are required to observe the most rigid rules of abstinence and fasting, never allowed to eat flesh, and strictly enjoined to allow no woman to enter their presence or cross the threshold of their establishment. A small, peaceful tribe of Arabs, residing in adjacent glens, are employed by these friars to convey their food and clothing from Jerusalem.

In a small, open square, they spread out upon the pavement their little articles of traffic, consisting of beads, buttons, crosses, walking sticks, etc., inviting us to make investments. About seventy of these anchorites live together in this building, where everything around exhibits an aspect of gloom and misery, as might be expected where nature is interrupted by the exclusion of the cheering, enlivening and happy influence of woman.

From Mar Saba we proceeded to our encampment, half a

mile distant, in a beautiful dell, encircled by stupendous mountains.

The following day, having nine hours' ride before us, we started before sunrise, our path extending over high, barren, rocky ridges, through a wild, desolate region, skirting fearful ravines, and passing along the brink of frightful chasms and precipices, occasionally catching a glimpse of the Dead Sea, through breaks in the distant cliffs; at length we behold the sacred Plains of Jordan, and there lies, in full view, the Dead Sea, with its waters sparkling beneath the bright and burning sun.

Having descended into the valley, while passing through a jungle of tall cane and thorns, those of our party in front suddenly encountered a band of armed Bedouins, whose fierce looks and threatening attitude prompted them to turn back very hurriedly. Antonio, our dragoman, immediately rushed up from the rear to ascertain the cause of interruption; on his approach, the Bedouins concealed themselves among the cane and bushes, except three, who stood their ground defiantly. Antonio, somewhat excited, hurried the company rapidly through the jungle, then galloped up to the three Bedouins, and, aided by his men, forced their arms from them, and took them as trophies of victory to the Dead Sea. The sheik being in the rear, and not appearing till the affray was nearly over, some conjectured that he dictated the ruse; our subsequent acquaintance with him, however, convinced us that this supposition did him injustice.

The Dead Sea is the most remarkable body of water in the world. It is ten miles wide, forty in length—lying in a deep ravine, about thirteen hundred feet below the level of the Mediterranean, enclosed by lofty cliffs of bare, white and grey limestone. We stopped on the shore near where the Jordan empties. We noticed here quantities of drift wood which had been accumulating for ages; but little else appeared except sterility, dreariness and death-like solitude.

We were informed that nothing was to be found upon any of its borders exhibiting life, except here and there where a brackish fountain, or little streamlet from the mountain, produces a small thicket of cane, willow and tamarisk. I think the water is more intensely salt than that of any other body of water except Salt Lake. It contains twenty-six per cent. of saline matter, which is sufficient to render it fatal to animal life. It is as transparent as the water of the Mediterranean. Its specific gravity is so great that the human body will not sink, and eggs float when two-thirds immersed.

After spending some time in gratifying our curiosity and in experimenting on the bathing qualities of its waters, we left its dismal shores, steering across a flat, sterile plain, some three miles distant, and stopped under some willows on the banks of the sacred Jordan, near the place where it is supposed the Israelites crossed, and where our Saviour was baptized.

But I am reminded of the increasing length of my letter, and although we are now in Jerusalem, intending to start in the morning to visit northern Palestine and Syria, my correspondence must leave us for the present in this Scriptural locality, with its impressively solemn associations.

LORENZO SNOW.

LETTER LXI.

Visit to the Jordan River—Sacred Localities—Singular Custom Among the Christians of Palestine—Fountain of Elisha—Valley of the Jordan—Brook Cherith—Plains of Jericho—The Jericho of To-day—Entertained by Bedouins—Bethany—Residence of Mary and Martha—Tomb of Lazarus—Garden of Gethsemane.

PALESTINE, March 6th, 1873.

EDITOR DESERET NEWS:

Our visit to the River Jordan was interesting. As we drank of its sweet and refreshing waters and washed in its sacred stream, our thoughts and reflections recurred to the days of childhood, when we were accustomed to peruse the Holy Scriptures describing the important events which transpired in this locality—the passage of the Israelites when the channel became dry, as the priests, bearing upon their shoulders the sacred ark, stepped into the flowing stream; the dividing of the waters by Elijah when he passed over the dry bed and was taken up into heaven from the plain on the opposite side by a whirlwind; and Elisha, as he returned, took the mantle of Elijah that fell from him, and smote the waters, saying, "Where is the Lord God of Elijah?" thus making the third time the Jordan was divided. But another event of much deeper interest is associated with this place—the baptism of our Saviour, referred to in the following language—"John came preaching in the wilderness of Judea, and Jesus came from Galilee to Jordan to be baptized of him;" and we were at or near the identical point where all these memorable events had taken place, standing upon the bank, looking down into the glen, and bathing in the same stream which had borne silent witness of these sublime occurrences.

This stream of Biblical history flows through a glen varying from two hundred to six hundred yards in width, and from fifty to one hundred and fifty feet in depth below the surrounding plain. The bottom of the glen is sprinkled here and there with shrubs; tamarisk, oleander and willows grow on the banks of the stream, which are generally very steep. The Jordan varies in width from eighty to one hundred and fifty feet, with a depth often of ten or twelve feet. It flows through the Sea of Galilee; from the great fountain at Dan, to where it empties into the Dead Sea, its distance in a direct line is ninety-two miles. The Sea of Galilee is about six hundred feet higher than the mouth of the Jordan, and sixty miles distant. This river has a rapid current, making it dangerous to bathers unacquainted with the stream. A gentleman from New York, who joined us at Jaffa, stated that on his previous tour to Palestine, while bathing here, he was suddenly carried down by the force of the current, and at the last moment was saved by a dexterous and extraordinary effort of his dragoman.

A singular custom prevails among the Christian churches of Palestine—that of bathing in the Jordan every year at Easter. They gather in multitudes, putting themselves under the protection of a Turkish escort, headed by the Governor of Jerusalem or his deputy, to protect them from the Bedouin robbers. Starting from the "Holy City," traveling on foot and upon mules, donkeys and camels, through the wild, mountain regions of Judea, they cross the Plains of Jordan, and on reaching its sacred stream rush indiscriminately into the flowing waters, young and old, men and women, regardless of propriety or even decency. Through this ceremony they anticipate peculiar favors and heavenly blessings.

Having sufficiently examined the Jordan and its surroundings, we proceeded across the plains, making our encampment at the Fountain of Elisha, near the ruins of Jericho. This fountain consists of several small springs which flow from beneath a large mound. These are the famous waters which were healed by Elisha, as spoken of in Scripture. A stream flows from them of considerable size, which waters a portion of the Plain of Jericho. The Valley of the Jordan, in the direction we crossed, is about ten miles in width, possessing a rich soil, and with proper tillage could be made abundantly productive. A great portion of it, however, is a dreary, desolate region. Some parts of the valley watered by the Brook Cherith and the stream issuing from Elisha's Fountain are covered with lotus trees interspersed with willows and a prolific growth of weeds. Some distance from these water courses, the trees and shrubbery are more thinly scattered, which viewed in the distance resemble an immense park, beautiful and picturesque. These plains were formerly celebrated for their richness and fertility—their palm groves and luxuriant gardens, producing honey and balm, reckoned the most fertile region of Judea. Now, nothing of this kind remains. The Plains of Jericho were formerly considered the garden of Palestine; their aspect now is strangely different, nothing is seen but small fields of grain intermixed with thorny bush. A small village, occupied by Arabs, is the only modern representative of the ancient Jericho. The houses are formed of stone walls, built up loosely without mortar; the roofs flat and covered with brush and gravel; the yards and wretched patches of gardens are enclosed by winrows constructed of the bows of thorns; the walls of the village, to protect its shiftless inhabitants from the raids of the Bedouins, are made of the same material. In riding through this disgustingly filthy town, we were lustily cheered by some dozen dirty, half-naked children, collected for this purpose, but more particularly for backsheesh. Sheep, children, goats, women and men, all indiscriminately huddled together, and no doubt this people deserved the profligate character given them, *i. e.* similar to that of Sodom and Gomorrah.

In the evening, some twenty Bedouins appeared in our camp, equipped and prepared to amuse us by their accomplishments in music and dancing, for the purpose of laying claims to our backsheesh. We considered it policy to accept the offer: accordingly we took seats before our tents. They posted themselves in a standing line immediately fronting us, each having a short sword girded under a ragged mantle, all scantily and shabbily clad, making rather a primitive appearance. They commenced their singular manœuvres by dodging forward and back at the same moment, clapping their hands, accompanied with rapid stepping of the feet and a strange chant, occasionally making a whizzing, thrilling whoop, the like of which was never heard but from the throat of a Bedouin, their chief standing in front, twirling and flourishing a naked sword in the faces of his comrades, keeping time with their fantastic motions, steppings, chantings, and whoopings, occasionally turning suddenly, he made the whole exceedingly impressive by flourishing the naked blade close to our faces. The drift of their songs, we were told, was highly flattering to the ladies, and complimentary to the gentlemen—the former for their extraordinary beauty, the latter for their anticipated liberality in bestowing backsheesh. We took the hint, and recollecting several robberies and murders which had occurred in the vicinity, we paid them for this wretched entertainment, constantly adding more, until we excited their admiration. We retired to our tents, reflecting on the strange difference between the present occupants of this locality and those who inhabited it when prophets converted bitter springs into sweet fountains, and smote impetuous streams, piling up their waters on either side and walked through on dry ground.

The following morning, after breakfasting and drinking the sweet waters of the Fountain of Elisha, we left the Plains of Jericho, and ascended into a wild, rocky, mountainous region, our path lying along the brink of the most sublime ravine of Palestine. It is many hundred feet deep, where but little else is seen than precipices of naked rocks, containing here and there a grotto seemingly inaccessible to anything but eagles; yet we were informed that these solitary caves were once occupied by hermits, some of whom reduced their bodies to a condition that four raisins per day supplied the cravings of appetite. Down to an immense depth, we discerned a small stream tumbling over the rocks, which we were told was the "Brook Cherith, that is before Jordan," where the prophet Elijah was fed by ravens, while the famine prevailed in Palestine.

We stopped for lunch under the shade of some crumbling walls and pointed arches, where our generous sheik left us, his services being no longer required. Before leaving, he inscribed, in beautiful Arabic, his official name in my journal. Mounting our horses, we soon reached Bethany, situated about two miles from Jerusalem. Its location is pleasant and romantic, being built on the eastern slope of Mount Olivet, partially surrounded by steep hills, encircled by old, decayed terraces, supporting a few scattered fig and olive trees. It is a poor, miserable village, with narrow, filthy streets; the whole presenting a dismal appearance, yet a place of sacred interest. Here dwelt the sisters, Mary and Martha, with Lazarus their brother. Here Christ raised Lazarus from the tomb and presented him alive to his weeping sisters. Here, too, was the house of Simon the leper, in which Mary anointed Jesus with precious ointment and wiped his feet with her hair. The sites of these events are still pointed out—the house of Simon, that of Mary and Martha and the tomb of Lazarus. The latter is a deep vault, partly excavated in the rock, and partly lined with masonry. We stopped our horses at the front of the entrance. This opens on a winding staircase leading to a small chamber whence a few steps more lead to a small vault in which the body is said to have been placed. We made but a short stay in this village, much to the disappointment of a crowd of dirty, ragged customers who clamored fearfully for backsheesh.

As we approached Jerusalem, we descended a steep hill, down a rocky, winding, shelvy path, past an immense cemetery and the Garden of Gethsemane, with its ornamental trees, gravel walks, flowers and shrubbery, then around the towering battlements of Jerusalem, and soon reached our encampment, well pleased with our three days' excursion.

LORENZO SNOW.

APOSTROPHE TO JERUSALEM.

Thou City with a cherished name,
   A name in garlands drest,
Adorned with ancient sacred fame,
   As city of the blest.
Thy rulers once, were mighty men,
   Thy sons, renowned in war:
Thy smiles were sought and courted then
   By people from afar.

A holy Temple, built as God
   Directed it should be,
In which His glory shone abroad,
   With heav'nly majesty;
Was great adornment to thy place,
   And lustre to thy name;
With much of grandeur, wealth and grace.
   To magnify thy fame.

The Lord was with thee then, and deigned,
    In speech well understood,
Thro' prophets, by His wisdom trained,
    To counsel for thy good.
Attracted by illustrious fame,
    As by a ruling star,
To study wisdom, people came
    From other climes afar.

Thine then, a chosen favored land,
    Was crown'd with plenty's smile;
The mountains dropped down fatness, and
    The hillsides wine and oil.
And thou wert like a golden gem
    Upon a nation's brow.
Jerusalem, Jerusalem,
    Alas! What art thou now?

Degraded, and on every hand,
    From wisdom all estranged;
Thy glory has departed, and
    All, but thy name is changed!
From God withdrawn—by Him forsook—
    To all intents depraved;
Beneath the Turkish iron yoke,
    Thou long hast been enslaved.

Divested of all heavenly rites,
    Thy crest has fallen low;
Around thy walls are squalid sights
    Of beggary and woe;
Thy streets are narrow, filthy lanes—
    Offensive to the breath;
Thy pools appear like sewer drains,
    That breed disease and death.

No Temple now, that God designed—
    No church by him approved—
No prophet to reveal His mind,
    By inspiration moved;
Where once, a royal banner spread,
    The "Crescent," waving now:
A sable wreath is on thy head,
    And blood upon thy brow.

The curse of God those changes wrought,
    Through crimes the Jews have done,
When they, His counsels set at naught
    And crucified His Son.
Since then, has retribution's hand
    Put forth its fearful skill,
Upon thy structures and thy land,
    A destiny to fill.

Thy children—seed of Israel,
    Of God's "peculiar care,"
On whom the weight of judgment fell,
    Are scattered everywhere.
    *   *   *   *   *   *   *   *
Thy sun has not forever set—
    God has a great design,
And will fulfil His purpose yet,
    Concerning Palestine.

Th'appointed hour will surely come,
    According to His will,
For God, with "Faithful Abraham,"
    His cov'nants to fulfil.
Thyself redeemed from deep disgrace
    Of filth and negligence,
These uncouth structures shall give place
    To taste and elegance.

Thy walls shall be of precious stones—
    Thy gates, of richest pearl;
And on thy tow'ring battlements
    Shall sacred Banners Furl;
The seed of Jacob, then shall dwell
    In bold security:
"More than thy former glory, shall
    Thy latter glory be."

                        E. R. SNOW

PALESTINE, March 6, 1873,

LETTER LXII.

Topography of Jerusalem—Hill of Evil Council—Mizpeh—Mount of Olives—Valley of Jehoshaphat—Hinnom and Kedron—Absalom's Pillar—Siloam—Mosque of Omar—Solomon's Temple—Hill of Zion—Tombs of the Holy City—Mount Moriah—Worship of Moloch—Scarcity of Water in Jerusalem—Political and Financial Condition of the Jews—Place of Lamentation.

PALESTINE, March 7th, 1873.

EDITOR DESERET NEWS:

I was much interested in the topographical appearance of the country around about Jerusalem. The city is situated on a broad mountainous ridge, between the two valleys of Hinnom and Kedron. All around, from one to three miles distant, are loftier summits, consisting of irregular broken ridges, varying from fifty to two hundred feet above the buildings of the city. They slope down, forming into small plains, low valleys, and steep, rugged ravines, presenting a panoramic view, beautiful and sublime. Along the western horizon runs a long range of hills, about the same height as that on which the city stands.

On the south, some distance from the city, is the "Hill of Evil Council," where it is said Caiaphas had a house where the priests and elders met to compass the destruction of Jesus; it is now covered with the ruins of some village. Northwards, rising conspicuously in the distance, is "Neby Samuel," the ancient Mizpeh, which is distinguished by its high towers. On the east, about half a mile from the city walls, the Mount of Olives rises from the Valley of Jehoshaphat, olive trees ornamenting its slopes, its summit crowned by a mosque, with its high tapering minaret. Some portions of these hills show little else but white rocks, projecting from the soil, which is almost as white as the rocks themselves; others are covered with fields of grain, and fig and olive orchards.

The plateaus and vales are generally cultivated, and covered with herbage, and fig and olive trees. The ravines, especially the Hinnom and Kedron, in places are so steep and rugged that nothing is seen, scarcely, but a few olive trees here and there, growing upon narrow terraces, built upon the rocks and cliffs. The summit of the Mount of Olives rises several hundred feet above the city, affording one of the most commanding views of Jerusalem and its surroundings.

I ascended this mountain, and obtained a favorable position upon the highest point on its summit, spent a happy hour in surveying the "Holy City," its environs, and the endless objects of rare and sacred interest, which formed the magnificent scenery around. Through the olive trees along the declivity could be discerned the white top of "Absalom's Pillar," and the grey excavated cliffs of Siloam; the high walls of Jerusalem appeared with their square towers; the Mosque of Omar, with its magnificent dome in the centre, occupying the site of Araunah's threshing floor, and Solomon's Temple, around it a grassy area, the whole encircled by olive and cypress trees; the two domes and the strong square tower of the Church of the Sepulchre, the massive towers of the citadel standing upon the Hill of Zion; in the distance a long line of high hills, and low broken ranges of mountains, with intervening vales, plateaus and wild ravines—the whole forming a marvelous picture of varied beauty and magnificence.

It is astonishing, the number of cemeteries we observed around about Jerusalem. It is truly said, that the "tombs" of the "Holy City" are more numerous than its buildings.

Nearly every hill and valley is studded more or less with these monuments.

The slopes of Mount Moriah and Mount Olivet, and portions of the deep valleys of Hinnom and Jehoshaphat form exclusive burying places. In viewing the multitude of tombs in the rocks and cliffs along the ravines of Hinnom, we were forcibly reminded of the prophecy of Jeremiah—

"They shall bury in Tophet till there be no place.

"They have built the high places of Tophet, which is in the valley of the son of Hinnom, to burn their sons and daughters in the fire."

Here, at the bottom of the defile, amid its cliffs and rocky steeps and gloomy scenes, the Israelites performed their worship of Moloch, alluded to by Jeremiah. These heathen rites consisted in making a burnt offering of children in the following manner—

A statue of Moloch was erected of gigantic proportions, consisting of brass, in the form of a man's body, with a head like that of an ox. The interior was hollow, in which was constructed a large furnace, by which means the whole statue could easily be made red hot. The children to be sacrificed were then placed in its arms, while drums were beaten to drown their cries. It is asserted, however strange it may appear, that Solomon was the first who formally introduced these fearful practices, though previous to this they had been performed occasionally by the Israelites.

Seeing no lake, pond, stream, rivulet, nor scarcely a living well or fountain, in or around Jerusalem, we naturally inquired how its inhabitants, especially its former dense population, were supplied with water. We were informed that within the walls of Jerusalem living wells and fountains, at present were comparatively unknown. Three small fountains, in the lower part of the valley of Jehoshaphat, are said to be the only waters that can be depended upon in the region around.

The city is chiefly supplied by means of its cisterns, every house of any importance having one or more of these, so arranged that the winter rains can be conducted into them, by means of pipes and ducts, from the roofs and court yards. With suitable care the water in them can be preserved pure and sweet during the whole summer. Besides these private cisterns, there are many public tanks, pools and reservoirs in the city and suburbs. We saw the ruins of aqueducts, cisterns and immense tanks, which showed that in former periods great attention and a vast amount of labor had been employed to secure supplies of water.

In every quarter of the site of the ancient city numerous reservoirs and cisterns are discovered—some of immense capacity, excavated in solid rock; others, formed upon the flat surface of the rock, built up around with stones, thickly lined with cement. One of these subterranean reservoirs was discovered eighty feet below the surrounding surface. Subterranean aqueducts lead in various directions from the cisterns, frequently formed in the solid rock, extending many hundred yards. How these numerous cisterns were supplied is still a great mystery. Some imagine it was effected by conduits connecting with secret springs and fountains a long distance beyond the city.

The Jewish rabbi, with whom we conversed, stated that many springs and fountains, which formerly supplied the inhabitants of Jerusalem, had long since ceased to flow, but he expected the time was near when they would be revived into living waters.

Jerusalem occupies but a small space—its walls are but a little over two miles in circumference. Its population has been variously estimated; the following particulars, I believe are tolerably authentic: Jews nine thousand, Mahommedans five thousand, Christians about four thousand, making a total of eighteen thousand.

The political and financial condition of the Jewish population is not very flattering or prosperous. The people are generally poor and oppressed, without means or opportunity of improving their circumstances. They receive large contributions from Europe and America, to aid in objects of charity, and in making small improvements in the way of public buildings.

In our interview with the chief rabbi, we learned that foreign influence is operating, in a small measure, in their favor toward softening the feelings and moderating the rules of the Turkish authorities; that they are allowed to purchase and hold title to real estate; but they have no money to expend in this direction, and if they had it would be discouraging under the present system of taxation. All kinds of property are heavily taxed, and all private and public enterprise is discouraged. A direct tax is levied on persons, cattle, land and fruit trees; tobacco and silk pay about forty-two cents per pound, and all other articles eight per cent., either in kind or money.

Near where the temple formerly stood, is a small paved area where the Jews have been permitted, during many centuries, to approach the precincts of the site of the Temple of their forefathers, and lament and wail over the ruins, and the desolation of their nation and sanctuary. In this retired locality, each Friday, Jews of both sexes, of all ages, and from every quarter of the world, are seen weeping, bathing the stones with their tears, and lifting up their voices in loud lamentation. No one can witness this scene without being touched with feelings of the deepest sympathy, and the poet may well say:

> "Oh, weep for those that wept by Babel's stream,
> Whose shrines are desolate, whose land a dream;
> Weep for the harp of Judah's broken spell,
> Mourn—where their God hath dwelt, the godless dwell!"

LORENZO SNOW.

LETTER LXIII.

Sacred Localities—The Stone of Unction—The Holy Sepulchre—The Chapel of the Angel—Hill of Calvary—The Hole in which the Cross was Planted—House of Pilate—"Behold the Man"—The True Cross—Opposition Gardens of Gethsemane—Rivalry of Christian Sects—A Terrible Massacre—Fighting Among Christian Zealots Prevented by Turkish Guards—Christianity Despised by Jews and Mahommedans.

PALESTINE, March 8th, 1873.

EDITOR DESERET NEWS :

Among the variety of objects which claimed our attention while at Jerusalem, was the Church of the Holy Sepulchre. It is an extensive building, with a host of sacred relics and holy places, grouped together within a few yards of one another; among others, the place of the Saviour's crucifixion; the spot where his body was anointed for burial; where the Virgin stood, and witnessed the crucifixion; the place where his body was wrapped in linen clothes; the rent in the rock produced by the earthquake; the place where the soldiers cast lots for his raiment; the column to which he was bound when scourged; the place where he was stripped by the soldiers; and the prison in which he was incarcerated previous to being led to the place of crucifixion, &c.

In front of this building is a small area, occupied by a sort of bazar for the sale of sacred relics, and used also as a place of gathering for all classes of pilgrims. Within this building, near the door, surrounded by a low railing, is the Stone of Unction, which consists of a marble slab, on which the body of the Saviour is said to have been anointed for the burial. This, we were told, however, is not the real stone, as that was concealed underneath to prevent devout pilgrims from carrying it off, or wearing it away by constant kissing, as was the case with the bronze toe at St. Peter's, at Rome. Several lamps are suspended over this sacred spot, and kept constantly burning. We proceeded to the apartment appropriated to the Holy Sepulchre, twenty-six feet long, by eighteen broad, ornamented by a dome. We entered, first a small apartment, called the Chapel of the Angel, where it is said he sat upon the stone which had been rolled away from the door of the sepulchre. A portion of this stone stands upon a low pedestal, though it is asserted that the real stone was stolen by the Armenians, and is now exhibited in their chapel. From this apartment, a low narrow door opens into the vault of the sepulchre. It has a dome roof sustained by short marble columns. The place where the Saviour's body is said to have lain, is covered by a marble slab, considerably worn at the edges by the continued kissing of pilgrims. A large number of gold and silver lamps are suspended over it, and kept constantly burning. It is fitted up as an altar; above it are costly gifts, thickly set with precious stones, presented by different sovereigns of Europe.

A Greek priest was officiating when we entered, who signified his recognition of our presence by scattering sweet perfumery in great abundance over our persons. All pilgrims were sprinkled in like manner, who were constantly crowding in upon their hands and knees, kissing the cold marble, sobbing and bathing it with their tears. This is said to have been hewn in the rock, but we could see no rock—the floor, tomb, and walls are all marble.

We ascended a flight of steps leading to an apartment or small chapel, which is said to cover the Hill of Calvary. Here was shown a rent or hole in the rock, as that in which stood the cross while the Saviour hung upon it. Many other places were shown, which it is needless to mention. After leaving this building, we went to the House of Pilate, which is said to occupy the same locality as that of the Roman Governor; we saw but little, however, to satisfy us of the identity of the Judgment Hall. We came to a building said to cover the place where Jesus came forth wearing the purple robe and crown of thorns, when Pilate exclaimed to the people, "Behold the man." The place was pointed out where the Saviour sank under the weight of the cross, when Simon the Cyrenian was compelled to take it up, and bear it after him; also the spot where Veronica appeared with a napkin to wipe the sweat off the Saviour's brow, when his portrait was miraculously impressed upon it. This pretended relic is preserved as one of the chief in the Basilica of St. Peter's at Rome.

Considerable mystery, contradictions and disputations exist in reference to the identity of these sacred relics and holy places. In regard to those embraced within the Holy Sepulchre, it is maintained by some intelligent writers that none of them are genuine. Doubtless some of them, if not many, are strangely misplaced.

Religious enthusiasts of opposite sects vied with each other in searching out relics, and places to be reverenced and adored by people of their respective persuasions, performing pilgrimages to the Holy Land, their zeal, in some instances, carrying them beyond the bounds of honesty, to practising deceit and imposition. Many of these places had been remaining for centuries beneath the gradual accumulations of debris, and could not be identified, either by history or tradition; consequently, divine intimations were sought, miraculous tests applied, and other methods resorted to in order to establish their claims to genuineness.

Helena, the mother of Constantine, when about eighty years old, in the fourth century, is said to have been divinely impressed to proceed to Jerusalem and make sacred discoveries—to search out the true cross, the holy sepulchre, and other relics and localities connected with the crucifixion of the Saviour. Accordingly, she went to Jerusalem and, enlisting the services of the inhabitants, instituted a search for the cross of the Saviour. Digging through the debris, some twenty feet or more, at length three crosses were discovered, together with the tablet, the nails and crown of thorns. The tablet or inscription, " This is Jesus the King of the Jews," being separated from the crosses, therefore the true cross could not be identified. At last a remedy was discovered. A lady of quality was confined upon her bed in Jerusalem, of a fatal disease. The three crosses were successively presented to her; the two first without effect, but on the approach of the third, she sprang from her dying couch perfectly restored. Thus the identity of the true cross was established. The pillar to which Christ is said to have been bound when he was scourged, is carefully secured, that it may not be stolen by pilgrims, who are only permitted to touch it with a small, round stick, some four feet long or more, kept for this purpose. This stick, after having one end put in contact with the sacred relic, is then kissed by the pilgrims with great fervor and vehemence. While present we witnessed many instances of this fervent and striking devotion.

We visited the reputed Garden of Gethsemane which belongs to the Latin Church. An opposition one has recently been established by the Greek Church. As soon as the trees have sufficiently grown, and other fixtures remained long enough to impart an ancient and venerable appearance, it will then be exhibited to devout pilgrims as the real genuine Garden of Gethsemane.

The low, sunken condition of Christianity in Jerusalem, is pretty clearly illustrated in the following description of scenes enacted in the Church of the Holy Sepulchre. On Easter eve, each successive year, it is pretended that holy fire descends from heaven, lighting up all the lamps in the Holy

Sepulchre. On this occasion multitudes of enthusiastic pilgrims are assembled from every quarter of the globe, awaiting with burning anxiety to participate in its benefits, and to receive its holy influences. Just before the prescribed moment for this miraculous descent, the Greek Patriarch enters the tomb, alone, and presently gives out through a hole in the wall, the holy fire, to the eager and excited multitude.

In former years all the churches participated in the performance of these rites, but latterly have desisted, one after another, till, at present, this practice is continued only by the Greek Church. At these extraordinary scenes, very serious accidents frequently occur—old men and women crushed and trampled to pieces, or perhaps quarrels arise between rival sects, resulting in shooting and stabbing one another. In eighteen hundred and thirty-four, deplorable and fearful scenes were enacted in that sacred building. While the church was crowded with Christian pilgrims, a contention arose, in which the Turkish guards engaged; the confusion soon became general, and directly grew into a terrible battle. The scene of horror can not be described. Numbers were bayoneted or knocked down with the butt ends of muskets, and their blood and brains scattered upon the wall and pavement, each seeming intent to destroy his fellow, or save himself from immediate destruction. Many were pulled down and trampled to death while endeavoring to escape from the building. When order was restored, the dead were lying in heaps around, and even upon the Stone of Unction the bodies of the dead were piled up, and in some places the wounded and dead were thrown together promiscuously, one upon another, five feet high or more.

The Turkish government is obliged to keep a guard constantly watching at the Church of the Holy Sepulchre, to prevent these contentions and fightings between the rival Christian churches.

These contradictions, contentions, impositions by the rival Christian sects, in Jerusalem, render the Christian religion a subject of scorn and contempt, both to the Jews and Mahommedans, and it is certainly a matter of serious regret that, in this enlightened age of Christianity, such things should exist in this sacred locality where our holy religion was established, and our Saviour martyred.

LORENZO SNOW.

LETTER LXIV.

Robbers' Glen—Bethel—Ancient Shiloh—Jacob's Well—Joseph's Tomb—Mount Gerizim—Ancient Shechem—Ancient Samaria—Tomb of John the Baptist—Dothan—Plains of Esdraelon—Mountains of Gilboa—Spring of Jezreel—Suite of Rooms of Joseph and Mary—Dining Room of the Saviour and his Apostles—An Assyrian Chapel—Mount Carmel, Nain—Church of the Annunciation—Assyrian Pilgrims.

Camp at Nazareth, Galilee, Palestine,
March 9, 1873.

President Brigham Young:

Dear Brother:—We broke camp at Jerusalem on the 5th inst., and rode over a rocky, barren and almost desolate country, and camped in a ravine called the Robbers' Glen, near a spring termed the Robbers' Pool. The country is generally too rocky, barren and dry to produce anything. In the afternoon we passed several large and thrifty fig orchards and some olive groves. We passed Bethel at some distance on our right, and other ancient sites, but saw nothing that we could date back to the Jewish era, some of the ruins belonging to the Roman, some to the Saracen, but more to the Crusader period; tradition alone indicates the location of ancient Jewish cities. On the 6th we passed the site of ancient Shiloh, where the land was divided by lot among the children of Israel; visited Jacob's Well, and near by what some claim to be the Tomb of Joseph, which has been recently repaired by the British Consul. At Jacob's Well we were shown Mounts Ebal and Gerizim; on the summit of the latter the Samaritans have a mosque in which they annually offer sacrifices; they are said to be the oldest and smallest sect in the world. There are said to be extensive ruins on the summit of Gerizim. We camped that night near the city of Nablus (ancient Shechem); the day's ride six hours. During the day the valleys were wider, better cultivated, and more fruitful than nearer Jerusalem.

On the 7th it rained most of the day, and during our ride we visited the site of ancient Samaria, for more than 200 years the capital of the ten tribes of Israel, and it endured a seven years' siege by the Syrians, and was miraculously relieved; and afterwards was taken by the Assyrians, after three years' siege, when they were carried away captive. We were on the site during a rainstorm and saw ruins and columns, apparently not dating beyond the time when Herod built a palace there; he also built a temple, and made other considerable improvements. The Tomb of John the Baptist, said to contain one set of his bones, dates back to the Knights of St. John, and is the best preserved ruin on the site. The site is not inferior to any I have seen in Palestine for a city, and could be easily defended against ancient warfare. In the rain we missed Dothan, where it is said Joseph was sold to the Ishmaelites, and lunched on some rocks, and after an eight hours' ride camped near Jonin, a small collection of Arab stone huts. Around it are lemon, orange, olive, dates, and fig trees, looking thrifty, and indicating fertility in the soil, were there sufficient rain.

At 7.30 a. m. we were in the saddle, and soon crossing

the Plains of Esdraelon. What the Bible calls a valley we term a ravine; and what is here termed a plain we call a valley. We were shown the mountains of Gilboa in the distance, where Saul was defeated and slain. After riding five hours, during which a short, sharp shower swept over us, we lunched on a hill side, and in half an hour rode through and camped on the east side of Nazareth. Brother T. Jennings made a detour and visited the Spring of Jezreel, the place of encounter between Gideon and the Midianites.

The last day's ride was through a country that could be made very delightful with plenty of rain. Some portions of the route from Jerusalem had what may be termed a rough road, more of it a pack trail, and much of it a very rough bridle path, and it is astonishing to us how the Arab horses manage to keep on their feet. It is also astonishing to see how thoroughly the prophecies in relation to the desolation of this country have been literally fulfilled. A little barley and wheat has been of late years raised in favorable spots without irrigation; wherever water can be obtained for irrigating, the soil is very fertile. Limestone is the prevailing rock from Jaffa to Nazareth, and it is certainly a stony land.

To-day we visited what was once a synagogue, said to be the one in which the Saviour preached, Luke iv, 16; it has been newly plastered. We then went to a monastery, and were shown what they said were the parlor, bedroom and kitchen of Joseph and Mary; then visited the site of what is claimed to have been the workshop of Joseph, a few stones of the old foundation being pointed out, also a wardrobe and cupboard said to have been made by Joseph; then a chapel containing a large limestone, apparently in its natural position, on which it is said the Saviour and his disciples frequently partook of their meals, both before and after his resurrection. I then went to a Protestant church and heard Dr. Zeller deliver a discourse in the Assyrian language to about

60 persons. The singing and all the service was conducted in that language, and the small audience appeared very cleanly, intelligent and attentive.

After dinner we ascended the hill, back of Nazareth, from which Mount Tabor is seen near by on the east, and beyond the mountains east of Jordan; Mount Carmel and the Mediterranean to the north-west, the hill of Nain to the south, the village of Cana and much of the Plain of Esdraelon and the country between the points mentioned. On the summit of the hill were several matrons, maidens and children; also a few Arab men, who were around a tomb they said was the tomb of a prophet, but we could not learn his name or faith. They all appeared to be very jolly, and one man offered to dance for half a franc, which was paid to him, and then one of the women danced for the same fee. Their mode of dancing required but little exertion.

This town is said to contain from 3,000 to 5,000 inhabitants, and the ways are very narrow, crooked, many of them steep, and very filthy. Sister Snow attended the service in the Greek church at 7 this morning, and Brother Schettler soon after; it is called the Church of the Annunciation. Late in the afternoon Brother Carrington and I went to the Church of the Annunciation, where we found a few persons attending service in a room very beautifully adorned, much after the manner of like churches in the Ionian Isles and Switzerland. A monk placed wax candles in our hands and showed us down several marble steps into a beautifully fitted up side-room, where he pointed to a covered spring, claimed by the Greeks to be the fountain where the angel Gabriel made the announcement to the Virgin Mary, and drew up a pitcher of water, of which we drank, finding it pure and good, as is all the spring water of these limestone regions. There are two other places here claimed by different sects as the localities of the Annunciation. A dime was the monk's fee for his services in showing us the fountain and drawing the water.

8

Near us was a large encampment of Assyrian pilgrims, men, women and children, who had come a forty days' journey on their way to Jerusalem; they also rested over the Sabbath. Neither our dragoman or guide, nor any one we could find, understood this language, so we could not converse with them. A mother in their party died Saturday night, and the funeral services seemed to partake both of the Moslem and Christian form; the child of the mother was the principal wailer.

Our camping places have frequently been near graveyards, and we have often seen bands of women, with white outer robes, wailing and lamenting over the graves of their relatives; they are generally professionals, hired to do the mourning, and are supposed to perform the service better than amateurs.

GEORGE A. SMITH.

LETTER LXV.

Church of the Holy Sepulchre—Sacred Localities—Religious Services on the Mount of Olives—Dedication of the Land of Palestine—Hospice of the Knights' Templars—Trades Among the Arabs—Arab Cookery—Visit to the Chief Rabbi—Valley of Hinnom—The Gibbeah of Saul—Bethel—Robbers' Glen—Mosque of Shiloh—Jacob's Well—Mounts Ebal and Gerizim—Sychar—A Gala Day—Dothan—Valley of Esdraelon—Mount Tabor.

NAZARETH, March 9th, 1873.

EDITOR WOMAN'S EXPONENT:

I wrote you on the 4th ult., the day before our final departure from Jerusalem, and so hastily that I said very little of that great centre of attraction. In the estimation of Eastern Christendom, the "Church of the Holy Sepulchre" is the most sacred place on earth. Within its idolized precincts, a Turkish guard is constantly stationed to prevent quarrels between the different sects of Christians—Roman Catholics, Greek Catholics, Armenians, etc., who have separate chapels in this extensive building, where they each perform their respective modes of worship. But, notwithstanding this precautionary measure on the part of the government, serious and bloody fights sometimes occur, which the Mussulman very reasonably considers uncomplimentary to the Christian religion.

We were shown through the varied departments of the edifice, our guide pointing out many "identical" places, where important events of Bible history transpired; and, although our credulity as to specified localities failed of being whetted to a point, we knew and felt that we were really where the ancient Jerusalem once stood, and consequently in the vicinity where those scenes transpired, and it did not matter essentially whether this or that, was the "Stone of Unction," whether Mary stood on this or that side of the sepulchre when Jesus manifested himself to her after his resurrection, whether the one secured in the wall, which we were permitted to touch with a rod, was the "True Cross," etc., etc. We knew by incontrovertible testimony, that here Jesus was crucified for the redemption of man, was resurrected, ascended, and, at no very distant day, "will in like manner descend."

On several occasions I took the liberty to question our guide respecting his own faith in some items which he seemed anxious to impress us with as "identical," and, to our great amusement, he shook his head with an expressive smile which he tried in vain to suppress.

Sunday morning, March 2nd, President Smith made arrangements with our dragoman, and had a tent, table, seats and carpet taken up on the Mount of Olives, to which all the brethren of the company and myself repaired on horseback. After dismounting on the summit, and committing our animals to the care of servants, we visited the Church of Ascension, a small cathedral, said to stand on the spot from which Jesus ascended. By this time the tent was prepared, which we entered, and after an opening prayer by Brother Carrington, we united in service in the order of the Holy Priesthood, President Smith leading in humble, fervent supplication, dedicating the land of Palestine for the gathering of the Jews and the rebuilding of Jerusalem, and returning heartfelt thanks and gratitude to God for the fulness of the Gospel and the blessings bestowed on the Latter-day Saints. Other brethren led in turn, and we had a very interesting season; to me it seemed the crowning point of the whole tour, realizing as I did that we were worshipping on the summit of the sacred Mount, once the frequent resort of the Prince of Life.

The next day we took another stroll through the city, visited the Mosque of Omar, which, by Mahommedans, ranks as the second of holy places; they claim that it contains the throne on which Mahomet will judge the world. It is the best edifice in Jerusalem.

The fallen Hospice of the Knights Templars, near the Church of the Holy Sepulchre, in its very dilapidated condition, affords shelter to many braziers, barbers and cornchandlers; one room in the great ruin is used for a bazar, another for a tannery, one for bathing, etc. Many common kinds of trade are carried on in the streets. A thoroughfare is frequently the only home of the Arab—there he eats, drinks, buys and sells; when he would rest, wash or pray, he retires to the court of his mosque, which is the true Moslem's safe resort, and from which no officer can drive him. There he is sure to find water, for every mosque is supplied with at least one fountain, where all must wash before prayers; and when he has finished his devotions, he may throw himself upon the mats and rest. With a bundle of sticks, the cook kindles a fire on a little cluster of stones, places over it a kettle or pan, into which he puts a few olives, lentils, a piece of fat and a handful of parched corn, stirs and simmers them together until it is delicious to an Arab's palate. Lepers, the personification of filth and wretchedness, were to be seen in huddles on the street outside the city wall, beggars, reminding us of the lazzaroni of Naples.

Although I felt satisfied with my visit to that world-renowned city of sacredly interesting histories of the past, and of bright prophetic anticipation for the future, and in spite of the deep sense of the curse of God resting on the land and on the people, my feelings during our stay had become so pleasantly associated with the scenic view of the surroundings of this ancient site of time-honored memories, that I realized a feeling of reluctance at bidding a final adieu.

On the 4th President Smith and others called on the

chief Jewish Rabbi, Abraham Askenasi, and in the evening we had a very interesting interview with him and three others, who called at our tents.

On the morning of the 5th, leaving our place of encampment in the Valley of Hinnom, we commenced an ascent, rising to an elevation which commands a fine view of the city, Mount Olivet and the variegated surroundings. Here I curbed my impatient steed while I treated my vision to a lingering, farewell gaze, and looked for the last time, with deep thoughts and with feelings of intense interest.

A little over two hours' ride brought us to Ischal, the Gibbeah of Saul. From there we rode to Bethel, the place of Jacob's vision, and, at night, after travelling through a narrow, crooked ravine, in a trail as rough as jagged rocks could make it, with mountains above, rising almost perpendicularly to a great height, we encamped near the Robbers' Glen, in a beautifully romantic spot, with a fountain of pure water flowing out of the rocks.

On the 6th we passed the Mosque of Shiloh. The face of the country here is picturesque. We stopped at Jacob's Well, and by bringing into requisition every bit of cord and rope attainable, succeeded in drawing water from the depth of 75 feet. This well is near the entrance to the valley between Mount Ebal and Mount Gerizim. The site of the ancient Sychar, is said to be a little to the north of, and in sight of, this well, which is supposed to be where Jesus asked the Samaritan woman for water. A short distance from Sychar, is Nablous, the ancient Shechem, the city of Joshua and the Judges, said to have been five hundred years older than Jerusalem, and to have claimed the precedence. Nablous is situated on the east slope of Mount Ebal, opposite Mount Gerizim, on which Moses called the hosts of Israel together, and said " Choose ye this day whom ye will serve." We found it surrounded by olives and palms, and refreshed by flowing streams. It was a gala day, and we saw multitudes in holiday costumes, promenading, singing, dancing and having a cheery time beneath the shade of rows of tall trees, the sight of which seemed a special luxury. We encamped near the town, very much admiring the natural grandeur of the scenery, combined with the fertility and rich productions of the soil, so strikingly in contrast with the general sterility. The fig, which grows here abundantly, is just putting forth leaves, signifying "that summer is nigh."

The next morning we started in the rain, which continued alternately during the forenoon, which whetted our appreciation of umbrellas. Our trail lay in a picturesque country, although extremely rugged at times, apparently where nothing but goats and reptiles could go, and we were led to wonder at the strange changes since the "iron chariots of Solomon," were in use here. It truly seems that a series of earthquakes, as well as of political revolutions are indispensably necessary before roads, instead of trails, will be the order in this judgment-stricken land. We stopped a short time at the miserable looking village which occupies the site of the ancient Samaria—passed the Mount Carmel range—Dothan, the place where Joseph was sold by his brethren; and entered the beautiful Plain of Esdraelon, (Megiddo) the great battlefield of ancient Israel. Nearly in the centre of this delightful plain, is an elevation of perhaps two miles in circumference at the foot, in regular conical shape, very smooth, having the appearance of an enormous mound, and sufficiently elevated on the centre to overlook the entire plain. What an enviable location for a splendid mansion! But it is minus all that kind of decoration—in this country, with very few exceptions, the houses are grouped, some on the tops and others on the slopes of rugged mountains.

We passed Mount Tabor on our right, and, after riding over a rocky winding path, came in sight of the memorable city of Nazareth, which, by straight line is sixty, by camel trail eighty, miles from Jerusalem. It is impossible for me to describe my thoughts and feelings as we rode slowly on its narrow, crooked and indescribably filthy streets, passing crowds of people outside of dreary-looking dens, (from the doors of many of which smoke was issuing, they being the only apertures for its escape) holding out hands and asking for backsheesh. I was forcibly reminded of the question of Nathaniel, " Can any good come out of Nazareth ? " Nazareth lives in the past: it was, for years, the earthly home of our Saviour—this gives it immortality. More anon.

ELIZA R. SNOW.

LETTER LXVI.

Farewell to Jerusalem—A Gala Day—Arab Agriculture—Nablous, Ancient Shechem—Among Ferocious People—Avengers of blood—Cultivation of the Olive—Samaria.

Syria, March 11th, 1873.

Editor Deseret News:

Leaving Jerusalem, we ascend by a steep, rocky, winding path to the commanding heights of Mount Scopus, where, turning backward, we take a long, lingering look at the " Holy City "—its noble domes, its high, tapering minarets, and its surrounding mountains. We descend the mountain into a naked, desolate region, our path lying over rocky plateaus, through deep ravines, and over barren hills covered with loose stones and sharp rocks. A small village is seen away to our left on a lofty hill, flags and streamers flying, guns firing, and groups of men and women gaily attired, in open air, rejoicing in the dance. We pass several towns perched among the gray rocks, on the mountain slopes, or crowning the summits of high hills, also several sites of ancient towns overspread with ruins. Sterility and barrenness form the general features of the country. The trees are few, gnarled and stunted, here and there sticking out from rents and holes in the rocks, and broken, decayed terraces, and still clinging to the cliffs.

The second day we found the hills and glens less rugged, the country improving in general appearance, the soil more fertile and better cultivated. We passed through many winding valleys with landscape beautiful and picturesque, the hills terraced from base to summit, supporting vines, fig and olive trees, the scenery enlivened by wild flowers, bright and gay, springing up from the green, luxuriant herbage. The Arab is seen with his primitive plow, and diminutive oxen, breaking up his ground; a Bedouin on his fleet steed, with his brass-bound gun suspended over his shoulder, galloping over the hills; the Mussulman, with his wives and children, scantily dressed, plucking the weeds from his patch of grain; peasants passing in their gay dresses of red and green; long strings of mules, donkeys and camels, winding along the tortuous path; the shepherd preceding his flock of sheep and goats, leading them along the mountain slopes, or standing with them clustered around a favorite fountain.

We are now approaching Nablous, a modern town on the site of the ancient Shechem, a name familiar to the biblical reader. Clambering up a steep, rocky path, we arrive at the crest of a lofty ridge, where we enjoy a lovely, romantic scene—the finest and most pleasing since leaving Jerusalem. Before us lies an undulating plain, stretching far away northward, encircled by picturesque hills, no object on its surface to break the view; around its borders are small groves of orange trees and here and there clumps and rows of olives, giving it the appearance of a European park. The villages here as elsewhere, instead of being located on the plain, are, for security, built on the crest of steep hills, or high up on the acclivities.

The people we now meet appear different in character, manners and dress from those occupying the country we have passed. They look daring and ferocious, ready to commence hostilities on the slightest provocation. Armed cap-a-pie with a long flint-lock shot gun, a huge dagger sticking in front of their girdle, pistols, and a large knobheaded club, they seem pleased in displaying these arms, and, judging from their sturdy, athletic appearance, I have no doubt they could employ them to great advantage. We frequently met these fellows armed in this manner, driving along a miserable looking, half-starved donkey, loaded probably with all he possessed, except his arms and shabby clothing. There is, however, a cause for this oddity. A bloody feud, most likely, exists between his family and some other family, which was commenced hundreds of years ago by their ancestors. Some person was killed, and one of that person's family killed another in return; then another was killed in revenge, and thus it has continued until the present. Every member of the family is in danger, and lives in dread—any moment the avenger of blood may pounce upon him. Therefore he is armed at all hours, and in all places—when leading his flocks on the mountain, his donkey on the road, or when plowing in the field, oft-times having to flee from house and home, and abide with strangers. This fearful state of things arises from the following law of the Koran, "O, true believers, the law of retaliation is ordained to you for the slain—the free shall die for the free." I suppose Mahomet drew this from the Old Testament, but failed to make the corresponding merciful arrangements—"cities of refuge."

The second night we camped in a lovely spot, in the suburbs of Nablous. This city, known in Bible history as Shechem, possesses the most charming and picturesque scenery of any site in Palestine. It is situated along the base of Mount Gerizim, on the south side of a verdant valley, sparkling with streams and fountains, and decorated with olive trees, gardens and fruit orchards. The cliffs, hills and mountain slopes, supporting terraces, rising one above another in regular gradation, growing narrow strips of waving grain, together with fig, olive and orange trees. The valley is clothed in the richest foliage and vegetation. Viewed from different points, the city, with its white-domed buildings, and its mosques, and towering minarets, presents a charming picture. Nablous contains eight thousand inhabitants, only five hundred of whom are Christians. The buildings are constructed chiefly of stone; in style and general appearance they are similar to those in Jerusalem. The streets, as in all other towns in Palestine, are narrow, crooked and extremely filthy. The houses project over and cover them, being supported on arches. The inhabitants have the reputation of mistreating strangers, especially ladies. Prompted by curiosity, no doubt, they visited our tents by multitudes. In turn, we perambulated their filthy city, experiencing no ill-treatment. In Shechem, as we learn from sacred history, Simeon and Levi avenged the dishonor of their sister Dinah, by murdering the whole population of the city, having first decoyed them into complete disability of defending themselves. It was the first spot where Abraham pitched his tent in Canaan—"Place of Shechem at the oak of Moreh." Jacob also, on his return from Mesopotamia, pitched his tent in this then pastoral region. This is the place where Jacob sent his favorite son, Joseph, to look after his brethren. "A certain man found him wandering in the field" and directed him to Dothan, about twelve miles north, where they had removed. Here Rehoboam was proclaimed king over all Israel; and not long afterwards the ten tribes revolted, and made Jeroboam, the son of Nebat, king, and established Shechem as the capital.

Soap, cotton and oil are the chief productions at Nablous. The olive is extensively cultivated, and is seen around every village and hamlet. Clothed in mid-winter, with their soft, grey foliage, they always impart beauty and add an air of cheerfulness to the landscape. The olive is slow in its growth, requiring from twelve to fifteen years before it begins to pay the expense of cultivation. It is long-lived—one thousand years and upwards. The older ones have a remarkably venerable appearance, with their great gnarled and furrowed stems, especially when representing the last stages of life's decline. Usually the fruit ripens in November and December, and is beaten off with long sticks, and the use of ladders, and gathered by women and children, who carry it away in baskets on their heads to the press, where the oil is extracted by an apparatus quite rude and primitive. The berries are placed in a round cavity excavated in a rock, when a huge stone is rolled over them by oxen, or manual force. The pulp is bound up in mats, placed under the press, which is forced down by a screw or heavy beam. The liquor is partially heated, the oil is then skimmed, and put into skins, or earthern jars.

From Nablous (Shechem) to Samaria, our next principal point, we pass through a lovely country—over terraced hills, and winding through partially cultivated valleys, with fields of grain two-thirds grown, and orchards of figs and apricots. Small villages are seen crowning summits of distant hills o perched high up their rocky sides, seldom appearing in the rich vales below.

Samaria contains about sixty buildings, with four hundred inhabitants. It occupies a narrow, rocky plateau, midway up the side of the steep, lofty hill. In the midst of a gentle shower, we rode up to the village through a narrow, winding path, climbing over large boulders, and forked, sloping, conical, shelving and slippery rocks. Halting a few minutes we then ascended to the summit, on which is an open area, formerly surrounded by columns, only a few of which are now standing. In descending the mountain, we reached a place on its slope, covered with magnificent ruins—a quantity of columns, some standing, others broken and lying in fragments over the ground. Sixty or more of these pillars, two feet in diameter, eighteen in height, are standing without their capitals, deeply sunk in the ground. It is supposed that these columns were designed to decorate the principal street of the ancient city. Large quantities of hewn stone are strewed around, over the plowed fields and the orchards in the valley below, and piled into the terraces which partially encircle the hill.

In viewing these immense ruins, I was reminded of the fearful prediction of Micah: "I will make Samaria as an heap of the field, and as plantings of a vineyard, and I will pour down the stones thereof into the valley, and I will discover the foundations thereof."

LORENZO SNOW.

LETTER LXVII.

A Famous Scripture Locality—A Village of Robbers—The "Fountain of Gardens"—The Battle Field of Palestine—Mounts Tabor and Hermon—Nazareth—The Holy Grotto—Workshop of Joseph—Table of Christ—Arab Ploughs—Cana of Galilee—An Arab School—Sea of Galilee—Tiberias—Bedouin Spinsters—Residence of Mary Magdalene—Serenaded by Bedouins—Backsheesh.

SYRIA, March 15th, 1873.

EDITOR DESERET NEWS:

Leaving Samaria, we wind up a rocky acclivity and pass through an avenue of olive trees, to a smart looking village, located on a stony ridge. Our road now lies over low hills covered with dwarf oak and hawthorn, through rich valleys abounding in wheat fields, fig orchards and groves of venerable olive trees, with gnarled and furrowed trunks, clothed with gray foliage, and along over hills whose terraced sides are covered with vineyards. Several villages are seen dotting the hillsides or crowning their lofty summits. We passed through some low, winding ravines. These are the passes so often defended by the "ten thousands of Ephraim and thousands of Manasseh" against their northern invaders. In the midst of these hills, the famous Gideon, the hero of Manasseh, was nurtured and reared; through these passes he marched at the head of his little army against the Midianites, who were lying in multitudes in the Valley of Jezreel.

We passed a large village surrounded by olive groves. Its inhabitants have a bad reputation. It is said that they will not miss an opportunity of plundering the solitary traveler when found in the neighboring glens.

Friday, 7th, we camped at Jenin, interpreted "fountain of gardens." It contains three thousand inhabitants, chiefly Mahommedans. The town is charmingly situated, commanding a view of the great Plain of Esdraelon. The low hills behind are overspread by shrubbery, with here and there patches of olives. Around the town the landscape is clothed in rich verdure, variegated with flowers of brilliant colors; also fine gardens encircled by hedges of cactus of immense growth, and palm trees here and there raising their graceful heads. The Plain of Esdraelon, the famous battlefield of Palestine, stretches far away, from fifteen to twenty miles to the base of the mountains, below Nazareth, on one side enclosed by the hills of Galilee, on the other by the mountains of Samaria, the whole forming one vast, unbroken expanse of verdure. In all this plain, not a village or hamlet appears, though they are seen dotting the slopes of the surrounding hills, or perched on their rocky summits. Long strings of Bedouin tents are here and there strung along its borders, and numerous flocks and herds are fattening on its luxuriant herbage.

Several fierce looking Arabs visited our tents in the evening, whose appearance failed to impress us favorably respecting their future intentions; our guards occasionally fired a gun during the night, indicating their presence and preparation for defense. The following morning we passed over the Plain of Esdraelon. We now have a view of Mount Tabor, dotted with oaks from base to summit, and Mount Hermon, panoplied in snow. After descending a steep, rocky ridge, we wind through a dreary glen, opening into the valley of Nazareth. We rode through the crooked, filthy and narrow streets of the city of Nazareth, and pitched our tents near its borders. The town is located in narrow ravines, and on the narrow, rocky declivities by which they are separated. A little valley opens out before it, about one mile long and one half mile in breadth, engirdled by high, bleak hills. The valley is divided into small, plowed fields, in the centre of which are patches of gardens, enclosed by hedges of cactus.

The Franciscan convent is the most prominent structure, then a mosque with its white tapering minaret looms up from among the low buildings. The city contains four thousand inhabitants, the larger portion of whom are Christians.

Nazareth is remarkable for being the home of the Saviour's boyhood—the scenes of his private life. Many objects and places are shown, associated with the Virgin and the Saviour—the "Holy Grotto," where the angel announced to Mary that she was favored of the Highest : the "Workshop of Joseph," in which Jesus worked; the "Table of Christ," &c., but having little faith in their identity, I waive description.

We remained over Sunday, and next morning pursued our way, leading over some fine valleys under moderate cultivation. Arabs were plowing the fields. Their plows, and mode of using them, are remarkably simple and primitive. This instrument consists of a crooked stick, four inches in diameter, shod with iron six inches wide, tapered to a point, a wooden peg through the top forming the handle. In the middle of this stick, the end of a small round pole is fastened, the opposite end is attached to the yoke by strings or ropes. The yoke is formed by a short, straight pole, with bows partly of wood and partly of ropes. It is placed upon the necks of two dwarfed, wretched oxen or cows, the size of our ordinary yearlings. In one hand the Arab holds the handle of his plow, in the other flourishes a long stick, by virtue of which the machine is put in motion, and its velocity regulated. It works into the soil about four inches, breaking the same in breadth. The land, under this mode of cultivation, will yield, per acre, probably six or eight bushels. Under proper management, it would produce five times the amount.

We stopped at an Arab village, known in Bible history as Cana of Galilee, consisting of a few low, dirty dwellings. We dismounted and entered a small, miserable structure, called a chapel, containing some old stone pots, which once, as we were informed, contained the water which Jesus converted into wine, at the wedding. Withdrawing from this place of relics, I entered a hall some fifteen feet in length by thirteen in breadth, divested of door and windows, occupied by Arab children as a schoolroom. Some thirty or forty boys, seated in rows upon the ground, each with a small tablet, covered with characters, were chanting their lessons very loud and with remarkable energy. This chanting and repeating together is the usual method adopted by the Arab teacher in instructing "the young idea how to shoot," it being maintained that it fixes more indelibly the principle in the memory. However this may be, I am certain the chanting scene was strikingly impressed on my memory, and the picturesque appearance and noisy characteristics of an Arab school cannot be forgotten.

At length we reach the summit of a lofty mountain and look abroad on the vale of Gennesareth, and down one thousand feet upon the Sea of Galilee, whose surging waves were once stilled, and the howling tempest silenced by the voice of the Saviour. Descending the steep declivity, we spread our tents among some old ruins, rent walls, and crumbling towers, directly upon the shore. The effects of the great earthquake of 1837 are everywhere distinctly visible.

The Sea of Galilee is about fifteen miles long, from six to seven broad, though, owing to the remarkable clearness of the atmosphere, it looks much smaller. It occupies the bottom of a deep basin, the sides of which shelve down with gradual slopes from the summits of the surrounding hills. On one side these hills or mountains rise nearly two thousand feet, intersected by deep ravines. The Jordan flows into it from the east, and passes out at the south. It is about seven

T

hundred feet above the level of the Dead Sea, into which the Jordan empties, after accomplishing a remarkably serpentine tour through the valley which bears its name.

We are tented in the suburbs of Tiberias, which is a small village of two thousand inhabitants. It numbers eight hundred Jews, poor, sickly-looking and friendless, an appearance, unfortunately, too applicable to the generality of this people whom we saw in the towns and cities of Palestine. They are permitted to occupy a small area in the middle of the town, where they have erected small synagogues, and established some common schools.

Close upon the shore is a Latin convent, which stands on the spot, as we were informed, where the scene of the miraculous draught of fishes occurred. Tiberias was built by Herod, the murderer of John the Baptist, in honor of the Roman Emperor, and was the capital of the province of Galilee.

The next morning we moved camp up the lake six miles. President Smith, Professor Carrington and T. W. Jennings, with two American gentlemen, taking boat and making the excursion by water; the remainder of the company, with myself, mounted horses and followed the shore. Our ride was interesting and cheering, under the influence of a smiling sun, and in an atmosphere of Egyptian balminess, far below the cold breezes of the hills of Galilee. We overtook some Bedouin ladies, each perched on the hump of a camel, traveling in the same direction, chanting their native songs very plaintively. Our young Arab guide, with becoming suavity, engaged them in an interesting conversation, the general features of which he afterwards explained. They informed him that they had no husbands, which circumstance they reckoned a great misfortune. This was attributable, they said, to one cause only. The laws and customs of their country permitted the father to dispose of his daughter for any stipulated amount, the price varying from five hundred to eight thousand francs, according to the beauty and accomplishments of the lady in question; that they could readily procure husbands, but the young gentlemen who fancied them, and whom they wished to favor, were not prepared to meet the exorbitant demands of their fathers; consequently they were not married, which they regretted exceedingly. It was the custom of the ladies, they said, to marry early, at the age of twelve or thirteen years; that they themselves were rising of twenty, a circumstance which made them uncomfortable and very melancholy.

We passed a cluster of low houses, resembling hovels more than human dwellings. This was formerly the residence of Mary Magdalene, whom the Saviour delivered from the power of demons. Our path now lay along the gravelly shore of the sea, and through tangled thickets of thorns, cane and tall nettles, occasionally passing clumps of oleanders, adorned with blushing roses, peeping out beneath their green luxuriant foliage. At length we reached our camping ground, a romantic spot—a pretty patch of green sward, formed of clover and other grasses, near a remarkably large fountain, whose sparkling waters burst forth beneath a large grey mountain and swept down into the sea, some yards below. A camp of wild Bedouins, on our approach, comprehending our wishes, generously consented to withdraw to a distant locality. Before leaving, however, they proposed to honor us with a serenade. Their instruments were strikingly rude and, as we presently learned, better adapted to loud, shrill noise than to musical harmony. Our animals were not excitable under ordinary circumstances, but this was a little too much for their nerves—looking towards the tempestuous sounds they commenced snorting, prancing, breaking away, and rushing off in various directions. In this state of things, we saw, that, however flattering the serenade might be to our vanity, it was a drawback to our progress as tourists; hence we intimated to our Bedouin admirers that though we appreciated the honors they were laboring to bestow, should it suit their convenience to terminate at once the peculiar entertainment we should consider ourselves eminently favored. They closed the amusement with a modest suggestion that some backsheesh was due for their services, which having paid, our muleteers hurried off in search of the animals.

LORENZO SNOW.

LETTER LXVIII.

Services in a Greek Church—Personal Cleanliness and Mean Dwellings of Turks and Arabs—Nazareth—Armenian Pilgrims—Hills and Plains of Galilee—Arab Villages—Communism—Novel Method of Churning—From Alexandria to Cairo—Sea of Galilee.

DAMASCUS, Syria, March 17th, 1873.

EDITOR WOMAN'S EXPONENT :

In my last I left you at Nazareth. Our encampment was near a Greek church, and the next day being Sunday, soon after sunrise, I strolled in the direction, and seeing the people gathering, went in where a large congregation appeared devoutly worshipping. Unlike the Roman, the Greek Catholics perform their services in the language understood by the people, modern Greek, and the difference in effect is strikingly visible in the countenances of the congregation. After listening some time to services, to me unintelligible—witnessing the usual ceremonies of kissing the picture of Jesus and his mother—sprinkling with "holy water" and kneeling and bowing before the cross; and seeing no one but myself in foreign costume, lest my presence should be intrusive, I withdrew, feeling thankful to God for the gifts and ordinances of the Everlasting Gospel—particularly that of baptism for the dead.

In my preceding letter I mentioned the dirty streets and dreary houses of this city; and while in the church, I noticed, as I have frequently done, what seems to be a general characteristic, *i. e.*, the appearance of personal cleanliness, being in contrast with the intolerably negligent and uncomfortable-looking houses the people occupy; this with both Turks and Arabs, but particularly the latter. I have, in a great many instances, seen men dressed in white from the waist to the ankle; and women from the top of the head to the feet (and it was really white) come out of the most untidy and forbidding-appearing dwellings; huts made of mud with a small opening for entrance, and entirely without windows —groups of women in white seat themselves on the ground which they do as readily as we sit on chairs and sofas, and yet look as clean as though the soil of the earth was not adhesive.

But a spectacle of a different kind was presented before me while at Nazareth. A short distance from our encampment, were a large company of Armenians on pilgrimage to Jerusalem, some of them partially tented—others grouped in squads under the precarious shelter of projecting rocks at the foot of a ledge that lined the mountain side.

They were forty days from Armenia; their appearance was deplorable. Prompted both by sympathy and curiosity, I walked into their midst and the closer view increased my heart-ache for poor degraded humanity! Old, middle-aged, and young, down to the little infant, miserably clad, and truly the personification of filth. The sight was a sad picture, for the expression of their faces corresponded with their outward condition. Their cooking utensils were few and simple, and what I saw of their food seemed less comfortable and sufficient than their clothing. But, whatever might have been the difference in circumstances and motives, these poor Armenians held one object in common with us—we were coming from, they were going to, Jerusalem.

Monday morning, the 10th of March, we left Nazareth, passing over the hills and plains of Galilee; saw many of the wandering Arabs, or Bedouins, who live in movable habitations, and change from place to place, as suits convenience, for grazing and agricultural purposes. Many of them have large herds of sheep, goats and cattle; cultivate the ground to some extent; and raise wheat, barley, beans, and sometimes other vegetables. Their houses, or rather tents, are constructed of flags made into long plats, similar to rush window blinds, but of a much coarser and stronger texture, and sufficiently wide for the height of the building. These are set upright in a square form or otherwise to suit the taste or convenience of the occupants, and covered with a very coarse kind of haircloth which is said to be impervious to water. These tents can be taken down at pleasure and rolled in packages for transit. Sometimes large villages are built in this manner; we passed through quite an extensive one, with some of these buildings in course of erection. I noticed several large ones that were connected together in line, making a long row, in front of which were several large soup kettles; and the apartments seemed to be filled with occupants, every appearance indicating a community style of living. I was quite amused with a churning operation. The cream or milk, whichever it might be, was confined in a goat skin which was placed on a rudely constructed swing, out of doors, and a woman was keeping it in motion, back and forth. These Arabs are apparently of a lower grade, and are much less cleanly in appearance than those who live in mud huts. In going by rail from Alexandria to Cairo, we found the country dotted with mud towns and villages. We passed through one of very small extent, said to contain twenty thousand inhabitants. It is very surprising to see how compactly these people are stowed in their small houses, and how closely the houses are huddled together.

I now leave you on the beautiful Sea of Galilee— a place of more than ordinary interest in Bible history.

ELIZA R. SNOW.

LETTER LXIX.

Cana of Galilee—Ancient Stone Jars — Jotapa—A Memorable Battle Field—Tiberias—Sea of Galilee—Ancient Ruins—Chorazin—Bethsaida—Site of Capernaum—Lake of Gennesareth—At Dan—Cesarea Philippi—Burial Place of Nimrod—Castle of Subeiteh—Damascus—Visit the American Consular Agent—Mosque of St. John—Interview with Abd-el Kader.

CAMP ON THE RIGHT BANK OF THE RIVER ABANA,
DAMASCUS, Syria, March 18, 1873.

PRESIDENT BRIGHAM YOUNG:

DEAR BROTHER:—On the 10th, a ride of five miles from Nazareth brought us to a small huddle of rude stone huts, said to be on the site of Cana of Galilee. A primitive looking house is shown, said to be on the site of that in which the wedding was held where the Saviour turned the water into wine. Two large, rough stone pots, much resembling the old hominy blocks of the early settlers of Missouri, were shown us by a monk, who, in very broken English, informed us they were the ones the Saviour used at the time; they will contain some twenty-four quarts, and are now used for baptismal fonts.

About two miles from Cana is the site of Jotapa, memorable in history for its desperate defense, under Josephus, against Vespasian, in the Jewish war. We passed through the Valley of Hattin, where Saladin, the Caliph of Egypt, gave the final blow to the power of the Crusaders in the Holy Land. The region traveled over is smoother and less rocky than any thus far this side of Jerusalem, except the Plains of Esdraelon. Camped inside the walls of Tiberias, which is on the west shore of the Sea of Galilee, or Lake of Tiberias, or Lake of Gennesareth, some four miles north of where Jordan leaves the lake. There are extensive ruins here that date back to the time of Herod the Tetrarch, the murderer of John the Baptist. The present walls were probably built by the Crusaders, and enclose much unoccupied ground. The place was damaged by an earthquake in 1837. The inhabitants are mostly of Jewish descent. Some hot sulphur springs, about a mile south, were formerly celebrated for their efficacy in rheumatic complaints and skin diseases. We saw three small fishing boats, one of which had just unloaded several fish resembling suckers, bass, shiners and catfish. There were very fair potatoes in the market, and our dragoman bought some. I looked through the principal shops for a pair of gloves, but they had none.

Our dragoman, Anthony Makloof, on the morning of the 11th, chartered a fishing boat, and Brothers Carrington and T. Jennings and I took a three-hours' boat row, some nine miles, to where the Jordan enters the Sea of Galilee, where we took a short stroll on the right bank of the Jordan; there was an encampment of Bedouins on each side of the river, with their goats' hair cloth and rush cane or flag tents, flocks and herds; several of the cattle, as they passed us, fat and jolly, curled their tails like young pigs. The river enters from between low hills, and has a small valley on each side by the lake, and is about three feet deep across the bar. We lunched under the shade of two large old trees, and then rowed southerly along the western shore about three miles, and landed at the supposed site of Chorazin, where are a few ruins. Another hour's row in the same direction brought us to the supposed ruins of the Bethsaida of Peter and Andrew, where are now some Arab mills, from which point a short row brought us to our camp, which had moved up the lake about six miles to the fountain of the fig tree (Ain-et-Tien), on the supposed site of Capernaum, where there is scarcely a ruin visible.

On the 12th, on our route, we ascended rocky hills several thousand feet and viewed the lake. Aside from the Bible associations, the lake is very beautiful; our guide books and maps state it to be from 600 to 650 feet below the Mediterranean; the hills surrounding it slope to its shores, except at the small crescent-shaped valley of Gennesareth. As the location of many of the Saviour's teachings it is an object of great interest to the Christian mind. While I was bathing in the lake I saw a pilgrim bow down to the lake and kiss the stones, from ignorant reverence. It is about six miles by thirteen, and is 165 feet deep. If abundant rains fell upon the country it would be fruitful. Our dragoman tells us that nearly all vegetation now looking so fresh will in a few weeks be dried up.

At several points, in ascending the rocky hills on the morning of the 12th, we saw traces of an ancient road, said to have been built by the Romans from Damascus to Tiberias, on which the rocks they had smoothed were so slippery that our horses could scarcely keep their feet. In the afternoon we passed some patches in cultivation, and a large spring named Ain Meltahah, on which is a rude mill, and camped at another large spring in the upper valley of the Jordan, the finest region we have seen this side of the Plains of Esdraelon. Some of our Bedouin neighbors visited us. A boy about nine read, apparently very well, in Arabic, what our guide said was a portion of the history of Joseph. Several were moving their tent villages, preparatory to farming; they have considerable herds of cattle and flocks of sheep and goats, and a few camels. Their ploughs are insufficient for good work; they plough with oxen. Frogs were numerous and musical.

Thirteenth.—Passing numerous Bedouin tents and herds, and crossing a branch of the Jordan on an ancient stone bridge, we lunched at Dan, under two large oaks. Here is one of the principal fountains or springs of the river Jordan; we drank the pure water, and thought of Abraham at Dan, in pursuit of the kings, to recover Lot, (when he pursued the kings to Hotab, on the right hand of Damascus,) and of the calf which Jeroboam set up here to prevent Israel from going to Jerusalem to worship. Unless there was better water at Jerusalem then than now, Jeroboam had selected the most pleasant site. In the evening we camped at Banias, the Cesarea Philippi of Herod Agrippa, where Paul was held bound and where Christ enquired—"Who do men say that I the Son of Man am?" Matthew XVI, 13. The place is now a small village of filthy, miserable Arab stone huts, and fragments of broken columns and pilasters occupy the site. Here we visited another of the main springs or fountains of the Jordan, which supplied the ancient city with an abundance of the best of water, and is now used for irrigation.

Fourteenth.—We rise about 5,000 feet over rocky steep paths and one snow bank on the spurs of the Mount Hermon range, rendered slippery by the rain of the previous night, and then a long rapid descent, rough and stony, brought us to an Arab village on a beautiful little stream in a deep rocky gorge, where we lunched, and we camped for the night at Kefr Hauar, another small Arab village on the bank of a pretty stream; here is the reported burial place of Nimrod. We have seen several small groves of timber being raised by irrigation. Our pack train starting some time after we did was caught some two hours in a rain and snow storm, while we were ahead of it. A boy came into camp with six perfect toes on each foot, and six fingers on each hand, including thumbs.

On a high peak above Banias are the ruins of the castle Subeiteh, which covered an area of 1,000 by 200 feet, and which we passed near by on our left; it dates to the period that Judea was a kingdom, and is said to be one of the most magnificent ruins in Syria.

FIFTEENTH.—As we advanced towards Damascus cultivation began to increase, and we passed some vineyards on light reddish soil, and lunched in a small grove of young thrifty trees carefully raised by irrigation. For some two miles outside the walls, on the side we entered, we passed between large fields, orchards and gardens made luxuriant by irrigation upon the plan in practice in Utah, and this belt of cultivation seems to extend around the city, while beyond the belt thus cultivated it appears barren. Our way to camp led directly through the city by narrow and ill-paved streets thronged with people. This city, said to be the oldest in the world, has made very shabby improvements. Eliezer, Abraham's chief steward, was a native of Damascus, about 1,913 years before Christ. It needs some Yankee enterprise to reconstruct this place, though its present condition demonstrates what irrigation might be made to do in this part of the world.

SUNDAY, 16.—We met in one of our tents and administered the sacrament in the afternoon.

MONDAY, 17.—We made a call upon the American Consular Agent, N. Meshaka, a native Syrian, who has never been in America. He treated us very courteously, and we conversed with him for some time. He asked us many questions in relation to our faith, being able to converse to some extent in the English language; he is not a Mahommedan. He informed us that the Mahommedans could marry four wives, and buy as many as they might be able or wish to. He said the Turks would not approve of allowing women the privilege of voting, that placing them too nearly on an equality with man. We walked through a portion of the street called

Strait, and through many streets and ways all narrow, and visited what our dragoman told us was the best private residence in the city. We came to the conclusion that Damascus is one of the shabbiest built cities we have ever visited; its great beauty consists in the possession of water and land for perhaps some twenty square miles, which has been reclaimed from the surrounding desert. It is wonderful to us how these crowded haunts of human beings are preserved from destruction by pestilence. The Consular Agent told us that at this season the city was healthy, but in summer and fall it is sickly. According to Dr. Burns, this city has some 150,000 human beings on an area of about a mile square, with 200 mosques thrown in, one of which is in an enclosure of 1,100 feet by 800.

At 3 o'clock Mr. N. Meshaka, accompanied by two of his friends, called upon us in camp. He informed us that if we wished to establish missions in this country it would be necessary to obtain permission from the Sultan. The Prince of Saxe Weimar has just passed our camp on his entry to Damascus, announced by the firing of artillery, and received by thousands of people lining the side of the road, giving us a good opportunity to see the people; some 3,000 troops, cavalry, artillery and infantry, had previously gone out to escort him; he is a young man in a plain light gray suit.

Monday, 18—This morning a servant of the Consular Agent, dressed in a ginger-bread Turkish livery, with a curved sword and whip, called at our camp by order of the Agent, and conducted us to the great mosque, or Grand Harem, or Mosque of St. John. In 705 it became entirely a mosque; previous to that it had been a Christian church, and from the time of the Saracen occupation half of it was Christian; before that, or originally, it had been a heathen temple, and some of its ancient columns are still remaining. They showed us a tomb containing a gold casket said to contain the head of John the Baptist; behind an iron grating the ankles of Mahomet are pointed out. We ascended one of the minarets and had a fine view of the city and its surrounding gardens, groves, cultivated fields, and the neighboring villages, beyond which is desert. We then visited Abd-el-Kader, rendered historic by his long and able defense of Algeria against the French, and also for his kind rescue of many Christians in the massacre of 1860. His Highness treated us with much courtesy, and our interview was very pleasant. He said it was 27 years since he went to France, and he had resided here 16 years. It is said that Mahomet when as a camel driver he first came in sight of Damascus, refused to enter it, saying; "Man can have but one paradise, and my paradise is fixed above;" this may illustrate the difference between the naked desert, and the portion irrigated by the waters of the Abana and Pharpar.

Brothers Snow and Carrington will take the post coach for Beyrout this evening at 6 o'clock, timed to arrive there to-morrow at 8 a. m., 14 hours' ride; we expect to reach there on horseback Friday evening, 21st, if the weather proves as favorable as hitherto.

The party are all well, peaceful, and in good spirits. Many thousand ladies visited our camp yesterday to see Sisters Snow and Little.

GEORGE A. SMITH.

AT THE SEA OF GALILEE.

I have stood on the shore of the beautiful sea,
The renown'd and immortalized Galilee,
When t'was wrapp'd in repose, at eventide,
Like a royal queen in her regal pride.

No sound was astir—not a murmuring wave—
Not a motion was seen, but the tremulous lave,
A gentle heave of the water's crest—
As the infant breathes on a mother's breast.

I thought of the present—the past; it seemed
That the silent Sea with instruction teem'd;
For often, indeed, the heart can hear
What never, in sound, has approached the ear.

Full oft has silence been richly fraught
With treasures of wisdom and stores of thought,
With sacred, heavenly whisperings, too,
That are sweeter than roses, and honey dew.

There's a depth in the soul, that's beyond the reach
Of all earthly sound—of all human speech,
A fiber too sacred and pure to chime
With the cold, dull music of Earth and Time.

'Tis the heart's receptacle, naught can supply
But the streams that flow from the fount on high,
An instinct divine, of immortal worth,
An inherited gift, through primeval birth.

* * * * * *

Again, when the shades of night, were gone,
In the clear bright rays of the morning dawn,
I walked on the bank of this self-same Sea,
Where once our Redeemer was wont to be.

Where, "Lord save, or I perish," was Peter's prayer,
Befitting the weak and the faithless elsewhere.
And here, while admiring this Scriptural Sea,
Th' bold vista of Time brought th' past up to me.

Emboss'd with events when the Prince of Life
Endured this world's hatred, its envy and strife;
When, in Him, the Omnipotent was revealed,
And, by Him, the wide breach of the law was healed.

The gates He unbarred, and led the way,
Through the shadow of death, to the courts of day;
And "led captivity captive" when
"He ascended on high, and gave gifts unto men."

E. R. SNOW

Damascus, Syria, March 17th, 1873.

LETTER LXX.

Leave Jerusalem—Bethel—The Robbers' Glen—Ruins of Shiloh—Jacob's Well—Gerizim and Ebal—Shechem—City of Samaria—Church of St. John the Baptist—Dothan—Valley of Jezreel—Endor—Nazareth—Church of the Annunciation—Cana of Galilee—Dwelling Place of Joseph and Mary—Tiberias—Where Nimrod was Buried—Cesarea Philippi—Damascus.

DAMASCUS, March 18th, 1873.

EDITORS SALT LAKE HERALD:

At 8.15 a. m., on the 5th inst., we left Jerusalem *en route* for this city. The weather was pleasant for traveling, and we reached Beeroth after a three hours' ride. After lunch we passed Bethel, where Jacob had his vision (see Gen. XXVIII, 10-22); rode through a canyon, which is called The Robbers' Glen, and camped for the night at the mouth of the same, where a number of years ago a traveling party had been murdered. During the day we passed through many olive groves and fig orchards, and in the valleys a good deal of barley was sown, and looked very well. The following morning we broke camp at 7.30 a. m., passed through the ruins of Shiloh at 9 a. m., where there is a very large and remarkable old tree (see Josh. XVIII, 1; XIX, 51; Jer. VII, 12-14). We lunched at Jacob's Well, (see John IV, 6), between the mountains of Gerizim and Ebal; this well is seventy-five feet deep. In the afternoon we rode on to Nablous, the Shechem of old, which was one of the cities of refuge (see Josh. XX, 7). It is quite a large city now, and there seems to be some business transacted here, but the streets are very narrow and filthy. On Friday morning it was raining and continued during the forenoon; the road was very much up and down hill, and in some places exceedingly rough, and also slippery on account of the rain. Our Arab horses are very sure-footed, and it is astonishing to us how safely they carried us over really dangerous looking places; thank the Lord, we have not met with any accident. We rode now over the hills of Samaria, and about 9 a. m., we passed the site of the ancient city of Samaria, which is beautiful for location. A large number of granite columns, a good many standing, and others prostrate, are found all over the hill. Here are also the ruins of the Church of St. John the Baptist, with his supposed sepulchre, and by reading Micah I, 5-7, it will be seen how literally the Divine judgments have been executed. In the afternoon we passed Dothan, where Joseph was sold by his brethren; crossed the frontier between Samaria and Galilee, and reached Jenin, near the entrance to the fields of Esdraelon, after eight hours' ride, at 4.15 p. m. We had stopped about one hour for lunch in the middle of the day.

Saturday the 8th, we left about 7.30 a. m., and passed over the fertile and well cultivated Plains of Esdraelon, called in the Scriptures the Valley of Jezreel and Plains of Megiddo, (see Judges VI, 33; 2 Chron. XXXV, 22), and had mostly good roads but they were muddy from yesterday's rain. To our right we saw the mountains of Gilboa, Little Hermon and Endor, in the distance, where Saul visited the witch under cover of the night. A little further on, Mount Tabor came in sight which makes a very striking appearance; and a little after 3 p. m. we reached Nazareth, which is nicely situated on a mountain slope, reaching down into the valley. Our tent ground was at the foot of the town, and close to the Greek Church of Annunciation. A large number of Armenians, who had come forty days by land to perform a pilgrimage to Jerusalem, were camping close by.

We spent the Sabbath in visiting the Greek Church of the Annunciation, where we were shown the fountain where Mary sat when the angel appeared to her; then we went to a Catholic church, which, it is said, was the synagogue in which Jesus preached to the Jews, (Luke IV, 16 to end); thence to a Latin convent, where a polite friar showed us several natural caves, generally called the "parlor, bedroom and kitchen" of Mary, where she is said to have lived with Joseph. He took us to another chapel, erected on the site of Joseph's carpenter shop, and showed us some antique furniture; and still in another chapel he showed a large natural rock, on which he said the Saviour had eaten, before and after his resurrection. To show us all these sights he had to take us through a number of streets, and we came to the conclusion that of all the narrow and dirty streets of the Palestine cities we had visited, the beautifully situated Nazareth could boast of the most crooked, the steepest and the filthiest.

Monday morning before leaving Nazareth we witnessed an Armenian funeral of a pilgrim woman, who had died the day before. We started at 8 a. m., and after riding about an hour and a quarter we reached Cana of Galilee, where Nathaniel was born and where Jesus worked his first miracle (see John II, 1 to end). Our road led alternately through fertile valleys and over high hills. At 3 p. m. we came in sight of the Sea of Galilee, also called the Lake of Tiberias or the Lake of Gennesareth, and at 3.45 we reached our tents, pitched at the north end of the City of Tiberias, within about ten rods of the shore of the lake, which is very beautiful. It is about thirteen miles long by six miles wide, and 620 feet below the level of the Mediterranean. We had a fine moonlight night, the moon being nearly over our heads, and we enjoyed the scenery very much. We visited the city, around which extensive ruins of its former greatness are found, and also two hot sulphur springs a mile south of the town, the temperature of which is said to be 144 degrees, Fahrenheit. Tuesday,

v

the 11th inst., we had a delightful morning and saw to the north of the lake Mount Hermon, ten thousand feet high, whose tops are covered with eternal snow. President George A. Smith, Albert Carrington and Thomas W. Jennings, with two other gentlemen, took a ride over the lake in a fishing boat to the mouth of the Jordan, while the rest of our party traveled along the shore about six miles north, to our next camping ground, at the supposed site of Capernaum, where we found a splendid spring of good water, shaded by a large venerable fig tree. The following day we traveled over some high hills to the plains by the waters of Merom, and camped near another spring, a few miles north of the famous fountain of Ain Mehalah. On Thursday we passed over very fine farming land, saw a number of Bedouin tent villages, large herds of stock and flocks of sheep and goats, lunched under two large shade trees at Dan, near one of the principal sources of the Jordan, and reached Banias or Panias, the ancient Cesarea Philippi, at 2.30 p. m. Here, from a cliff of limestone about 100 feet high, bursts forth another source of the river Jordan; and broken columns and many ruins all over the neighborhood speak of the former greatness of this place where the Apostle Paul made his celebrated defense before King Agrippa, (see Acts XXV and XXVI.) During the night we had a heavy thunder storm, and one of our tents fell down.

Friday, the 14th, we traveled over the spurs of Mount Hermon, rising to an elevation of more than 5,000 feet, and traversing very hard and stony ways. We reached the Arab village Beit Jenin, at noon, and stopped there for lunch and rest for about two hours, near a nice spring. Two and one half hours more riding brought us to the Arab village Kefr Hauar, which is said to be the burial-place of the "mighty hunter" Nimrod. This was one of the hardest day's riding we have had, and our pack train, that had taken another road, was traveling for three hours in a rain and snow storm. Next morning we left a little before 8 a. m., our road leading us through fertile and well cultivated plains, and we soon saw the minarets of ancient Damascus in the distance. The road was excellent all day, and soon after nooning we were approaching the luxuriant suburbs, passing through fields, gardens, vineyards and orchards, which extend round about Damascus for miles, and are watered from the streams Abana and Pharpar. The gardens and orchards are fenced with walls of dried mud, cut in immense square blocks, and the walls are from eight to ten feet high. All the apricot trees were in blossom, and the whole region looked very fertile. We entered through the eastern gate, and rode through the whole city, as our camping ground was outside the western gate. The streets and suburbs of the city were crowded with people, and a great number of women were out in their white robes, as it was "Miram," one of the Mahommedan holidays of Lent. Damascus is generally admitted to be one of the oldest cities of the world, and is said to have been founded by the grandson of Noah. It contains now about 150,000 inhabitants, mostly Mahommedans, and but very few Europeans are seen in the streets. The Scriptural references to this old city may be found in Gen. XV, 2; 2 Sam. VIII, 6; 1 Chron. XVIII, 6; 1 Kings XI, 24; 2 Kings V, 12; VIII, 7; XIV, 28; XVI, 9; 2 Chron. XXVIII, 5; Isaiah VIII, 4; X, 9; XVII, 1, and Jer. XLIX, 23, 24.

We have called upon the American Consular Agent, Mr. N. Meshaka, a Syrian, with whom we had quite a lengthy and pleasant interview, and he returned the call at our tents with some of his friends. We also took a stroll through the city, looked at the numerous bazars, saw the extraordinary old plane tree, the trunk of which is forty feet in circumference, passed through the street called "Straight," (see Acts IX, 10, 11,) and intend to visit some more places of interest.

We are all in good health, and expect to leave to-morrow for Beyrout.

PAUL A. SCHETTLER.

LETTER LXXI.

Start for Beyrout—At Damascus—An Excellent Road—Massacre by Turks—Rain—At Kob Elias—Arrive at Beyrout—Sacred Relics—Monkish Rivalry—Physical Contrast Between Arabs and Jews—Silk Culture—Groves of Figs, Oranges, Olives and Dates.

New Oriental Hotel, Beyrout, Syria,
March 24, 1873.

President Brigham Young:

Dear Brother—On Tuesday evening, 18th inst., Brothers Snow and Carrington took post coach for Beyrout, where they arrived on the morning of the 19th, and posted the letters I wrote to you at Nazareth and Damascus, and other letters forwarded by them, to go by the steamer on the 20th. During the time we remained at Damascus, several thousand women came out to look at our camp, and great numbers of them kissed Sisters Snow and Little, and seemed much interested in seeing them.

Our programme included a visit to the ruins of Baalbec, but it was not deemed best to make it. This arrangement proved to be well-timed, as I learned from a Mr. Todd that his party to Baalbec were exposed for several hours to a cold, severe and drenching storm of hail and rain on Wednesday and Thursday. Where we were the weather was favorable.

The French company's road, 112 kilometres of five-eights of a mile each, is well macadamized, and kept in excellent repair. It crosses the Anti-Lebanon and Lebanon ranges of mountains and the beautiful plain or valley between them, which is irrigated by abundant streams flowing from the two ranges, and is well cultivated. The massacre of the Christians by the Turks at Damascus, in 1860, caused six European powers, including Turkey, to send some 6,000 French soldiers to Damascus, to protect the Christian interests; probably from this move sprang the excellent road between Damascus and Beyrout, made, kept in repair and owned by a French company, who have a charter for fifty years, at the expiration of which time the road is to become the property of the Turkish government; should that event transpire, Mr. N. Meshaka, U. S. Consular Agent, said the road would at once be allowed to go out of repair. A change from rocky trails to this smooth road seemed very agreeable, though the descents were fatiguing.

During the night of the 18th we had a rain, which changed our rather damp camp ground into a swamp, making our start on the morning of the 19th an agreeable change. The day threatened rain but it passed to the north of us. Camped at Dimas, in the Anti-Lebanon range.

Thursday night, 20th, we camped at Kob Elias, an Arab town at the east base of the Lebanon range. The valley between the two ranges is one of the most fertile and best cultivated that we have seen, water for irrigating being supplied by streams fed by rains and melting snows.

We arrived at Beyrout at 2.45 p. m., Friday 21st, and stayed in camp until the 22nd, when we went to the New Oriental Hotel, the hotel where Brothers Snow and Carrington were being full. Our dragoman, Mr. Anthony Makloof, proved himself efficient in conducting us from Jaffa to this place, and in providing very comfortably for our wants.

We have had but part of a day's rain during our journey from Jaffa—on the 22nd of February. We were provided with good horses, and they performed their part well. We all arrived here in good health.

In my letters to you I have reported rather minutely what

has been told us by our guides and the monks, &c., in relation to the old sacred sites and relics, which may be illustrated in the case of John the Baptist. At the Church of San Lorenzo, in Genoa, we were shown the chain with which he was bound, and a casket which contained his head; Pope Innocent having decreed that no woman should enter the chapel containing these relics only on one day in a year, Sisters Snow and Little were not admitted into the chapel; the monk informed us there could be no mistake about their identity. When at Samaria, in the Church of St. John the Baptist, erected by the Knights of St. John in the 11th century, and much dilapidated, we were allowed to look into the tomb and see the bones of St. John and his family. When visiting the Grand Harem at Damascus, once the Church of St. John, and now the Mosque of St. John the Baptist, we were shown an enclosure containing the head of John the Baptist in a golden casket. When in Venice, in a church, I was shown a piece of marble upon which the guide assured me the head of John the Baptist fell when it was cut off, and a casket containing his remains, which he assured me were brought from Palestine about 800 years ago. I suppose it would be sacrilegious to doubt the identity of all these sacred remains. I visited the Garden of Gethsemane, was shown by a monk the spot where the Saviour was arrested and the tree under which he sweat great drops of blood. The garden is surrounded by a good, newly built wall; the olive trees are very old. The Greek monks have another garden near by, which they assert with equal positiveness to be the true one.

Owing to a mis-date, accidentally made in advising the Liverpool office, we get no mail matter here, but expect to receive it at Constantinople on the 31st. On our way there the ship makes short stops at Cyprus, Rhodes and Smyrna, giving opportunity for going ashore.

At Beyrout, there are some schools and missionary establishments belonging to Catholics and Protestants, but we are told they are sustained by large contributions from abroad. Most of the business here is conducted by foreigners; and as many as possible, both natives and foreigners, get appointed to some public office of a foreign government, or a dragoman or servant to some officer of such government, to avoid many of the exactions of the Turkish government.

So far as could be observed in a hasty ride through the country the Bedouins and others of Arab descent seem to be tall, lithe, well-proportioned and athletic, indicating a goodly degree of physical purity; our dragoman informs us that adultery is punished with death, which aids in preserving from physical corruption and degeneracy. The Jews seem to be a down-trodden race.

In this vicinity the cultivation of the mulberry and the production of silk are carried on to a considerable extent; and in many places the slopes of the mountains are extensively terraced and cultivated and dotted with small villages; and in an intervening valley some good sized groves of pine are well cultivated, while figs, oranges and olives are raised in large quantities, and date trees are tolerably numerous.

GEORGE A. SMITH.

LETTER LXXII.

Sea of Galilee—Tiberias—A Daughter of Juda—Visit Jewish Residences—Human Beings and Asses Dwelling in one Room—The Cleanest Town In Palestine—Mouth of Jordan—Chorazin and Bethsaida—Ruins of Magdala—A Ramble on the Sea Shore—Mount Hermon—Damascus and Its Forty Thousand Dogs.

BEYROUT, March 24th, 1873.

EDITOR WOMAN'S EXPONENT:

Aside from the deep interest with which sacred history clothes the Sea of Galilee, it is beautiful. We camped within the walls of Tiberias, a small town situated on the sea shore. As I walked along the edge of the water, a young daughter of Judah came — filled a large earthen jar with seawater—placed it on her head, according to the usual custom, and started home. Prompted by her gracious and friendly greeting, I followed, and by signs (how much bother that confounding at Babel has occasioned!) made her understand that I wished to accompany her home. She seemed pleased, and on entering, set her jug down in the front room, and leading the way into the second and only remaining one—which was parlor, sitting and sleeping room, as I understood by being shown where the mats for lodging were deposited—she introduced me to an elderly woman, who received me very cordially. The room was very small and neatly spread with rush or flag rugs over the earth floor. The two Jewesses motioned me to follow them through a small opening—the only one except the door—into a little garden containing a few "petatis," one or two low trees, a few shrubs, mint, etc. I had some pretty wild flowers in my hand which the young lady threw down very significantly, at the same time plucking and presenting me green branches from a hyssop bush, the most flourishing shrub in the yard. To this, although destitute of fruit and flowers, they seemed to attach a great deal of consequence. The garden, or yard, had no egress but the one through which we entered, consequently, we crawled back into the house, when the young Jewess took me across the street into another house, where we found a neatly-dressed Jewess, with but one room, and I think at least one-third of that was appropriated to donkeys, their portion being defined by a narrow ditch, which served as a trough, in which they were feeding. She was tending an infant, and rising, saluted me politely, and urged me to occupy her stool, which was the only seat present. The floor was hard, smooth ground, destitute of carpet or rug; an iron tripod about five inches high was standing over a fire in the lady's portion of the room, on which something was boiling; and although whatever smoke existed must have circulated through the room it was not perceptible. Despite all the peculiarities, there was an order and an air of neatness in this house that really surprised me. I give these descriptions as samples—these houses appearing to be about the average type. The population of Tiberias is mostly Jews, and it has the distinguishing honor of being the cleanest town in Palestine.

The next day President Smith, Professor Carrington, Brother Jennings and two American gentlemen traveling with us, wishing to enjoy a boat-ride on the sea, were rowed across to the mouth of the Jordan, supposed to have been near the locality of Chorazin and Bethsaida, while the rest of the party preferred riding on horseback to the place of destination, occupying two hours along the sea side. We passed the ruins of Magdala, said to be the place where Mary Magdalene formerly lived, and preceded the boaters nearly four hours. In the meantime, Miss Little and myself took a seaside walk in search of shells for our friends at home; but after promenading the shore and scrutinizing the water's edge for a long distance, pronounced it a failure—selected a few pebbles and returned to camp, tired if not fatigued.

Of the Sea of Galilee I shall probably say more hereafter. At this point the snow-crowned Mount Hermon is in plain sight, the spur of which we traveled over on the 14th after encamping at Banias, the ancient Cesarea Philippi, the preceding night. We ascended to the height of five thousand feet, over the roughest passes and trails imaginable—sometimes over rocks apparently as smooth as glass, and the greatest wonder was that our animals kept in standing position. But they are trained to rocky, difficult passes—they know but little of roads; this I learned after leaving Damascus, from which place to Beyrout is a splendid macadamized road, on which between these two points the "diligence" for passengers, and a mail coach run daily. Until on this road, I had not discovered that my horse was skittish, but here—feeling out of its latitude, it was afraid of everything, and although I had to be all the time on the watch, I was much amused; the rest of the animals manifested in a greater or less degree the same strangeness of feeling.

Before we reached Damascus, for a long distance, the way was lined on each side with fields of grape vines, apparently well cultivated. We rode through the city and camped on an open square washed by the beautiful river Abana; and the next morning I expressed my willingness to admit the statement that Damascus keeps forty thousand dogs—their noise in proof.

Here, as has been customary with the party whenever consistent, we had the sacrament administered on Sunday. Monday we accompanied President Smith on a visit to the sub-American Consul, N. Meshaka, a native Syrian, who spoke English tolerably. He received us with marked kindness—asked President Smith many questions concerning our people, politics, religion, etc., spent an hour or more in earnest conversation, and expressed himself much gratified with the call, which he returned in the evening. Before we left, an attendant served to each a tiny cup of coffee, containing about half a gill, which, as a national token of friendship, courtesy prompted us to accept.

ELIZA R. SNOW.

LETTER LXXIII.

Leave Damascus—The only Wagon Road in Syria—Fine Scenery—Mountains of Lebanon—Beyrout—Finish of Camp Life—On board the "Mars"—Island of Cyprus—Rhodes—Patmos—Scio—Smyrna—Lesbos—Tenedos—Dardanelli—Abydos—Gallipoli—Sea of Marmora—Golden Horn—Constantinople.

HOTEL D'ANGLETERRE, CONSTANTINOPLE,
April 4th, 1873.

EDITORS SALT LAKE HERALD:

We left Damascus on the morning of the 19th of March, having given up the idea of visiting the ruins of Baalbec, and took the nearest route for Beyrout, which is a fine macadamized wagon road, 112 kilometers, or about 67 English miles long, built by a French company, and kept in excellent condition. This is in fact the only wagon road in Palestine and Syria, all the rest being pack trails and bridle paths, and no vehicle could pass over them for any distance.

The scenery we passed through was very fine. Our road

led for miles through gardens and orchards, and then through some romantic mountain gorges, that reminded us much of our canyons at home; and we camped for the night near the Arab village of Dimas, situated on the spurs of the Anti-Lebanon. The following morning, before we left, several thousands of black goats came out of the different parts of the village to be driven to the surrounding hills for pasturage. After passing through a few more canyons we descended the Anti-Lebanon, into a large plain or rather highly cultivated valley, situated between the Lebanon and Anti-Lebanon ranges of mountains. We stopped for lunch near the river Lithany, and camped for the night near Kob Elias, on a spur of the mighty Lebanon. Friday morning, the 21st, was very cold, and we had to ascend for about two hours before we reached the summit, which is here 6,825 feet high. For the rest of the day the road was continually descending towards Beyrout, which made this last day of ours in the saddle rather fatiguing. We had a beautiful view of the "Glory of Lebanon," and the nearer we approached Beyrout, the more the fertility of the soil and the beauty of the scenery increased. We passed through beautiful vegetable gardens, fig orchards and a large number of thrifty mulberry plantations, till we reached our camp ground at Beyrout, at 2.45 p. m.

On the afternoon of the 22nd, we moved to the New Oriental Hotel, close by the Mediterranean, as our time for Palestine camp life had expired. The time of our departure by steamer was fixed for the evening of the 24th, but she was about twenty-four hours behind time, and we had to lie over another day. At four p. m. we went aboard the steamer *Mars*, 400 horse power, 3,356 tons, and as it had been blowing hard a few days ago, the ship rolled considerably, and quite a number of the passengers got sea-sick. Next morning the sea was calm, and we reached Larnaka, the principal city on the Island of Cyprus, at 8.30 a. m., and stopped there till 4.15 p. m. to load and unload freight (mostly fruit) and passengers. During the night and next day we steamed northwest, and had heavy headwinds, so that we could not make up for lost time, as was intended. At 5.30 a. m., the 28th, we dropped anchor at Rhodes, and stopped there about three hours, but the surf was so high that the captain advised the passengers not to go ashore, except those who had to stop here. Five boats had been upset the day before, and three men drowned. Some parts of the island looked very romantic and fertile. From here we steamed in a northerly direction through the Grecian Archipelago, and passed a number of beautiful islands, among them, a little after dark, the celebrated Island of Patmos, where John the Revelator had his wonderful visions. Early the following morning we reached the Island of Scio, where we took aboard a large number of cases of oranges and lemons. At 9.15 we left, and reached Smyrna, at 4.15 in the afternoon. Sunday morning we went ashore for about three hours, and walked through the principal parts of this ancient city, but we had no time to go to Ephesus by rail, to visit the ruins of the lately excavated temple of the Diana of Ephesus, which we very much regretted. We departed at 11.15 in the morning, and passed a number of islands. In the evening we arrived at Mytilene, the ancient Lesbos, and the following morning at Tenedos. At 10 in the morning we stopped one hour at Dardanelli, passed a few miles further to Abydos, where Leander used to swim across to visit his beloved one. At 2 p. m. we reached Gallipoli, stopped a couple of hours and then entered the Sea of Marmora. Early on Tuesday, the 1st of April, we reached the Golden Horn, and as the sun was rising we had a beautiful view from the deck of our steamer of the city of Constantinople, with its many mosques and minarets. This city occupies one of the finest natural situations in the world, being built upon a tongue of land of a triangular shape, which lies upon the west side of the southern entrance of the Bosphorus. On the northern side of the city is a branch of the Bosphorus, called the Golden Horn, which forms a magnificent harbor. Beyond this are the suburbs of Pera, Galatea and Sophana, the former of which is the principal seat of trade. We put up at the Hotel d'Angleterre, where we found a number of letters and papers from home, which were very welcome to us, as we had not received any letters since the 24th of February. In my next I will give you a description of our visit at Constantinople. To-morrow morning we expect to leave for Athens, reaching there on the morning of the 7th, and stay about five days in Greece. Mr. Feramorz Little with daughter and Mr. Thomas W. Jennings intend to leave our party at Syra, and go direct to Trieste, to reach there next Thursday, the 10th.

PAUL A. SCHETTLER.

LETTER LXXIV.

Damascus—Reception Rooms Of a Prince—River Abana—At Dimas—Large Flocks of Goats—In Camp on the Anti-Lebanon Mountains—The Scenery of Lebanon—Contrast Between Art and Nature—Beyrout—Silk Industry—Entertained by Turks—Adieu to Tent Life—On Board the "Mars."

Constantinople, Turkey, April 8th, 1873.

Editor Woman's Exponent:

The city of Damascus has a venerable appearance—it is very shabbily built, and whatever taste may be internally displayed, its private buildings exhibit none on their exterior. We visited what had the reputation of being the best apartments in the place—just fitted up for the reception of a German prince, whose arrival was hourly expected. The reception room was a cushioned siesta, open in front and facing a square, or open court, in which was a large fountain. From this we were conducted into a large, square room, which, strange to say, was well lighted with glass; the front part was floored with variegated marble, on which stood a white marble basin, four feet in diameter, into which the water was gently flowing from a fountain. The back part of the room was raised some six inches above the front, carpeted, and amply supplied with lounges, sofas, etc., all in veritable eastern style, and exceedingly neat. This same young Prince of Weimar and suite have been several times on board steamers with us—we saw them in Jaffa and Jerusalem, where, as well as in Damascus, they were received with a display of public honors.

On the morning of March 19th, we left the old city of Scriptural celebrity—the scene of many former striking incidents, particularly that of the miraculous conversion of Paul, and having walked on the "Street called Straight," (which judging from the gate leading into it was much broader formerly than now)—with its one hundred and fifty thousand inhabitants, without shedding any tears of regret. Now, instead of narrow trails, we travel on the broad, smooth "diligence road," through a narrow gorge between high rocky ridges, overlooking narrow strips of fertility along the beautiful Abana river, which skirts the almost perpendicular bluffs for several miles, and at night camp at a village of hovel-like dwellings, called Dimas. The next morning, while waiting the adjustment of tents, baggage, etc. on the pack mules, we were much interested in seeing the numerous goat herds with their large flocks of goats, starting out to the mountains which surrounded us on all sides; and, particularly to our amusement, numbers of these goats issued from the doors of the houses, to which there was but one opening. As the goats came through the doorway, they were intermingled with men, women and children. Our encampment was on a ridge of the Anti-Lebanon range.

The next day we traveled over an extensive valley lying between the two ranges, which as we approached the great range was highly cultivated, and crowned with luxuriant fields of grain, with houses representing civilization, if not refinement. Leaving this delightful landscape scenery, we ascended a steep ridge, where we camped for the night, in sight of lofty peaks of the celebrated Mountains of Lebanon, covered with snow; and felt the atmosphere cooled by its frosty breath. The next morning, as we ascended the highest elevation, we found the cold intense—banks of snow, from time to time, lying on the roadside, much to the annoyance of our animals—they seemed to be making its acquaintance for the first time.

At several points on this Lebanon range the view is beautiful beyond description—not only beautiful, it is grand and magnificent, combining a portion of sublimity, that, while you are struck with admiration, a feeling of awe instinctively entwines around your imagination. I was so captivated with the wild, bold, majestic scenery of nature, exhibited in an interminable variety of forms, before, behind, all around me, that many times I stopped my horse, that I might feast my eyes on the surrounding beauties of nature—the almost uncultivated "Glory of Lebanon." Some of the mountain slopes presented an appearance of having been terraced long ago, and in many places the vine is seen in rows, apparently struggling against the wash of storms and the waste of years.

The place where for the last time we dismounted for lunch I shall not readily forget. It was on a high elevation overlooking a cluster of ridges which rise in proud loftiness over deep ravines, that, viewed from our stand-point, produced a sense of giddiness from their immense depth. Although the sides of their eminences are very steep, they are terraced, and, from base to summit, highly cultivated, and covered with many varieties of vegetation, and exhibit, in a striking illustration, the effect of the skilful power of art in softening and in transforming the rough and wild condition of nature. To complete this strange, picturesque scene, the broad, smooth road, paved with white limestone, commences a descent directly from our lunching place, and, instead of crossing the ravines and running in a straight line, it winds and zigzags around, low down at the foot of these eminences, its whiteness forming a marked contrast to the green verdure of vegetation, the luxuriant foliage of shrubbery and shade trees, and the gay colors of the flowers, already in full bloom.

After leaving this point, which is about ten miles from Beyrout, the road runs in a straight direction, and, for a long distance, is lined on both sides with fields of mulberry. These trees have an old appearance—the trunks being very large, and the branches young and small from constant pruning. The manufacture of silk is quite a business at Beyrout, this place having superseded Damascus, where formerly it was carried on extensively.

Before our arrival in Beyrout, our dragoman, having special business in the city, left us in charge of a Turk who could not speak English, and understood it but little; and as we preceded our pack mules with tents, etc., he took us to a house where we were received with tokens of kindness: everything was done that hospitality need suggest—we were seated in the best room on cushioned seats, were served to tiny cups of coffee, glasses of lemonade, etc., were shown into their weaving establishment with many specimens of silk manufacture—all this time without understanding what prompted these expressions of friendship, for we could not comprehend a word of each other's language. After some time Antonio, our dragoman, came and relieved our curiosity, by informing us that the people of the house were relatives of the man who introduced us to them. Presently our tents were pitched and we left the hospitable roof, and invited the lady of the house with two or three others to accompany us, which they did. The distance was short, but others seeing these, joined in, and then others joined them, and by the time our tents were reached, we had a large procession. At this time there was a public demonstration in favor of a German Prince, just entering the city, but we concluded that ourselves drew the most attention. The next forenoon we were visited by multitudes; some of the ladies urging Miss Little and myself, we accompanied them to their homes, which we found, though simple in style, very neat.

In the afternoon—the 22nd of March, we mounted horses for the last time—bade adieu to tent life, and rode to the hotel, and on the 25th went on board the steamer *Mars*, of the Austrian Lloyd line, *en route* for Constantinople.

ELIZA R. SNOW.

LETTER LXXV.

Four Days at Constantinople—Visit the German Minister—Embark on the "Mars"—Arrive at Athens—Famous Grecian Ruins—Religious Toleration.

HOTEL DES ETRANGERS, Athens, Greece,
April 10th, 1873.

PRESIDENT BRIGHAM YOUNG:

DEAR BROTHER:—Our short stay of four days at Constantinople gave us but little time to form an acquaintance with a people so reserved and exclusive in their domestic affairs as are the Turks. The more we examined the city, the more we appreciated its fine situation. The quarters called Galatea and Pera, between the Golden Horn and the Bosphorus, are being built up much in the European style. Many parts of Constantinople proper, called Stamboul, have been burned at different periods; and much of the remainder would be improved by clearing off the old rickety wooden buildings, widening and straightening the streets and erecting more sightly and substantial buildings. Its population, including immediate suburbs, is stated to be 1,078,000, and under a liberal government it would become one of the largest commercial cities in the world.

Its possession has been fiercely contested within the period of history, it being recorded to have been besieged twenty-four times, and taken six times. The Latin Crusaders under Dondolo, the blind Doge of Venice, in 1203, conquered and pillaged this city, not even sparing the tombs of the Emperors. The sacred ornaments of the Church of St. Sophia were carried to Venice. Its final conquest, by Sultan Mahmoud II, was in 1481. The Mosque of St. Sophia, stripped of its images, its crosses and paintings mutilated, remains in good preservation to this day; four stately minarets have been erected to give it the character and appearance of a mosque. To build that church Justinian plundered the temples of Asia, Egypt, Greece and Rome. It measures 235 feet north and south, by 350 east and west, and was built in the Byzantine style. When it was taken by the Turks it was filled with a worshipping congregation of frightened men, women and children, who hoped they would be protected and their lives preserved in the church; history states they were massacred in the building by the soldiers. Our guide told us that a clergyman was performing service at the time, and was but half through; that the marble opened when the Turks entered, and enclosed the minister and his boy assistant; and that when the Christians again take the building, the marble will open, and the priest and boy come out and finish the service. The guide did not seem to credit the legend, but said it was believed by many.

A considerable portion of the inhabitants of Constantinople are Greeks. General Baker, the American Minister, with whom we had a pleasant interview, stated that the Turks at the present were far more tolerant towards the Christians than the Christians are towards each other. He expected to soon receive instructions to sign a protocol which will authorize American citizens to purchase and hold real estate, and enjoy the rights and protection of citizens.

We called on the German Minister and were courteously entertained.

We witnessed the procession of the Sultan going to the mosque on Friday, the Turkish Sunday, accompanied by his son. A magnificent boat, richly gilt, with a highly ornamented throne under a canopy, rowed by 26 oarsmen, a smaller boat with the son, rowed past seven steamships of war formed in line, with their masts and rigging covered with men; during the time 21 guns were fired by the ships; he was received at the mosque by some 1,200 infantry, and a large number of officers in gay uniform; he stepped from the boat to the platform, and walked up the steps into the mosque. On his return the firing was omitted.

Constantinople is somewhat remarkable for a large number of very fine horses, well fed and cared for.

On our visit to the Sweet Waters we saw hundreds of carriages, a large number of which contained Turkish ladies, only their eyes unveiled, though most of the veils were thin. The turn-outs were most of them first-class, the sexes of the natives riding separately.

On the morning of the 5th we went on board the steamship *Mars*, and arrived at Syra on the evening of the 6th, where Brother and Sister Snow, Brother Carrington and myself reshipped on the steamship *Wien*, while Brother Little and daughter and Brother Jennings, not wishing to visit

Greece, stayed on the *Mars* on their way to Trieste and Venice, expecting to stop a day or two at Venice, from which place Brother Little and daughter purpose proceeding to England.

We arrived at Piræus, the port of Athens, which has a beautiful land-locked harbor, on the morning of the 7th.

On the 8th visited the Temple of Jupiter Olympus; sixteen of the original 120 columns are standing; a fallen one shows the mode of their construction; also the Arch of Hadrian near by, which formerly was on the line between the city of Theseus and the city of Hadrian, who reigned in Rome A. D. 118. Then drove to the Monument of Lysicrates, said to be the most ancient monument in the Corinthian style, B. C. 335. Then to the Dionysiac Theatre, on the east corner of the south-east slope of the Acropolis, built B. C. 340. Then to the Odeum of Herodes; from there the guide pointed out the so-called Museum Hill, the prison of Socrates, the Pnyx, and Mars Hill, all near by. Then to the propylean entrance to the temples on the Acropolis; on the left was the pedestal of the Statue of Agrippa; to the right the ruins of the Temple of Nike Apteros, or Victory without wings, erected in honor of the Greek victory at Marathon; from thence the guide pointed out the Island of Salamis, and the Straits of Salamis, where the Greeks defeated the Persians in a naval battle. We then went into the Parthenon, or Temple of the Virgin; then to a point where we had a fine view over Athens, and much of the surrounding country. Then to the Erechtheum, a temple just north of the Parthenon, and near the north wall of the Acropolis. Then we drove to the Pnyx, and stood on the stone platform from which it is said Demosthenes and others used to address the people assembled in the open air. Then we drove to the Temple of Theseus, in which are many specimens of statuary more or less injured, and many other antiques. Then to an old cemetery recently laid bare in part, where are some fine specimens of burial monuments. Then we were shown one side of the Magazine of Hadrian, which had some fine columns. Then an ancient market gate, near which was a stone column on which was chiseled an ancient price list. Then the Temple of Eolus, or the winds, and from thence to the hotel, after an interesting and instructive out of nearly four hours.

Last evening, agreeable to invitation, we took tea at the American Minister's, and spent some two and a half hours very agreeably.

This city is said to contain 48,000 inhabitants, and Piræus 11,000, the two connected by a five-mile railroad, the only one in Greece. There are two other good, small harbors near the Piræus.

Christian religions are tolerated, but no proselyting is allowed, except to the established oriental Greek Church. The King, though a Lutheran, has his children baptized by immersion by the Greek Patriarch, constituting them members of the Greek Church, as is their Russian mother.

The orange trees are loaded with ripening fruit, and are both useful and ornamental. What our guide called pepper trees are much used for shade, and are very handsome.

Only a small part of Greece can be cultivated, the residue being mountainous and swampy. Barley is headed out, and looks very luxuriant. The beef is excellent, also the butter and honey. One thinks of these things after being some weeks in Turkey. It is asserted that there is no brigandage in Greece now; as an evidence, we are told if we were to visit the field of Marathon, or take a drive in the regions adjacent to this city, we must give a day's notice, and a guard of soldiers will be sent with us at the expense of the government, which at least shows a determination to protect travelers.

I have not seen an American flag in the Mediterranean, but yesterday I met the Admiral of the U. S. Mediterranean fleet, and the Captain of the *Wabash* and several other officers of the U. S. navy. They told me there were six U. S. ships of war in the Mediterranean, but for some time past they have been off the coast of Spain, watching American interests there. The *Wabash* and another ship are now in Greek waters.

When Athens contained 500,000 inhabitants, with the temples on the Acropolis in their splendor, it was probably worth visiting, especially if men spent their time as St. Paul describes in Acts, chapter xvii. The ruins show an extensive knowledge of architecture and the mechanic arts. An immense Venetian tower somewhat disfigures the outlines of the Acropolis. There are marks on the columns of the Parthenon of the cannonade during the war of Greek independence, and there is a pile of shells and cannon balls near the Propylea, or entrance to the temples.

Though not with you in person at the Conference, we were with you in spirit; and while traveling to acquire general information and to improve health, we exercise our faith by constant prayer to our Father in Heaven, that a double portion of the Holy Spirit may rest upon you and President Wells, and all the priesthood of Zion, and feel confident that Zion's cause is daily strengthening, while Satan's kingdom is growing more rotten and divided.

Our party all unite with me in a hearty God bless you and all Israel.

GEORGE A. SMITH.

LETTER LXXVI.

At Athens—Plains of Attica—Hill of Mars—Galilee—Scriptural Reminiscences—Fountain of Dan—Cesarea Philippi—Damascus—An Unfortunate Architect.

ATHENS, GREECE, April 10th, 1873.

EDITOR DESERET NEWS:

We are in the city of Athens, surrounded by the ruined temples and crumbling walls of ancient Greece—have stood on the lofty summit of the Acropolis, beside the marble columns of the Parthenon, in the midst of broken pillars and fallen temples, looking down on modern Athens, the Plains of Attica, the famous Hill of Mars, and off on the "Flowery Hymettus." We have met the King of Greece on the sidewalk of Athens, cane in hand, and in simple costume, like an ordinary gentleman, have seen the nation's deputies debating in parliament, and have spent an evening at tea with our American Minister, have sailed on the classical waters of the Mediterranean, up the Archipelago, among its beautiful islands. We have viewed Constantinople, its numerous mosques with swelling domes and pointed minarets, and promenaded its dark, winding avenues, through its wilderness of bazars, have seen the Sultan—all, and a thousand things else, since leaving Palestine. Therefore it is possible an apology is due for so long continuing descriptions of the Holy Land. Syria and Palestine, in many respects, we have found the most interesting of any country we have visited. As regards the character and condition of the people, its natural scenery, its having formed the great theatre where were displayed, during many centuries, the dealings of God with favored Israel, as well as its being the opening scene of the gospel dispensation; besides embracing the sites and melancholy ruins of ancient cities, so familiar to the biblical student.

I now return to Galilee. I ascended the mountain above "The Fountain of the Fig Tree," to a point overlooking our camp and commanding a view of the Plain of Gennesareth, the Sea of Galilee, and the towering summit of Mount Hermon. Here I employed the passing moments in serious reflections on the associations called forth by the peculiar circumstances around. A great portion of the Saviour's life was spent in the region around the Sea of Galilee. After having been expelled from Nazareth, his native city, by his own townspeople, he came down from the hilly country of Galilee, and made his home upon these shores, chose his Twelve Apostles, taught the people in their towns and villages and on the seaside, as they flocked around him in multitudes. He performed his mighty works in the cities of Chorazin, Bethsaida and Capernaum, which stood on these shores, filled with inhabitants. Eighteen centuries have wrought marvellous and fearful changes in the scenery and condition of this locality. When the Saviour and his apostles were coasting along these shores, addressing anxious multitudes, healing the sick, unstopping the ears of the deaf, giving sight to the blind and raising the dead, Tiberias, adorned with its numerous palaces and temples, stood in the zenith of its glory, its citizens reveling in splendor and luxury, and its many priests, in imposing costumes, full of studied systematic knowledge of the law and the prophets, and glowing with pious zeal to entrap and destroy the Apostles and the Saviour of the world. Infamy covers the memory of those priests, and not a single building of that magnificent city remains, and nothing is seen but patches of low decaying walls, a few heaps of hewn stone, and granite columns strewed around. The country about the Sea of Galilee was then densely populated—cities and towns occupied its shores, the summits and slopes of the surrounding hills. Bethsaida, Capernaum, Chorazin and many larger cities, were teeming with inhabitants, and in the height of prosperity. The Plain of Gennesareth, under the finest state of cultivation, appeared like a paradise of gardens, growing luxuriantly the choicest of fruits. This plain is now overspread with thorns and tall nettles, and everywhere marked by the finger of desolation. Those cities are now left without an inhabitant, and their places covered with heaps of decaying stones and prostrate walls. Capernaum is so nearly annihilated that even the place it occupied is subject of keenest dispute among travelers; and even now, I see before me in the vicinity of our tents, decaying relics, considered by some to designate the locality of that ancient city.

We left the Sea of Galilee, and continued our route through an improving country, crossed an old Roman road, through fields of grain, beans and lentils, passing several large camps of Bedouins, and for the night pitched our tents at a large fountain, near which a company of Arabs were engaged in digging a sect, to water a rich plain below. This night was characterized by a concert of striking wildness, performed by a great multitude of musical frogs in adjacent marshes, joined by howling dogs in an Arab camp, mingled with loud responses of the hoarse voices of our pack-mules, combined with a hideous chorus of sharp yelping jackals in the neighboring glens.

The next day we passed several long lines of black tents of the Bedouins, and numerous herds of cattle feeding in the plains and rich valleys. They were dwarfed, and were degenerated like the inhabitants of the country. We lunched at the "Fountain of Dan," one of the great sources of the Jordan, in the shade of a venerable tree, remarkable for the immense area covered by its branches. On our departure, two Arabs stopped to enjoy their bread and cheese in its cooling shade. While thus occupied they were surprised by a marauding party of Bedouins, who relieved them of all their little conveniences. While sympathizing in their misfortunes, we were somewhat pleased that we had escaped their experience. We camped at Cesarea Philippi, on the bank of a rushing stream, in the midst of a beautiful grove. Here is the great fountain which forms the main source of the Jordan, the most celebrated of rivers. From this immense fountain the waters collect, and soon form into a rapid torrent, rushing along with great impetuosity, tumbling over rocks, foaming and scattering its spray in all directions. At this place, that remarkable conversation occurred between Christ and his apostles, in which Peter affirmed that Jesus was "the Christ, the Son of the living God." And Jesus answered and said unto him, "Blessed art thou, Simon Barjona, for flesh and blood hath not revealed it unto thee, but my Father which is in heaven: And I say also unto thee, that thou art Peter, and upon this rock I will build my church and the gates of hell shall not prevail against it." Thus securing to every person the privilege of obtaining a like revelation.

Concerning this city, Cesarea Philippi, we record the same fate as followed the ancient city of Palestine—fragments of walls, here and there a stray granite pillar, partially concealed in the debris, hewn stones crumbling to pieces, lying in heaps, or scattered over the ground.

The modern village consists of some forty houses massed together with flat roofs, on which the dirty and filthy inhabitants sleep in the summer season, to prevent being eaten by flies and bedbugs, and bitten by scorpions, which they are too lazy to destroy.

The following morning, leaving Cesarea Philippi, we

pass over a well watered country, whose inhabitants possess more energy and enterprise, improving, in a small degree, a few of the natural advantages which surround them. We camped at night near what is said to have been one of the burial places of Nimrod; and the next day, after an interesting ride of a few hours, on ascending an eminence a panorama of great beauty and magnificence burst upon our view—the city of Damascus, "the Pearl of the East," its wide extended plains, on which are a hundred villages, numerous mosques looming up here and there, above the immense spreading mass of broad, white roofs, their great swelling domes, and tapering minarets, adorned with golden crescents, the great Plain of Damascus, ornamented with rich fields and beautiful gardens, groves of poplar and walnut, orchards of figs, apricots and pomegranates, and numerous vineyards, sprinkled here and there with tall, conical cypresses, and now and then a palm lifting its graceful head, stretching east far away till lost beneath the gray horizon northward, till reaching the mountains of Anti-Lebanon, and away south, where it is bounded by the river Pharpar, of scripture memory. The picturesque appearance of the circling hills and mountains casts an air of singular enchantment around this profoundly magnificent scenery—the long, bare ridge of Anti-Lebanon, the snow-capped peak of Hermon, distant some forty miles, a multitude of beautiful conical hills; and still beyond, a long ridge of pale blue mountains, the "Hills of Bashan."

Passing along this plain, we entered Damascus, rode through some of its principal streets and camped outside the walls, on the banks of the Abana. Much of the richness and beauty of the Plain of Damascus is owing to the invigorating influences of this stream of Bible celebrity, which flows through it from west to east, and is conducted from its channel, and carried on to the plain. Another mode of irrigation, however, is adopted in places where the Abana cannot be reached; it being rather peculiar, I will describe it. A well is first dug till water is discovered; the slope of the plain is then followed, when another is sunk, forty or fifty yards distant; the two are then connected by a subterranean channel, leaving sufficient fall for the water to flow. In this manner a long line of wells is constructed, and the stream of water thus secured is at last on a level with the surface, when it is ready to be used. The plain has a great number of these curious aqueducts, several of which extend along from two to three miles under ground. Where the waters of one are spreading life and verdure over the surface another below is gathering a new supply, obtaining it, in some measure from the surplus of the former, which soaks through the soil.

We called on the American Consul, who treated us courteously and assisted us in accomplishing the object of our visit to Damascus. Before we left, he spent an hour under our tent in conversation mutually agreeable. We visited Prince Abd-el Kader, who, during the invasion of Algiers by the French, fought so valiantly to preserve the freedom of his country. The interview was pleasant and interesting—Mocha, in elegant cups, served in Oriental style, illustrated his good feelings and respectful consideration.

Damascus is supposed to be nearly four thousand years old, the oldest city in the world. Some affirm that it was founded by Uz, the son of Aram. Atleast, it was a noted place in the days of Abraham—the steward of his house was mentioned as "Eliezer of Damascus." The city is about four miles in circumference, and contains one hundred and fifty thousand inhabitants—about eighteen thousand of these are Christians, six thousand Jews, and the rest Mahommedans. The Christian population, previous to the massacre of 1860, numbered about thirty-two thousand. During the three days of those bloody and heart-rending scenes, it is supposed that nearly three thousand Christians were murdered. Their private dwellings and churches were burned, their property destroyed, and the survivors driven forth from their homes penniless, with no means of support. Women and girls were seized and compelled to suffer the most fearful of all forms of slavery. Many of the buildings of these sufferers still lie in ruins. In walking the streets of Damascus, among the staring crowds, I imagined there was discernible, in the sombre countenances of many of the people, similar feelings to those which prompted the massacre of 1860, and that they were only waiting an opportunity.

Damascus is noted for the number of its mosques. We gained access to the principal one, partly through the courtesy of our American Consul, and partly through the stimulating influence of a golden Napoleon. On entering we pulled off our boots and put on slippers. In Catholic countries, on entering places of worship, taking off the hat is the invariable requisition, while in Mahommedan jurisdiction the temple of devotion cannot be entered without taking "off the shoes," while the *chapeau* may remain undisturbed. This ancient structure, the "Grand Harem," as it is termed, is second only to the Mosque of Omar. The Mosque and square cover an area in length of eleven hundred feet, and eight hundred feet in breadth. It has three styles of architecture, and is of great antiquity. It was originally Pagan, then Syrian Christian, and now Mahommedan. On one side it has a court surrounded by cloisters with arches in front, resting on columns of granite, limestone and marble. It has three minarets—the "Western Minaret," the "Minaret of the Bride," and the "Minaret of Jesus." According to Mahommedan tradition, when Christ comes to judge the world he will first appear upon this minaret, bearing his name, he will then enter the mosque, and summon to his presence men of every denomination. Under this mosque is a cave containing a casket of gold, in which is said to be the veritable head of John the Baptist. Any doubts we may have cherished of its identity we refrained from expressing, the same as when shown similar curiosities in the more enlightened Christian churches. We ascended one of the minarets, where we had a splendid view of Damascus and its environs.

A gentleman who spent several weeks in Damascus, hunting relics and curiosities, related to me the following anecdote concerning the founding of an ancient mosque, which stood in sight of our encampment. The Sultan, wishing to erect a mosque, engaged a distinguished architect, giving him instructions as to the dimension, style, and location, fixing the site in the centre of Damascus. The architect, having completed the work, repaired to the Sultan to report his proceedings, and claim his reward. The Sultan enquired if he had followed his directions. He replied that he had built the mosque according to instructions in every particular, that it was beautiful and magnificent, and he felt assured the Sultan would be highly gratified; but he had ventured to depart in one item from his instructions—considering that Damascus had a tendency to spread in one particular direction, he had located the mosque a short distance towards that point, from the centre of the city. The Sultan graciously complimented him on his peculiar foresight, dismissed him with flattering expressions, told him to go home, and a commissioner should be sent to examine his work, and if approved, he should be abundantly rewarded. No sooner, however, had he returned, than an order was sent by the Sultan to have him beheaded immediately, and the following inscription engraved upon his tomb, "Let this architect's head be restored when this mosque becomes the centre of Damascus." The gentleman said he read this inscription, in Arabic, on a decaying tomb near the mosque.

The external view of the private dwellings of the people is not inviting. The rough mud walls and projecting upper chambers, supported by decaying timbers, have a singularly rickety appearance. The entrance is by a miserable looking doorway through a narrow, winding passage, and not unfrequently through a stable-yard; and around the whole is cast an air of peculiar squalidness. The inside, however, exhibits a better complexion, many are neat and comfortable, and some approach to splendor and even gorgeousness, have an open court with ornamented pavements, a marble basin in the centre, surrounded with *jets d'eau*, citron, lemon and orange trees, and flowering shrubs, affording shade and filling the air with perfume. The apartments are furnished with chairs and sofas, with soft cushions, sometimes covered with embroidered silk and satin, the walls wainscotted, carved and gilded, and the ceiling covered with ornaments.

A fine macadamized road leading over some fifty miles, from Damascus to Beyrout, constructed by a French company, is the only decent road in Syria or Palestine. We passed over this thoroughfare through an interesting country, possessing natural scenery of peculiar beauty and grandeur, arriving at Beyrout, a seaport on the Mediterranean, in renewed health and vigor, gratified and instructed by our tour through Syria and Palestine.

LORENZO SNOW.

LETTER LXXVII.

Leave Constantinople—Piræus—Classical Ruins—The Greek Parliament—The Acropolis by Moonlight.

ATHENS, GREECE, April 11th, 1873.

TO MY BELOVED FAMILY:

I was in Constantinople only four days—sight-seeing is hard work when well followed. That is a great city, containing many objects of historic interest.

We left Constantinople on the 5th, arriving at Syra on the evening of the 6th, being on the same steamship we had sailed on from Beyrout to Constantinople. We have had very fine weather and smooth sea. We arrived in the Piræus on the morning of the 7th. It is a beautiful land-locked harbor, which has been rendered famous by history and song, since the days of Theseus. Five miles' carriage ride on a good road through cultivated but unfenced lands, brought us to our hotel in modern Athens. The city contains about 50,000 inhabitants, has many well built houses, and wide, well paved, clean streets, which contrast favorably with the narrow ways and crooked filthy streets of Jerusalem and Damascus, and other Turkish towns.

To-day I visited the Stadium, the place where the Olympic games were formerly performed once in four years. King George has renewed these games, and about 20,000 people witnessed the performance of wrestling, boxing, jumping, leaping, foot-racing, pole-climbing, &c. The successful competitors received their prizes from the hand of the Queen.

The amphitheatre is dug in an oval shape, with seats like stairs on each side, and could seat 50,000 or 60,000 people, and all see the exercises. I also visited the old baths, which have recently been dug up—immense floors of mosaic have been uncovered; they were some five feet underground. They were a very convenient set of baths.

I then went to the Areopagus, climbed to the summit of Mars Hill, which was somewhat difficult, the stones having been worn so smooth they were slippery. I stood on the stone which our guide said St. Paul stood on when he preached to the Athenians. Acts 17th chapter. I found a French barber and had my beard sheared.

I re-visited the Temple of Jupiter Olympus; sixteen columns fifty-two feet high still remain. Originally there were 124, ten feet square at the base and six and a half in the shaft. It was commenced 536 years before Christ and finished 130 after Christ, making over 600 years in building.

I then visited the Temple of Theseus, which retains a portion of its marble roof, which is the best preserved of any ruins I have seen.

I then went to the Greek Parliament, which is in session. We presented a note from the American Minister, Mr. John M. Francis, of New York. We were immediately seated in the Diplomatic Gallery. About one hundred deputies were in the seats, the King's ministers were occupying their desks. A spirited debate was in progress in relation to a claim on the National Treasury, the payment of which was contested. The President governed the Assembly by ringing a bell, instead of using the gavel. The appearance of the Deputies was quite democratic, each one seeming to dress according to his taste or his custom at home. Some of them wore white skirts, which our guide told us was the Albanian dress. Dark hair and eyes predominated. The galleries, except the one we occupied, were crowded to suffocation. The question at issue seemed to excite deep interest both with the Deputies and in the galleries. The President had to jingle his bell several times, to prevent interruption of the Speaker.

A handsome new building is nearly finished to accommodate the Parliament, which when done will make them much more comfortable.

This evening, I have arranged to visit the Acropolis by moonlight. I do not intend to imitate Mark Twain in stealing anybody's grapes, and consequently have no fear of being overtaken by the police.

On the evening of the 9th we were invited to tea at 8 o'clock p. m. at the residence of Mr. Francis, the American Minister. We met there Mr. Goodenough, the American Consul General of Constantinople. We had a pleasant visit. Eliza had a long conversation with Mrs. F., I with Mr. G., Brother Snow with Mr. F., and Brother Schettler with Charles S., son of the Minister. They all seemed deeply interested in our conversation, "Mormonism" being the sole topic of the evening. To-day Mrs. Francis called on Sister Eliza.

I expect that we shall leave here to-morrow about 4 o'clock p. m., and arrive at Trieste on the 17th, when I expect more letters.

Carriage hire here with good horses and seats for four, is three francs per hour. A guide who speaks English, eight francs per day. Hotel des Etrangers gives us two meals per day, room and lights for about three and a quarter dollars. Every place we visit costs extra—for instance, when we visited Parliament, the man who unlocked the box must have his fee. Beggars are not near as numerous as they were in Italy and Turkey. The Greek kingdom has doubled its population since its organization. The King and Queen are well liked and are doing all they know how to do, to develop the interests of the country. His garden contains some beautiful orange trees, loaded with ripe fruit, also date palm trees.

GEORGE A. SMITH.

LETTER LXXVIII.

Beyrout—Protestant College and Schools—Embark For Constantinople—Island of Cyprus—Mount Olympus—Sea of Marmora—Arrival at the Turkish Metropolis—Leave for Athens—Greek Independence Day.

ATHENS, GREECE, April 12th, 1873.

EDITOR DESERET NEWS:

In my last I closed with our arrival at Beyrout. The locality of this city is very beautiful: it stands on a promontory of a triangular form, the apex projecting into the Mediterranean, and its base extending along the foot of the Lebanon mountains. Groves of pine and mulberry are seen on the rising hills, and covering the mountain acclivities; and here and there groups of palm and cypresses. Our hotel, situated close upon the shore, commands a splendid view of the Bay of St. George, on which are floating ships and steamers, the Mediterranean, the finest portion of the city, and some of the picturesque scenery of Lebanon. It is a mental luxury to look from my window, or out from the open balcony, and contemplate these lovely scenes, wrought by the hand of God, and by his inspirations in man.

The city contains over fifty thousand inhabitants—one-third of these are Mussulmen, the rest Christians, Jews and strangers. Its numerous shops, capacious warehouses, its busy quay and numbers of bazars, ships and steamers, exhibit life and commercial enterprise, forming a striking contrast with the old, threadbare, worn-out, and moth-eaten systems of doing business, still practised in the towns and cities of Palestine. With regard to foreign trade and commerce, Beyrout stands foremost in Syria; the largest imports are for Damascus, it forming the seaport for that city. The chief article of export is raw silk, the trade in which is fast increasing, and every year becoming more important. In the vicinity of the city, and through the region of Lebanon, the country is being filled with mulberry orchards; and little doubt is entertained of its proving a permanent source of business and profit.

The new portion of the city is handsomely built, the private dwellings and public edifices are chiefly constructed of stone, substantially built, with some artistic display. Some of the streets are broad and well paved, and nearly everywhere signs of improvement and enterprise are visible, insomuch that one could almost fancy himself in a European city.

American and English missionaries have established a Protestant college and several schools in Beyrout and in Lebanon. These institutions are accessible to students of every sect and party who are willing to conform to the regulations, which are skilfully arranged with a view to proselyting. All boarders are required to be present at morning and evening prayers, and attend Protestant worship, and college classes upon the Scriptures, during the week. The Bible is also used as a text book for common instructions, &c. These educational departments are sustained by contributions from Europe and America. Some seventy students attend the Protestant college. The British Syrian schools at Beyrout number over six hundred scholars, and including the branch schools in Lebanon, rising one thousand.

March 25th, we embarked on an Austrian Lloyd steamer, for Constantinople. We passed the Island of Cyprus, had a view, from the deck, of Mount Olympus, the summit of which was once crowned with the celebrated Temple of Venus; passed the Island of Rhodes, where we saw the fortifications of the "Knights of St. John," their bastions, battlements, overhanging buttresses and lofty towers. The Island of Patmos was pointed out in the distance, where the Revelator John received his wonderful visions. We called at Smyrna, the city honored with many euphonious names—"The Ornament of Asia," "The Crown of Ionia," "Sweet smelling Smyrna," &c.; passed the Island of Mytilene, Tenedos; went through the Dardanelles, and were shown the place where Leander, and afterward Lord Byron, performed feats of swimming; then steamed over the Sea of Marmora, and at length arrived at Constantinople, the celebrated capital of the Ottoman Empire.

The port was crowded with ships, steamers, barges, ferries and small boats, so numerous that they appeared as if swarming on the waters, numbering many thousands. This magnificent bay accommodates twelve hundred sail, and is sufficiently deep to float ships of war of the largest magnitude.

For advantages of trade and commerce, and for beauty of situation, Constantinople undoubtedly excels all other cities in the world. It stands upon two continents, Europe and Asia, and upon two seas, the Black Sea and the Sea of Marmora. Its population is variously estimated at from five hundred thousand to eight hundred thousand; of these about three hundred thousand are Greeks and Armenians, sixty thousand Jews, and thirty thousand Europeans. It contains forty colleges, one thousand mosques, many Jewish synagogues, and numerous Catholic churches.

We visited the American Minister, and spent a few hours in his company very pleasantly. President Smith has made it an invariable rule to call on our American Ministers and Consuls, and with an exception, we have been courteously and kindly received, and in several instances our company has been solicited. Our cards, and our letters of introduction from President Young, on every occasion, have been noticed and honored.

While in Constantinople we visited the principal mosques, the tombs of the sultans, the offices of the Sublime Porte, the Treasury, Armory, Mint, Repository of Antiquities, the bazars and the Palace of the Osmanli Sultans, the Royal Seraglio. The Mosque of St. Sophia, which we inspected, in several respects is the most remarkable edifice in the Turkish Empire. It is three hundred and fifty feet in length, by two hundred and thirty-five in breadth. It was built for a Catholic temple in the sixth century, by the Emperor Justinian, and was sixteen years in course of construction. At that time it was celebrated as the most remarkable and magnificent temple in the whole empire. In the fifteenth century, it was converted into a mosque, through the conquering sword of Mohammed the Second, at the capture of Constantinople. It has two flags suspended on either side of the pulpit, indicating the victory of Islam over Judaism and Christianity, and the Koran over the Old and New Testaments. The roof is constructed in such a manner that it exhibits nine cupolas, the great dome forming the highest summit and so arranged that it appears as if suspended in the air; the whole seen together presents an appearance of singular grandeur and magnificence. The walls and numerous arches are built of brick; the interior of the building is adorned with the richest and most costly materials—granite, marble and porphyry of every description; black marble with white veins, white marble with rose-colored stripes, green and blue marble, and Bosphorus marble with black veins. We counted eight large porphyry columns which were taken from the "Temple of the Sun," at Baalbec, and six or eight of green columns of porphyry, which our guide informed us were from the Temple of Diana at Ephesus. The floor is formed of variegated marble with waving lines, imitating the movings of the ocean. The tiles which cover the arches of the cupolas were made at Rhodes, of chalk-white clay of peculiar lightness, being only one-twelfth of the usual weight; and had inscribed upon them,

"God has founded it, and it will not be overthrown: God will support it in the blush of the dawn." It has sixteen gates of bronze, adorned with crosses; the spaces between them are decorated with beautiful marble, and above them are mosaic pictures. The central dome is one hundred and seven feet in diameter, with a rise of forty-six feet, and with an elevation of one hundred and eighty feet above the ground, with semi-domes on two sides, of equal diameter. The grand dome is supported by arches resting on four immense piers, supported by abutments. Its numerous arches, pillars and cupolas, are all inlaid with marble mosaics of the most beautiful designs. In the cupola, are inscribed the following words from the Koran: "God is the light of the heavens and the earth." On ceremonial occasions, during the night, these expressive words are illuminated by thousands of lamps, suspended in circles, one above another, which, aided by attachments of ostrich eggs, and quantities of tinsel, and numerous artificial flowers, are said to produce a wonderful effect.

One hundred architects, during the construction of this mosque, superintended ten thousand masons, five thousand working on one side, the other half at the same time, engaged on the opposite side of the building. It is said, of the Emperor, that during the progress of the work, he paid occasional visits, to inspire the workmen, dressed in coarse linen, a cloth around his head, and a rough stick in his hand. When the walls had reached about six feet above the ground, an expenditure of about twenty-two tons of gold had been incurred; and a traditionary account is given, that when this extraordinary structure had been completed as far as the cupolas, the funds were exhausted, and the people groaning and murmuring under the heavy burden of imposed taxes; whereupon an angel appeared, and, leading the mules of the treasury to a subterranean vault, loaded them with four tons of gold!

We went aboard an Austrian Lloyd steamer, April 5th, and steered for Athens, the capital of Greece. In going down the Archipelago, the usual dulness and monotony of ocean life was partially relieved by the changing scenery and charming views, constantly exhibited on the numerous islands we were passing. Syra especially attracted attention—the picturesque appearance of its capital city of thirty thousand people, drew expressions of surprise and admiration. Stopping a few hours at anchorage, gave opportunity of inspecting this locality. The city is built on a gigantic, conical hill, rising steeply from the shore in a semi-circle, over a mile in width, extending to an immense height; its narrow and pointed summit crowned with a large cathedral; the whole hill, with its indentures and depressions, covered from base to summit with elegant buildings painted white, with green window shutters, blue cornices and balustrades.

It chanced to be a holiday with the Greeks—they were celebrating their independence. Flags were floating from the tops of buildings, and tall masts of the ships in the harbor. At night, before our departure there was a grand illumination in which the entire city, and ships at anchor, participated. The appearance, altogether, was very striking.

We arrived at Piræus, the seaport of Athens, 7th ult., having experienced a favorable passage. We took carriage and drove to Athens, five miles distant, over a beautiful road, skirted with poplar and pepper trees.

LORENZO SNOW.

LETTER LXXIX.

Palestine Tour Completed — Beyrout—Constantinople— Reminiscences of Crimean War—The Piræus—Athens, Ancient and Modern.

ATHENS, GREECE, April 12th, 1873.

EDITOR OGDEN JUNCTION:

Presuming that you feel a kindly interest in the progress of President Smith and party, I take the liberty of dropping you a few hasty lines—the gentlemen being too much engaged otherwise.

We completed our Palestine tour, arriving at Beyrout on the 21st of March, after having experienced the comforts and discomforts of tent life twenty-nine days and horseback riding twenty-one. We were two weeks earlier than common tourists, and, as the season proved, much to our advantage. Had we ordered the weather to suit our particular circumstances, it could not have been more favorable. Most of the storm was in the night, and our tents were sufficiently protective to meet emergencies. One forenoon was rainy at intervals, which, with the exception of one slight shower, was all the storm we had when out; and the temperature was just the thing for horsemanship, with, in two or three instances, slight specimens of the scorching heat that late tourists must undergo. We were told that where we beheld fresh, luxuriant herbage, six weeks later would present nothing but dry, parched and crisped vegetation.

Beyrout is quite an improvement on all the towns and

cities of Palestine and Syria we have seen. It contains many fine buildings, and some of its streets are, at least, respectable. There the mulberry is extensively cultivated, and this city has superseded Damascus in silk manufactures.

On the 25th we left for Constantinople, where we arrived on the 1st of April, having passed the islands of Cyprus, on which we had a view of Mount Parnassus, the ancient site of the celebrated Temple of Venus—Rhodes, Cos, and Scio—Samos, the birthplace of Pythagoras, and, for a long time, the residence of Herodotus, and where he composed most of his history. The steamer anchored at Smyrna, which afforded us a short visit to that place of Bible celebrity.

Constantinople, with its Golden Horn and the Bosphorus, with their ship-crowned bosoms, is magnificent, and occupies a position of which any earthly monarch might be proud as a site for a capital. It has a splendid harbor, but like all Eastern ports is destitute of a landing—probably this seeming negligence on the part of the Government is a policy for the support of the boatmen of the eighty thousand small boats or gondolas that ply on these waters. We were told that a somewhat similar protective system exists in Constantinople in behalf of the water-carriers, *i. e.* a tax on aqueducts, cisterns, pipes, &c., for the general supply of water.

The city and environs, including Constantinople proper, Pera, Gallatin and Sophana, these three being on the opposite side of the Golden Horn, contain one million and seventy-five thousand inhabitants—many very large and beautiful buildings, but the streets, after the order of those in Palestine, a sheer disgrace. We had a fine view of the exterior of the Sultan's Palace, which is very attractive—the style, though very ornamental, is exceedingly chaste. It stands on the shore of the Bosphorus, opposite Scutari. The city is liberally ornamented with mosques, domes and minarets, the usual diadems of Turkish towns, and is also much beautified with many tall cypress trees; most of them are in the burial places, it being here a Moslem requisition that both at the birth and death of a child a tree shall be planted, which accounts for the multiplicity which decorate this city.

We left on the morning of the 5th, and as the steamer clipped its way into the broad waters, I stood on the upper deck, and as I took a most delightful view of the city and surroundings, my attention was attracted to the Asiatic side, where, in full view, stands the immense barracks, which, during the Crimean war, was used for a hospital, and in which Miss Nightingale performed those benevolent nursing services for which she has been justly celebrated.

Early on the morning of the 7th the steamer cast anchor in front of the Grecian Piræus, and, as usual, we were rowed ashore, took carriage, and rode five miles to the beautiful city of Athens, which, once a place of great renown, sank into obscurity, weltering under the hand of oppression, but recently has been so far restored as to present altogether the appearance of a fine European city. We are informed that the rebuilding of Athens has been done mostly by Germans, who constitute most of the present foreign population.

We have seen some grand ruins—enough to give a person of large and active imaginative powers a *faint* idea of the wonderful magnificence, beauty and splendor of ancient Athens.

ELIZA R. SNOW.

LETTER LXXX.

The following is a portion of a letter from President George A. Smith to a member of his family—

Sunday at Sea—The Austrian Lloyd Steamers—An Immense Ship of war—Leave for Verona—The Quadrilateral—Field of Solferino—Tomb of Romeo.

HOTEL AU GRAND PARIS, VERONA,
Italy, April 20th, 1873.

We were five days on the waters between Athens and Trieste; we spent all day Sunday on the steamer in the harbor of Syra, waiting for the arrival of the *Jupiter* from Constantinople, and changed to it late in the evening; it was dark and the water somewhat rough, and the process of changing steamers in a small boat was somewhat difficult, but was made without accident.

We have had exceeding fine weather at sea, being altogether some fifteen days since we left Brindisi *en route* for Egypt, and I feel to speak well of the Austrian Lloyd steamers, slow and poking as they go, paddle, paddle, they carry us safely around. For about fourteen hours after I left Syra I was sea-sick, after which my disposition to cast up accounts ceased; this was caused by a fresh breeze ahead. We spent one day at Trieste, partly rainy, in visiting the wonders of that commercial port of the Austrian Empire. A number of steamers and a great number of sailing vessels are constantly there. The Austrian government is building an immense ship of war, the largest of her navy, which looks like a floating palace, and seems to be a heavy drain on the Imperial treasury to very little purpose. The streets are well paved, mostly with good square stone blocks, which contrast finely with the rough, narrow, ill paved streets of Turkish cities. Our hotel de ville was good, but we had to go up five flights of marble steps to the last floor, they saying they had to put us there because they had 300 guests. We visited an old cathedral very richly furnished and decorated, the columns being clothed in red velvet jackets. We also visited an old Roman tower, a collection of marbles recently dug out of the ground, the dockyard of the Austrian Lloyd's Company, where was the iron frame of a large steamer in course of construction. This company are said to have 80 steamships afloat, and purpose increasing to 100.

On the morning of the 19th we took car for Verona, passed through a very delightful country in a high state of cultivation, producing a great variety of choice things. It seemed a pleasant change to again get on a railroad; we had to change cars twice during the day, and at one station had our baggage examined by the custom officers of Victor Emanuel; they were very polite and gave us as little trouble as possible consistent with their duties. We have had no occasion to find fault with the treatment of customs officers during our journey, and I have only once been asked to show my passport, which was on landing in Egypt.

Ever since I landed in Palestine I have been exceedingly free from colds, affections of the throat, and rheumatic affection in my shoulder and arm, of which I complained last winter, in Utah; the affection of the throat that I complained of at Corfu soon passed away. Sight-seeing is hard work, and I am heavy, and tire out without being able to accomplish as much as I would like to. It takes considerable time to form acquaintance with the people and institutions of any country we visit, and on that account our acquaintance is necessarily limited.

This place is one of the four which were at the angles

of what was termed the "quadrilateral;" it was anciently fortified by the Roman emperors; portions of their walls and gates remain to the present. In 1815 it was in possession of the Austrians, who fortified it with the greatest care and skill they possessed. From a hill in a highly cultivated garden we had a view of the positions of these forts, which seem to have done them very little good in maintaining their supremacy in Italy. In plain sight from the hill was the field of Solferino, where Napoleon III and Francis Joseph of Austria contested in a great battle, engaging some 400,000 men on both sides; the result ceded this region to Victor Emanuel, and it now belongs to the kingdom of Italy. We also had a view of another great battle field of 1866, between the Austrians and Italians, and though the Austrians were victorious, the Italians, being the allies of Prussia, secured as the result of this campaign, the cession of Venetia, and Italian unity. We visited the old Roman amphitheatre, a large portion of which is still preserved; the marble seats now remaining would seat over 20,000 people, and when perfect it was said to accommodate, sitting and standing, some 75,000; it is said to have been built somewhere between A. D. 80 and 284. We have also visited several fine gardens, in one of them was said to be the tomb of Romeo, the fabled hero of one of Shakespere's plays.

We take rail for Munich, in the morning.

GEORGE A. SMITH.

LETTER LXXXI.

At Athens—Classical Ruins—Peculiar Customs Among the Greeks—Funeral Ceremony.

MUNICH, BAVARIA, April 22nd, 1873.

EDITOR DESERET NEWS:

I wrote you last, on our arrival at Athens. The whole of that modern city has been built within the last forty-five years. It is situated about five miles from the sea, on the Plain of Attica. Many of the buildings possess some architectural beauty, which, combined with their yellow-washed stucco, present an agreeable and lively appearance. Olive groves, the scene of Plato's meditations, stretching along the plain, the trees and shrubbery in the Queen's garden, an orange grove fronting the King's Palace, pepper trees skirting the boulevards, a few cypresses and Italian poplars, form the principal foliage which is seen in and around Athens. The Queen's garden attached to the Palace is a beautiful enclosure of several acres, extending along the boulevards, and partially encircling the Palace, and adorned with rich shrubbery, flower-beds, luxurious foliage, grass-plats, artificial waters, and winding gravel walks. Fronting the palace, is a small, enclosed area decorated with orange trees, in the centre is a fine fountain surrounded with seats for the convenience of promenaders. The trees were constantly dropping their golden fruit here and there, on the gravelly walks, but left untouched by the multitude of pedestrians. The King's Palace is the most conspicuous building in Athens. It is located on a gently rising eminence at the foot of Mount Lycabettis, and facing what is termed the "Square of the Constitution." On this square, September, 1843, the people and troops assembled, and continued ten hours without any act of violence, waiting for King Otho to grant the request of their leaders in signing the Constitutional Charter, to which, at last, he reluctantly consented. The front of the Palace has a portico constructed of marble—the walls of the building are composed of broken limestone faced with cement.

The Acropolis is a vast rock, rising to the height of three hundred and fifty feet above the plain, with a flat summit, about one thousand feet long by five hundred broad. The Areopagus, or Hill of Mars, is a lower eminence, forming a kind of offshoot to the Acropolis. The remains of the celebrated Temple of Jupiter Olympus occupy a broad square of ground a little eastward of the Acropolis. Fifteen Corinthian columns of immense size are now standing, out of one hundred and twenty-four, which formerly covered a space of three hundred and fifty-four feet, by a breadth of one hundred and seventy-one feet. These marble columns are fifty-five feet in height, and six feet four inches in diameter. One of the marble beams, supported by these gigantic columns, is said to weigh twenty-three tons. We noticed one of the pillars which had been thrown down in a high wind—it is formed of eighteen sections. It is estimated that three thousand dollars would be required to set up these sections, and restore the pillar to an upright position, which will afford a faint idea of the cost of erecting the entire building.

We ascended the Acropolis to inspect its stupendous and melancholy ruins. When it stood in the fulness of its splendor, the whole summit was occupied with temples, sanctuaries, statuary and monuments—only sufficient now remain to show their former grandeur and magnificence.

There were the marble temples of Minerva, Propylaca, Wingless Victory, the Erectheum and the Parthenon—also gigantic statues of Grecian deities, from forty to sixty feet in height, on lofty pedestals decorated with ivory and gold, glistening in the sunlight. Some of these colossal statues could be seen from the decks of vessels, standing a long distance out at sea. A few massive columns of temples are seen sustaining huge marble beams, over twenty feet in length. In the Propylacan Temple, quantities of black marble were used in its construction, and, the same as other heathen sanctuaries, was adorned with costly paintings and historical decorations. The entire expense of this building has been estimated at about two and a half millions of dollars. The Parthenon is built entirely of marble, and is two hundred and twenty-eight feet long, by one hundred and one broad. Its ceiling is supported the same as that of the Propylacan, by huge marble beams, resting on massive columns. One of the door-ways is thirty-three feet in height and sixteen feet wide; the head of the door-way is formed of marble lintels, nearly twenty-seven feet in length. The Erectheum has a number of standing columns, supporting massive marble beams and lintels over door-ways; most of this temple, however, lies in a heap of superb ruins. The frieze of this building was composed of black marble, adorned with figures in low relief, in white marble. The surface of the Acropolis is mostly spread with ruins, broken pillars, pieces of entablatures and sculptured fragments.

The Greeks have some very peculiar customs. When, after a lengthy absence, friends meet, or when parting for a considerable time, it is usual to kiss one another on the cheek. I have noticed in Athens, the same as in Italy, two gentlemen meeting on the public street, with hats off, demonstrating their affection by hugging and kissing each other in the most violent manner. Many of the Greeks have a habit of carrying in the hand strings of glass or wooden beads, which they manipulate or work with their fingers, while walking the streets, or in conversation, the same as the gentleman his watchguard, or twirls his cane, or the lady flirts her fan, having no religious reference, as the Catholic in counting his beads.

It is customary to make the sign of the cross in the following manner: Uniting the tips of the thumb and first two fingers of the right hand, and touching alternately the forehead, navel, right breast and left breast, three times in rapid succession, whenever passing a church, seeing the cross, or hearing the name of the Saviour spoken. They have a singular form for burying the dead. I witnessed the ceremony of burying two persons, who apparently had occupied respectable positions in society. The processions were preceded by boys in white robes, carrying a crucifix and other ecclesiastic insignia of considerable splendor, followed by priests, chanting in a low, monotonous, melancholy tone, while all hats were off, and every hand was making the sign of the cross, as the solemn train was passing along the crowded thoroughfare; the corpse, with ghastly features exposed to full view in an open coffin, covered with white cloth, variously decorated; the lid of the coffin painted with a large cross was carried along in the procession, in an upright position. The corpse was dressed in the clothing customarily worn while living; the head partially elevated, and the hands folded in front of a picture of the Virgin, placed on his breast.

Returning from the Museum, we met the King of Greece, who was walking leisurely along the sidewalk, among the citizens, dressed in plain, ordinary costume. His appearance is rather prepossessing; his figure is slight—of medium size, light complexion, and eyes expressive of both kindness and determination. He has the reputation of honesty and frankness—without affectation, and his domestic life above reproach, and makes the welfare and improvement of his people a direct aim and constant study. He is about twenty-eight years of age—married the daughter of the Grand Duke Constantine of Russia, and has a family.

The Greek Church and Greek nation may be considered synonymous words, as one cannot exist without the other, being interwoven like cotton and woollen threads in a garment. It is a strong prevailing feeling in the people, that, as the church cannot exist without the people, so the people cannot exist as a nation without the church. The banners of the Revolution were constantly blest by the Bishops, and among the first victims of that Revolution was the Greek Patriarch of Constantinople. In fact the first Article of the Constitution makes the Greek Church the corner stone of the political fabric. It is as follows: "The dominant religion of Greece is that of the Orthodox Oriental Church of Christ. All other recognized religions are tolerated, and the free exercise of worship is protected by law. Proselytism and all other interferences, prejudicial to the dominant religion, are forbidden." Therefore any attempt made by Protestants, in the way of proselyting, is regarded with suspicion.

President Smith called on Mr. Francis, the American Minister, who received him courteously, and requested him and party to spend an evening at his residence. We had a pleasant time with the Minister, his lady and son, also Mr. Goodenough, the Consul General of Constantinople, who was spending a few days in Athens. In conversation with these people, we gathered interesting items in reference to modern Greece, the king and government. Mr. Francis' fine abilities and conversational talent draw around him many visitors, especially Americans. Mrs. Francis is a lady of intelligence, of lively disposition and polite manners.

We left Athens on the evening of the 12th ult., on an Austrian Lloyd steamer for Trieste, Austria, where we arrived on the 17th, after a pleasant passage. This is a charming town, built in the form of a crescent, on rounded and conical hills and mountain acclivities. It is surrounded with beautiful scenery. The city has a population of about one hundred thousand. We were shown many objects of attraction and curiosity.

The 19th, we took train for Munich, the capital of Bavaria, through the Brenner Pass, by the way of Verona, a town in Italy. Our route led through an interesting country under an excellent state of tillage—the landscape covered with verdure, and rich in luxurious foliage, the apple, plum, apricot, cherry and chestnut adorned with blossoms, and the vine clothed with leaves, patches of clover, grain in full growth, green pastures and meadows, and off in the distance a long high range of mountains, with summits mantled in snow. We arrived at Verona in the evening and remained over Sunday.

The country from Verona to Munich is in the highest state of cultivation, abounding in fields of grain, vegetable gardens, fruit orchards, and vineyards; nearly the whole region is dotted with walnut, apple, cherry, apricot, plum and mulberry, the grapevine stretching from one tree to another, clinging to the branches, while below flourish luxuriant gardens, or waving grain. We passed over a narrow, winding vale, extending over seventy miles, skirted by lofty mountains, and adorned with towns and villages, and churches, here and there, on high plateaus above the plain; streamlets are seen now and then dashing and foaming over rocky steeps, producing cascades of great beauty and grandeur. We noticed images of the Saviour, nearly life-size, representing his crucifixion, and secured to posts placed here and there along the public road. Women were laboring in the fields, driving plow, spading ground, scattering manure, and some in tops of trees, trimming the branches.

Monday evening, 21st ult., we arrived in Munich.

LORENZO SNOW.

LETTER LXXXII.

Brigandage in Greece—The Classical Ruins of Athens—Leave the Piræus—The Austrian Lloyds—At Trieste—Verona—Ancient Roman Amphitheatre—The Tyrol—Munich.

Hotel Four Seasons, Munich, Bavaria,
April 22nd, 1873.

President Brigham Young:

Dear Brother—On the 10th inst. I wrote to you from Athens. We completed our visit to that memorable capital, and read up in the news received just as we were leaving Constantinople, and closed our correspondence to date. The Turks and Greeks have failed to agree on a plan to exterminate brigandage, as we learn from the Levant *Herald*, a paper published in English in Constantinople. The Greek government is doing all it can to make travel through the country safe. We were assured by the authorities that it was safe; that if we wished to visit the field of Marathon, Eleusis, the Straits of Thermopylæ, or Corinth, if we would give one day's notice, they would furnish a guard of soldiers free of cost. We saw proper not to run any risks, as we were told that the brigands had simply fled across the line into Turkey, and passed back and forward at their pleasure.

It is considered quite a treat to visit the Acropolis and other ruins by moonlight; the evening we visited the ruins the moon was nearly full, and shining clear and bright. The fifteen standing columns of Jupiter Olympus display their architectural modesty very soothingly to the eye by moonlight. The sixteenth column, which was blown down in 1852, or, as the guide said, was thrown down by an earthquake, was composed of fifteen pieces, and in all was some 58 feet high, and about six and a half in diameter. When the 124 pillars of this temple were all standing, the architrave in place and the marble roof in perfect order, as it was when completed and dedicated by the Emperor Hadrian, it must have been a magnificent structure; and it had been about 600 years in building. The view of the Acropolis by moonlight was very pleasant, as also the view of the city, which has been mostly rebuilt in the European style within the last 30 years. The Greek government keeps a night and day guard around these old temples, and is making numerous excavations in different parts of the city and vicinity, having disentombed parts of the ancient walls of the city, numerous burial places and tombs, baths, and the stadium of Lycurgus, discovering statues, monuments, and ornamental work, with inscriptions, from which they can determine dates, and the names of parties and other interesting facts. A building is in course of construction, into which it is designed to gather such of the more valuable of these marbles and other works of art into a national museum of antiquities, which will give additional advantage to the student of archæology.

Much of Greece would be very fruitful if it had rains, but it is a very dry and hot country in the summer, but said to be very pleasant during the winter. Where water can be procured for irrigation, it produces a great variety of choice fruits, vegetables, and ornamental trees.

We steamed from the harbor of Piræus on the evening of the 12th. We had a nice view of the Straits of Salamis, remembered as the site of the defeat of the fleet of Xerxes by the Greeks in the Persian war. We changed from the steamer *Wien*, at Syra, to the *Jupiter*, and at about midnight on the 17th we arrived at the *Hotel de Ville* in Trieste, Austria. The Austrian Lloyd steamers, in which we have traveled since leaving Brindisi, Italy, are slow, but safe and well conducted. Although that company run eighty steamships, many of them large, all freight and passengers are put on and off in small boats and barges, which is a slow process, and very disagreeable and often dangerous to passengers when the sea is rough. We should have gone ashore at Cyprus and other points, had it not been for the danger of being upset. Our steaming upon the Adriatic, Mediterranean, Ionian, Ægean, Archipelago, and the Sea of Marmora and their tributaries was about fifteen days.

On arriving at Trieste we received the *Weekly News* of March 5th, 12th, and 19th, and a *Herald* of the 22nd with letters from our families. On the 18th we drove through that commercial town, which shows manifest signs of prosperity and a live business, it being the principal commercial outlet of the Austrian Empire, and is said to contain 105,000 inhabitants.

On the 19th we traveled through a very fine country, highly cultivated, to Verona, in Italy, where we spent the Sabbath. Verona is one of the four fortified places formerly termed the quadrilateral, and is fortified for miles with every skilful device that the military engineers of Austria could suggest, and was supposed to be impregnable. From a high point, in a beautiful garden in the city, we saw the field upon which was fought the battle of Solferino, which resulted in transferring all these forts to the newly formed kingdom of Italy. The country is very handsome, fertile and well tilled. We visited a Roman amphitheatre about 1,700 years old, which still contains seats of Verona marble sufficient to accommodate over 20,000 people, and when complete must have been ample, including standing room, to accommodate 70,000. The gates of the ancient city, portions of the wall, and some old palaces also remain of the Roman works. The town now contains less than 70,000 inhabitants, but its complication of forts, walls, arsenals, barracks, magazines, embankments, palaces, and churches renders it a place of considerable interest.

Our journey from that place to this was accomplished in seventeen hours by rail up the river Adige and its tributaries over the Tyrolese Alps at the Brenner Pass, and down the river Inn and its tributaries. The road is excellent, the cars comfortable, and the route naturally very favorable for a road over so mountainous a region. The beauty of the mountain scenery would reward a lover of the picturesque for a journey through it, as it contains rich and highly cultivated valleys and mountain sides until they are so steep as to make it necessary to stake the soil down or terrace it, above which an immense forest of timber is crowned with snow. Numerous cascades and waterfalls add beauty and variety to the scenery.

While in Greece I was conversing with some gentlemen who spoke English, in relation to the Americans and English sending missionaries there to convert them. They enquired, "Why don't they send their missionaries to the heathen, and convert them to Christ? We are Christians already, and what sense is there in their spending their time and money to convert us over again? We are agreed now and have one religion, and that the ancient Greek Church. If we follow these American and English missionaries, we shall have no religion and be in dispute with each other, and what good can that all do us?" According to the provisions of the Greek constitution no person has a right to proselyte from the Greek Church; all have a right to enjoy their faith, and teach it to any one not of the Greek Church; but as all Greek children are baptized into the Greek Church, the field for missionary labor in that kingdom is very limited.

I visited St. Paul's Church, which is the cathedral of that kingdom, and is a new and handsome building. Though small in comparison with St. Peter's in Rome, it contrasts favorably with it in not being infested by beggars.

Sister Schettler, wife of Paul A., came to our hotel to-day; she had been visiting her friends for about two weeks, and is in good health and spirits.

Munich is a live city, the streets are clean, well paved, and many of them wide and handsome. It contains many public edifices, all permanent, and many of them handsome buildings. Its public institutions are numerous, with ample pleasure grounds and groves around it. Bavaria is a Catholic kingdom, Louis II its ruler, but it forms a prominent part of the newly organized German Empire. School buildings, and buildings for universities and seminaries of learning are numerous. Hospitals, museums, libraries and theatres, on a grand scale, are also here. Roman Catholic churches are numerous, and many of them are quite ornamental and, we are told, rich in relics.

GEORGE A. SMITH.

LETTER LXXXIII.

Constantinople—Island of Syra—Athens—The Acropolis—The Areopagus—Visit the American Minister—Trieste—Verona—Munich.

Munich, Bavaria, April 22nd, 1873.

Editor Woman's Exponent:

Constantinople, with its many waters and variegated land scenery—combining beauty and commercial advantages, surpasses all other locations I have ever seen. From an outside view, as we beheld it from the steamer's upper deck, before, and at sunrise, one cloudless morning, when the atmosphere was clear of smoke, this great capital of Turkey is magnificently beautiful. But, like most eastern cities, in consequence of narrow, crooked, filthy streets, it will not bear an intimate acquaintance. It contains many fine edifices, of which its many minaretted mosques are considered its greatest ornament; and to a Saint of God, who understands that He accepts no church, mosque or temple, unless built by his special direction, these are of little or no interest, only as a matter of curiosity. The tall, graceful, dark green cypress trees, of which there are great numbers, especially in the burial grounds of Constantinople, add much to the picturesque scenery, and are highly valued as being productive of health, by absorbing malarious effluvia from the atmosphere.

I was interested, and much amused with the novelty of the bazars—so very unlike anything I had seen. In the first place, you enter a narrow street or defile, with rows of small shops with open fronts, ranged along on each side, with articles for sale on shelves at the back and sides, and strung up in front—a vendor standing in the center, ready to wait on you. After going a short distance, other alleys or lanes lead off in various directions, then others branch out from them, and so on, till, without a pilot, you may be entirely lost in a forest of bazars, and your sight bewildered with their dazzling displays.

The exterior of the Grand Sultan's Palace is a rare specimen of taste, chaste beauty and elegance.

On the 5th of April, again on the upper deck of the steamer *Mars*, I took a farewell view of the Turkish capital, while its hills and dells, minarets, domes, towers and masts faded in the distance, as well as that immense structure on the coast of Asia Minor, celebrated as the place where Florence Nightingale bestowed her womanly and heroic aid in behalf of the sick, wounded and dying.

Near the shore of the beautiful Island of Syra, we changed steamers, and on the morning of the 7th, landed at

Piræus—took carriage—rode five miles, which brought us to the city of Athens. I am not an enthusiastic admirer of ruins, and time-worn relics of what is dead and obsolete, especially when they have no possible bearing upon present progress, yet, in spite of my positive predilections, my attention was strongly rivetted to some of the stupendous remains of the ancient splendor and magnificence of a city that figured so much in the classics and political history of Greece.

But, as I am not a professional archæologist, I shall leave the description to others. While visiting the Acropolis, on the lofty height of the plateau, a natural enormous rock foundation of the original Athens, we had a charming view of the present.

Anciently the Areopagus, or "Mars Hill," was a judgment seat, where the most important civil and ecclesiastical cases were tried and sentences pronounced. On this hill the Apostle Paul stood and addressed the people. I almost fancied him occupying that strikingly peculiar position—in close proximity to, and almost surrounded by temples of the greatest possible brilliancy, dedicated to, and containing vast numbers of, those venerated deities, the very gods which he repudiated in the audience of their worshippers; boldly telling his idolatrous hearers that "God dwelleth not in temples made with hands"—" we ought not to think that the Godhead is like unto gold, or silver, or stone, graven by art and man's device," etc.

We were invited to tea at the residence of the American Minister, Mr. Francis, and lady, where also we met Mr. Goodenough, American Consul General to Constantinople, and spent a couple of hours very sociably and agreeably. We saw George First, King of Greece, on the sidewalk, in plain citizen costume and were told that he is doing all in his power to better the condition of the people. His wife, Olga, is niece of the Czar, Alexander II, of Russia, thus uniting Danish and Russian element.

We left Athens on the 12th, arrived by steamer at Trieste, Austria, the 17th; at Verona, Italy, the 19th, and on the 21st at Munich, Bavaria.

Of all sight-seeing and entertainments, nothing has pleased us more than the packages of letters and papers which we met at Constantinople and Trieste, from Utah, informing us of "home, sweet home."

ELIZA R. SNOW.

LETTER LXXXIV.

The Nile—Heliopolis—Goshen—Red Sea—Holy Places—Sea of Galilee—River Jordan—Mountain of the Temptation.

Hotel Four Seasons, Bavaria,
April 22nd, 1873.

Elder John Taylor:

Dear Brother:—Your very welcome favor of March 3rd, per hands of Mrs. Little, was handed to me this morning by Mrs. Schettler, and read with much gratification.

I recognize, with yourself, the hand of the Lord in directing the channels of means, and doubt not he orders all things well. It would have afforded me much pleasure to have had you accompany me in my travels.

We are pleased to learn that so many are disposed to do right, and hope those who are worldly-minded will at once be disposed to reconsider their ways.

Our want of time and lack of knowledge of the languages of the peoples visited, of necessity curtailed our facilities for becoming very conversant with their customs and institutions.

We went up the Nile no further than Heliopolis, where a beautiful obelisk is all that remains, except tumuli and fragments. This place is said to be On, the residence of my great grandfather Potiphar, priest of On, and that obelisk is said to be one of the monuments of his temple. I took pleasure in the reflection that Asenath, the wife of Joseph and the mother of his race, walked over that ground, and looked upon that obelisk when Egypt was in its glory; and being of the family of Joseph, my interest on that occasion was intense. I presume we passed over the land of Goshen, and that we visited the Red Sea near the spot where Pharaoh was destroyed. I have but little confidence in the grouping by Helena, of the identical holy places within the walls of the Church of the Holy Sepulchre, but I have little doubt that we saw the top of Mount Moriah. We had a pleasant ride on the Sea of Galilee, and I was baptized for my health in the Jordan, where it is said John baptized the Saviour, and near where Joshua is supposed to have crossed with the children of Israel. I saw the mountain upon which our guide said the devil took the Saviour when he showed him all the kingdoms of the world and the glory of them. I did not feel enough interested to ascend it, and if I had I would not have seen all of Palestine.

Brother and Sister Snow, and Brother Carrington, unite with me in our hearty God bless you for ever and ever, and all Israel.

GEORGE A. SMITH.

LETTER LXXXV.

At Munich—Visit to a Kindergarten—Employments and Pastimes of the Children—Contrast between Children of Germany and France—Convenience of the Kindergartens.

Munich, Bavaria, April 25th, 1873.

Editor Juvenile Instructor:

I wrote you a description of one of the schools we visited in Paris. In that letter I promised to write you again when I had seen one of the German kindergarten schools; and now I have taken up my pen to fulfill that promise.

Mr. Geirisch, the gentlemanly brother of Sister Paul A. Schettler, who is here on a visit to her relatives, and now with us, obtained a card of admission from the Department, and President Smith and party, yesterday, visited one of the many Universities in this city. The one referred to is a normal school, expressly for educating ladies for teachers, with the kindergarten school attached. We are informed that the city of Munich is divided into districts, like the Wards in Salt Lake City, and that each district contains one of these kindergartens, and some of them are very large. I counted upwards of thirty in the one we visited—boys and girls, from three to six years of age.

They were not apprised of our visit, and when the porter opened the door for us to enter, the children were singing and marching, two and two, hand in hand—the matron, an amiable-looking lady, walking before them. As soon as we entered they halted in silence, till we had positions assigned and then, the lady going in front, a little rosy-cheeked, laughing boy followed as file leader, and the rest, two and two, hand in hand, resumed their march, stepping as true to time as a well disciplined body of soldiers, and occasionally changing time, by the matron's dictation, without the least disorder. In the course of the march, on intimation of the matron, they united their sweet infantile voices in harmonious singing, in their own language, which we did not understand.

When the marching exercise ended, they all repaired to their seats, and each was presented with his and her labelled portfolio, which the matron took out from a drawer which constituted a portion of a sideboard, the upper part of which was of glass, exhibiting specimens of the children's work in almost endless variety. The portfolios were neat and simple, made of blue pasteboard, each containing little specimens of industry, the unfinished piece of work, on which they severally were soon busied.

Some were weaving paper of different colors, some perforating white pasteboard in various delicate patterns, one little boy was intently at work, perforating a lamp shade, of which the design was beautiful, and, so far as completed, very accurately executed. Some were working with wool, others with silk; and what must be a great stimulus to these children, is, their work is not useless—they are all, even the least of them, working for a purpose. Whatever their piece of work, when it is completed, it is converted into something of real value, either for use, or for ornament. The lady informed us that many articles, made by these tiny artists and manufacturers, had been sent to Vienna for exhibition.

Our time was limited, and we did not hear their exercises in reading and spelling; but were shown their tiny, miniature gardening implements, consisting of hoes, spades, shovels, rakes, wheelbarrows, etc. The day being stormy, the children were all in, but we were told that in fine weather they are much out in their little garden, adjoining the school-room.

After six years of age, these children are removed into other and higher departments, and, as in France, the boys and girls are educated separately.

We noticed a striking difference between these and the little ones we saw at school in Paris, as it regards healthfulness of appearance these are robust and ruddy, with none of the sallow complexion and delicate, thin features of the Parisians.

These children are under immediate tuition five hours of the day, three in forenoon and two afternoon, but they are all day in care of the matron, who relieves the mother of all responsibility of charge, and she can go out to work during the day, if circumstances require her to do so, without any encumbrance or anxiety. Not only the poor, but many wealthy parents avail themselves of having their little ones kindly cared for and trained by these skilful matrons. The rosy-cheeked boy, who led in the march we witnessed, is son of the proprietor of this great hotel in which I am writing.

ELIZA R. SNOW.

LETTER LXXXVI.

Munich—Visit to a Royal Palace—Statue of Bavaria—Imperial Wedding—Vienna—The Arsenal—Summer Palace—The Great Exhibition.

VIENNA, AUSTRIA, May 6th, 1873.

EDITOR DESERET NEWS:

We spent a few days very pleasantly, and I hope profitably, in Munich, the capital of Bavaria. Our hotel accommodations, politeness of host, and the attention of servants, has been nowhere excelled. The general appearance of the people in respect to style of dress, their moral character and education, will bear comparison with that of the first cities in other European countries. The streets, public gardens, parks and squares, possess many attractions, but unfortunately the weather was unpropitious for the full appreciation of sight-seeing.

Munich is situated in a barren plain, upon both sides of the river Iser. It contains about one hundred and seventy-five thousand inhabitants, and is considered the fourth city in Germany in point of population. Many of its parks, squares, and public gardens are adorned with fountains, lawns, shrubbery, cascades, grottoes, equestrian figures and colossal statues. In one of these squares is a large obelisk, erected in honor of the Bavarians who were slain in the Russian campaign of 1812, bearing the inscription, "To the thirty thousand Bavarians who perished in the Russian war; erected by Louis First, King of Bavaria, completed Oct. 18, 1833. They died for the deliverance of the country." The park, called the English Garden, nearly five miles long by a half mile in width, is ornamented at vast labor and expense. We visited the Royal Palace, and spent some two hours in walking through the imperial apartments, inspecting the numerous objects of interest and curiosity—the Audience Hall, embellished with twelve portraits of Roman Emperors; the Green Gallery, with a great number of Dutch and Italian paintings; The Bed-chamber, containing curtains of gold brocade, valued at the enormous sum of four hundred thousand dollars; and the Mirror Room, adorned with precious vases of gold and silver, together with chandeliers of immense value. Also the Hall of Marriages, appropriately decorated with fresco work; the Hall of the Emperors, adorned with paintings by the most celebrated masters; the Hall of Charlemagne, with numerous pictures of gigantic size, commemorative of the most remarkable events in his life. The Throne Hall is one hundred and sixty feet long, and seventy-three wide, ornamented on either side by twelve

Corinthian columns of white marble, supporting galleries. Between these columns are twelve statues of princes in gilded bronze, each of which weighs nearly one and a half tons—the simple cost of gilding was about twelve hundred dollars each.

The Royal Library is a very beautiful building, comprising seventy-seven rooms, in which are contained more than eight hundred thousand volumes. The Royal Bronze Foundry is much celebrated—monuments have been cast in this foundry for nearly all parts of the world.

In the south-west of the city, on an eminence, in a large meadow, stands the colossal statue of Bavaria. It is placed upon a basement, which is ascended by a flight of forty-eight steps—the height of the statue itself is thirty-two and a half feet, and pedestal twenty-eight and a half. This female statue represents the Protectress of Bavaria, with a lion at her side. In her right hand she holds a sword, and in her left a chaplet. This immense statue was cast at the Royal Foundry. The interior of the figure contains a staircase of sixty-six steps, which ascend through the pedestal to the height of the knees, and from thence by a spiral stair to the head, within which eight persons can be seated.

One day, hearing that the king, with his suite and royal equipage, was out on an imperial wedding, I set forward, on foot, in company with my sister, to witness the immense attraction, which was drawing all Munich into the streets by tens of thousands. Having submitted to half an hour's journeying, pressing and smashing, by the patriotic and enthusiastic citizens of Munich, finally we secured the honor of gazing a moment on the passing pomp and glory of His Royal Majesty the King of Bavaria, and occupying a point toward which he *smiled* and *civilly bowed*. After narrowly escaping being trodden down by the crowd, I returned to my hotel, wondering how much mathematical skill or philosophical wisdom would be required to determine the exact value of what was gained by this exposure.

We left Munich on the morning of the 29th, and arrived in Vienna by train, the following evening. Vienna, the capital of Austria, is situated at the foot of the Vienna Mountain, in a plain, near the right bank of the Danube. It contains a population of about eight hundred thousand.

A boulevard encircles the city, planted with trees, and bordered with very elegant buildings, and beautiful gardens. The city exhibits some very remarkable edifices—the Castle, Cathedral of St. Stephen's, Imperial Palace, and many palatial residences of ministers and ambassadors. The suburbs of the city are very populous, containing many splendid edifices, fine promenades, and ornamental gardens. Many of the squares are decorated with various statues and monuments, displaying great skill in design and execution; among these is an equestrian statue of the Emperor Joseph III, who is represented on horseback, stretching out his hand, and blessing the people. Also an equestrian statue of the Arch-Duke Charles, erected in 1860—he is represented at the battle of Aspern, in the attitude of raising the flag, to lead the grenadiers to the attack. Also the Column of the Trinity, erected in 1679, on the cessation of the plague. This column is composed of white Salsburg marble, and is over seventy feet high; on the pedestal is a rock, upholding Religion, a cherub, overcoming the Master of the Plague, also some bass-reliefs, representing incidents of sacred history. The Emperor appears in the attitude of kneeling on the summit of the column, and angels rising toward heaven. Another very fine monument, built by Charles VI, consists of a canopy, sustained by Corinthian columns, beneath which is a group, representing the marriage of the Virgin. We noticed, in various parts of the city, many splendid fountains, fine bridges, broad, well paved streets, bordered with linden and chestnut, and skirted with magnificent buildings; and in the city and suburbs, many ornamented squares, public gardens and extensive parks.

Vienna has numerous cathedrals, some of which are fine specimens of Gothic architecture. The Church of the Saviour is an elegant structure, decorated in Gothic style—built in commemoration of an attempt to destroy the life of Francis Joseph, in the year 1853. The first stone was laid by the Emperor, which was obtained from the Mount of Olives, in Palestine, in 1856.

We visited the Imperial Arsenal, considered one of the grandest buildings in Vienna; it is very extensive and surrounded by ornamental grounds. It comprises numerous workshops, foundries, machine shops, and a Museum of Arms, containing specimens of weapons of all periods; artillery of brass and iron, and vast quantities of projectiles. It has nine steam engines, and two thousand men are kept employed within the buildings. It casts eighty cannons per day, and usually makes a run two days in a week.

The Imperial Summer Palace, a short distance from the city, is charmingly located beside a large public park, encircled by ornamental grounds, and has an orangery of seven hundred and forty trees, and a grand parterre, decorated with thirty-two statues, and a large basin, with two splendid fountains. The palace contains fifteen hundred chambers.

Of late years, great alterations and improvements have been made in Vienna, by tearing down old fortifications, erecting public buildings, straightening and widening streets and thoroughfares, and multiplying, enlarging and ornamenting public grounds.

We have spent some days in the buildings of the great exhibition. Everything in relation to it is upon the most magnificent scale; but I presume another month will be requisite to complete the arrangements to get the articles for exhibition unboxed and in their appropriate places. At present, great confusion exists in nearly every part of the buildings. It is supposed that it will exceed, in splendor, variety, extent, perfection of articles, correctness of arrangement, magnificence and universality, any previous exhibition. For the present, however, I will defer observations on this subject.

In Austria, as in all other countries which we have visited, soldiers, in military costume, are seen almost everywhere, in great numbers.

Perhaps you are weary of these descriptions of what we are seeing in the world—gorgeous churches, museums, picture galleries, mosques, zoological gardens, relics, ruins, antiquities, crumbling temples, statuary, obelisks, sumptuous palaces, odd customs, singular manners of people, religious fanaticisms, trickery and impostures, &c., but in sight-seeing we are confined within the limits of what the pride and vanity of the world have labored to exhibit, rather than what, in many instances, we should have preferred seeing. It would have been more gratifying to record our inspection of systems, on magnificent and universal scales, designed to remove poverty and distress, which, to a greater or less extent, everywhere prevail; and to give all an opportunity, irrespective of creeds, geographical lines or nationalities, of providing for their own wants and comforts, and of elevating themselves to the highest spiritual, physical, moral, and intellectual plane.

LORENZO SNOW.

LETTER LXXXVII.

Stormy Weather—No Beggars—Royal Marriage—Instruments of Torture—Visit the American Legation.

HOTEL KLOMSER, VIENNA, AUSTRIA, April 30th, 1873.

PRESIDENT BRIGHAM YOUNG:

DEAR BROTHER:—While we remained in Bavaria we had a constant series of storms, rain and snow, which reminded us that we were in latitude 48 N., materially abridging chances for sight-seeing and forming acquaintances.

About 11 p. m. of the 28th, Brothers Erastus Snow and his son E. W., W. C. Staines, J. G. Bleak and Joseph Birch arrived at our hotel in Munich.

There is one Protestant church building in Munich, all the rest are Catholic, and religious matters are held with a very tight rein in Bavaria.

I was informed by Mr. Geirisch, Brother Schettler's brother-in-law, that nearly all the people in Bavaria lived on rye bread and beer; but few could afford cheese, and very few meat.

The streets of Munich are clear of beggars; I am told it is a result of police regulations. A great many women work in the fields as farm laborers. In several instances I saw hale-looking women drawing loaded wagons in the streets of Munich; one span were drawing water, another a load of flour sacks, others were drawing single drays.

On the 28th, Prince Leopold arrived in Munich with his bride; a highly ornamented carriage, drawn by six horses in gilded harness, was in waiting to receive them at the station. One or two regiments of infantry and some horsemen escorted them to a public square, where they were received by the magistrates. The square and streets for a mile were crowded with gaping citizens. All the public buildings and many of the private ones were ornamented with flags. They were escorted to rooms in the royal palace, prepared by his bachelor cousin, King Louis II, for their reception. He is a general in the Bavarian army, and served in the Bavarian army in the late Franco-Prussian war.

The Hotel Four Seasons, at Munich, is one of the largest, finest and best conducted we have been in. I believe all the public improvements we have visited are very substantial, and but few in any way gaudy.

The railroad and cars from Munich to this city are good, and the business is well conducted.

The normal school in Munich is not superior to the one I last year visited in Potsdam, New York, but is really a very fine school, annually turning out thirty teachers.

A collection of instruments of torture in the National Museum were enough to curdle a man's blood; they were doubtless the invention of men professing to be the servants of Christ.

I visited the American Legation this morning. The weather is cold and unpleasant; it has been raining and snowing.

T. W. Jennings is with us. Mrs. Schettler remained in Munich with her friends. Brother L. Snow and Eliza, and Brother Carrington are here and well.

GEORGE A. SMITH.

LETTER LXXXVIII.

Principal German Cities—the King's Palace—A Famous Glass Factory—Glass Window Curtains—Visit the Universities—Marriage Festivities—Vienna and Its Great Exhibition—"No Place Like Home."

VIENNA, AUSTRIA, May 4th, 1873.

EDITOR WOMAN'S EXPONENT:

DEAR LULA:—My last was written after our arrival in Munich, which, after Berlin, Vienna and Hamburg, is first of importance in the German Empire, and contains about one hundred and seventy-five thousand inhabitants. It is a handsome, live city—has many beautiful buildings, and some wide, clean, well-paved streets and side-walks. This is the place of nativity of Mrs. Paul A. Schettler, whom we had the pleasure of meeting here, she having preceded us about two weeks, on a visit to her relatives. We are much indebted to the kindness of her brother, Mr. Gierisch, who tendered us assistance in gaining admittance to places of interest. He conducted us through the King's Palace, and being in His Majesty's service and confidence, showed us into apartments not accorded to the inspection of general visitors, many of whom were in some portions of the Palace with us. We visited several rooms which represent the sixteenth century, remaining in the original style of that period; others of later, and down to present date, some of which are only used on special royal occasions. We passed through a large hall which was being fitted up on the occasion of the Prince of Bavaria wedding the Princess of Austria, who, with some of the Austrian Court, are to arrive in two or three days, when a grand reception is to be given in this hall.

When in Venice we visited a glass manufactory, where glass was spun into very fine threads, and worked into any desirable form, as readily as silk; and, in this Bavarian Palace, we saw magnificent brocade window curtains, of beautiful colors, made entirely of glass. Some apartments were ornamented with gold in great profusion. Professor Carrington thought it a pity that so much of the precious metal should be useless, which might be better employed in behalf of suffering humanity. The four walls of one room were hung with portraits of ladies, called the "Beauties of Munich"—Mrs. Schettler and I thought Salt Lake City could furnish as many equally as beautiful.

The next day Mr. Gierisch obtained cards of admission, and conducted us to one of the many universities in the city, which we found to be a normal school for the education of teachers, which graduates about thirty annually. The ground floor of the building is appropriated to the kindergarten, a description of which I forwarded to the *Juvenile Instructor*. We visited three of the normal departments: in one, a lady was superintending, while amateur young ladies were taking practical lessons in teaching the classes, under her supervision. The other departments were under the immediate tuition of gentlemen teachers. In one of these, I remarked to one of the professors, who accompanied us, that the young ladies' appearance indicated energy of character, a requisite attribute for teachers, to which he assented, adding that they were also good natured, which elicited a hearty responsive smile of gratification from the young ladies, and produced a pleasant, general sensation.

In the last department, the number was small: in this, the students were completing their education, which we were informed is very thorough.

We were shown into the professor's studio, and also into the Superintendent's laboratory, where were chemical apparatus and botanic specimens, some of which were enlarged illustrations, for the benefit of students—a mannikin, also separate specimens of human bodily organs, much enlarged, etc. We were informed that no young lady can obtain a diploma as teacher, until she is a proficient in all of these branches; connecting the physical with the mental is certainly a healthful consideration in the educational process. A cultivated mind in a sound body can be much more effective in doing good than in an unsound one; which makes it requisite that school teachers, as well as parents, should understand the physiology, and the anatomical structure of the human body, in order to promote its healthful condition and adaptation, while cultivating the mind.

In France, boys and young men only are trained in gymnastics; but here they are practised by both sexes. They have appointed times for these exercises—we did not witness them.

The afternoon of the 28th was a gala time in Munich. At half past three, the Bavarian groom and Austrian bride would arrive at the depot; and with their suite, ride in carriages to the Palace. Of course all Munich must see them, and that portion, minus contiguous porticos, windows, etc., were on the streets and sidewalks, ourselves with the rest, to the number, as was judged, of from forty to fifty thousand. We were fortunately in a position to receive, or rather share, their gracious smiles and bows; but after all had passed, we began to think of returning to the hotel. It was of no use to make an effort, and we stood as still as the pressure of the crowd would admit, for some time, bracing ourselves as much as possible, to prevent being carried on the waves of the streaming multitude. All were smiling with pleasure; but this gave me a striking idea of the horrors attendant on a riotous uprising, where people are subject to be trodden to death without the possibility of escape! Such was the eagerness of the people to get a glimpse of the pageantry of royalty, on this auspicious occasion, that mounted officers were constantly on duty, pressing them back sufficiently for the procession to pass. This young Prince is cousin to the present King of Bavaria, who is not married.

The evening before leaving Munich, we were joined by Honorable Erastus Snow and his son Erastus, who has been on a mission in England, Missionary Agent of New York, W. C. Staines, Elder J. G. Bleake from the Liverpool office, and Elder Birch from St. George. Having from some unknown cause, failed of getting our mail, the arrival of these brethren, and the information they brought, was like "light shining in a dark place." We all left Munich on the morning of the 29th, when twelve and a half hours by rail brought us three hundred miles to Vienna. This is truly a beautiful city, said to contain 640,000 inhabitants. The streets are broad, with many open squares for free ventilation and are kept clean; the houses are many of them five stories high, and neatly built. By ascending some four hundred and twenty steps in the spire of St. Stephen's Church, we had a magnificent view of the city and surroundings, including the exterior of the unrivaled Palace of the Exposition, or "World's Fair," which, in the distance of two miles, appeared as if washed by the noble Danube, on which we saw little boats moving, apparently in miniature.

The Fair was formally opened on the 1st of May, as per announcement, but it will be one month at least, before its arrangements are completed. Many hands are constantly at work making preparations for and unpacking boxes of articles. The American Department is very little arranged, and I think no one is complete; and yet there is very much of the useful and ornamental already on exhibition; enough to illustrate the magnitude of design, and the order and magnificence of the arrangements. The Crystal Palace in London is a splendid affair, but will not bear comparison with this in Vienna.

Since leaving home I have seen many places and many

people—people in contrasts of circumstances, with wide extremes of habit and customs—have seen the rich in pomp and grandeur, and the poor in beggary and wretchedness—have associated with the highly educated and refined, and with the ignorant and semi-civilized—have visited magnificent royal palaces, and wretched abodes—have traveled over fertile plains and sterile deserts, verdant valleys and snow-capped mountains; and, although I have cherished a constant determination to enjoy everything enjoyable while abroad, and have really done so, I still think, as I have hitherto invariably thought, that home, with the Latter-day Saints, is the place of the highest happiness attainable on earth.

ELIZA R. SNOW.

LETTER LXXXIX.

At Vienna—Berlin—The Royal Palace—A Large Banquet Hall—Beautiful New Chapel—Monuments—Visit the U. S. Minister—Freedom of Parliament—Multitudes of Soldiers—Unhealthy Moral Condition of Berlin—Hamburg—Church of St. James—In London Again.

BERLIN, PRUSSIA, May 12th, 1873.

EDITOR DESERET NEWS:

On the 9th ult. we started from Vienna by train, and arrived here the following afternoon.

The country between Vienna and this, the capital of the German Empire, some five hundred or more miles, is delightful. Its immense undulating plains, here and there forming into low hills and rising mounds, all under a high state of cultivation, present a lovely, picturesque scenery. The whole country appeared to be filled with industrious and enterprising inhabitants. Elegant mansions peeping out amid the green foliage of romantic groves, villas, with their respective chapels surmounted with broad domes, or glittering steeples, and cities occasionally appearing in the distance, crowning the rising hills, altogether, form a panoramic view that is almost captivating.

On our arrival here we engaged quarters in the most fashionable and aristocratic hotel in the city, in a very pleasant and stirring locality.

Berlin is situated on a sandy plain on the river Spree, and is considered, in several respects, one of the finest and most interesting cities of Northern Europe—the metropolis of knowledge for Northern Germany, and the cultivated nursery of German arts and sciences. It contains about eight hundred and thirty thousand inhabitants.

Many of the streets are broad and straight—the buildings, frequently four and five stories high. The finest street passes our hotel—it is called "Unter den Linden," and is decorated with four rows of lime trees. In the centre of this street is a broad avenue for pedestrians, and on each side, arrangements for footmen and carriages. This magnificent thoroughfare extends from the Royal Palace, to the "Brandenburg Gate." This gate is constructed in the style of the Propylacan at Athens. It is sixty feet in height and one hundred and ninety in width, embracing five passages for carriages and footmen. It is surmounted by a figure emblematical of Victory seated in a chariot, drawn by four horses. The height of the group is nearly twenty feet. The expense of erecting this gate was in the neighborhood of a half million of dollars.

The Royal Palace is an extensive building—six hundred and forty feet in length, by three hundred and seventy-six wide, containing six hundred apartments. It contains a chapel, which is remarkable as being the place where the baptismal ceremony of Frederic the Great was performed.

The Picture Gallery, which is now used for a Banqueting Hall, is over two hundred in length, and one hundred and twenty-five feet wide. The largest room in this palace is one hundred and five feet in length, by fifty-one in width—decorated with a great variety of costly statues, and portraits of celebrated individuals. These palaces contain a new chapel, built in 1849, with a cupola measuring eighty-six feet in diameter. The altar is surmounted by a cross of silver seven feet in height, studded with gems, the cost of which is estimated at four hundred thousand dollars. There are several other palaces in the city, and some at Potsdam, a few miles distant, which is called the "Versailles of Prussia."

We have seen several splendid monuments, some of which we think as fine as any we have seen in Europe; also many equestrian statues of skilful and elegant workmanship.

We called on Mr. G. Bancroft, the American Minister—known as the American Historian—were kindly and warmly received, and enjoyed a very pleasant and sociable interview, at the close of which he cordially proffered his assistance, to the extent of his influence, in rendering our stay in Berlin profitable and interesting. He subsequently visited us at our hotel.

Here, we were fortunate in meeting Dr. Schleiden, member of the German Parliament, whose acquaintance we had formed in Salt Lake City, and which we renewed in New York, as mentioned in a former communication. This excellent gentlemen was delighted to see and introduce us to his intimate friend, Mr. Kapp, also a member of Parliament. These gentlemen have called upon us on several occasions, and have accorded us free access to the House of Parliament now in session; and have taken much pains in showing us objects of interest, and through interesting localities.

We were surprised to see the multitude of soldiers constantly parading the main thoroughfares and streets in this city. Every day they are marching past our hotel, in battalions, regiments, brigades and divisions, in the most imposing style, with magnificent flags and banners displayed—all led by instrumental bands of musicians in rich shining costumes—the whole performing their evolutions in the strictest order, skill and precision, presenting the finest and most splendid appearance of troops in any country we have visited.

Those fashionable institutions, "houses of ill-fame," are said to flourish and command the patronage of nearly all classes here, as in Paris, the gay metropolis of France; and some of them are built at an immense cost, and fitted up in fabulous splendor and sumptuousness. The people of Berlin, viewed superficially, are remarkably intelligent, and appear interesting, lovely, beautiful and happy, as though all were conscientious, moral, upright and pure; but, in this city, as well as in most others we have seen, corruption, rottenness, demoralization and misery are underneath.

Considerable sensation was created among the aristocrats in our hotel, through the calls of distinguished gentlemen, on our party. Our celebrity reached the public press, where we were creditably noticed, and perhaps somewhat flattered.

LONDON, May 19th.

We arrived here yesterday. Before we left Berlin, Elder Erastus Snow and son bid us adieu, *en route* for Scandinavia, and Elder Schettler in another direction, to attend to some necessary business, while President Smith, my sister and I left for London, *via* Hamburg and the German Ocean.

The country from Berlin to Hamburg is not prepossessing in its appearance. It exhibits no variety nor beauty of scenery—the face of the country is generally low and flat—similar to that of Holland, though not abounding in canals and windmills.

Hamburg contains a population of two hundred and twenty-five thousand, and is the principal place of commerce, and one of the most beautiful cities in Germany. It is situated on the river Elbe, about eighty miles from its mouth. The port is very extensive, and crowded with shipping of various tonnage.

The Bourse, the great rendezvous of merchants and capitalists of every rank, presents a lively, stirring business aspect, between the hours of one and two o'clock, p. m., when three or four thousand business people may generally be seen thronging the apartments.

This city affords a beautiful, fashionable commonage along the quay, which surrounds the basin formed by the River Alsten.

The Church of St. James is much noted: it is surmounted by a steeple three hundred and fifty feet in height. The great Church of St. Nicholas is also considerably celebrated—it is ornamented with a magnificent steeple, four hundred and fifty-six feet high, which affords a wonderful panoramic view from its summit. The Zoological and Botanical Gardens are represented to be among the finest in Germany.

We left Berlin on the 15th, and arrived in Hamburg the following evening, with the intention of remaining one day only. At the railroad station, the proprietor of a commodious hotel, in the most respectful manner, solicited our patronage—conducted us into his best apartments, and bestowed upon us more than ordinary attentions. The next day, he officiated gratuitously as our guide through the city—taking particular pains, and manifesting deep interest in pointing out and explaining every object of interest and curiosity. At first, we were a little suspicious that these extraordinary attentions were designed to establish heavy claims on the purse, but the mystery was at length revealed—this gentleman had read the German papers, and, at once recognized us as the "Distinguished Mormon Delegation" from Salt Lake. Our notoriety here brought us acquaintances.

A gentleman who, for many years, had been successfully engaged, on a large scale, in emigration, obtained an introduction, and very earnestly solicited our patronage, believing that, very soon, we should have a heavy emigration business in that country.

We left Hamburg on the 16th ult., on the steamer *Iris*, making our way over the German Sea, and arrived at Blackwall, London, on the evening of the 18th, after a pleasant and prosperous voyage.

LORENZO SNOW.

LETTER XC.

Leave Vienna—Bad Weather—Berlin—The Thier Garten—Bismarck and Moltke—Prussian Ladies—Hamburg—The Hollanders—A Land of Soldiers.

HAMBURG, GERMANY, May 16th, 1873.

EDITOR WOMAN'S EXPONENT:

DEAR LULA:—We left Vienna on the 9th, and arrived at Berlin, the capital of Germany, the next evening. The cold, stormy weather which overtook us at Munich, followed us to Vienna and from there to Berlin, where we had but one sunny day, which we improved in out-door sight-seeing. Walking down the principal promenade in the city, called Linden Street, (Unter den Linden) so named from being lined with four rows of lime trees, we strolled into the Thier Garten, an extensive public ground with artificial forests and shrubbery—garden plats, with statues in the centre surrounded with flower beds in full bloom—broad streets for carriages and omnibuses—side-walks for pedestrians and on opposite sides, roads for equestrians. These streets, many in number, cross at right angles, and extend far away in the distance, forming delightful avenues through the tall trees with their fresh, shady foliage. This furnishes a healthful exercise and innocent recreation for thousands. Here we saw multitudes of people of all classes—promenading, riding on horseback, in carriages, omnibuses and coaches; while others, seated on rustic benches—formed to correspond to the surrounding scenery, were enjoying the social chat under the shade of waving branches. It was truly delightful; and I thought that Salt Lake City, with its ample streets, beautiful streamlets and the many advantages it possesses, is quite deficient in this respect—it greatly needs cultivated public grounds—not only as being ornamental, but also of real utility.

One of the stormy days we visited the great German Parliament, where we saw Count Bismarck and General Moltke, of Franco-Prussian war celebrity; both are members of Parliament, and have seats near each other. We also saw Dr. Schleiden whom we met in New York. The Parliament House is not so large as the one occupied by the French Assembly in Versailles, but showed a fuller attendance than when we visited the latter. The gallery was crowded with spectators, both gentlemen and ladies, the latter, by the expression of countenance, manifesting as deep feeling of interest as the more lordly portion. We listened intently to two earnest speeches, but not comprehending the dialect, could not decide on their merits.

I much admire the appearance of the Prussian ladies. Generally speaking, they exhibit the most womanly good sense in their style of dress of any nationality I have seen for several years past. In spite of the prohibition against judging from appearances, the exterior unavoidably makes an impression with regard to the interior; and inasmuch as dress is acknowledged to be a legitimate index to the mind, I feel authorized to pronounce in favor of these German ladies —that they are truly worthy of being the mothers, wives and daughters of the staunch, athletic-looking soldiers of the Prussian-German Empire, whom I saw every day in full uniform, marching past my hotel, by thousands. These ladies dress with taste, and dress well, but with less disfiguring than fashionables do elsewhere, and in appearance are genteel, dignified and graceful. I have, here, seen scores of plain dress skirts worn by ladies apparently of the first class in society. Good sense is also combined with taste in the fashion of the ladies' riding suit. The skirt is what Webster would have called "a sort of betweenity," in length, between the short and the very long now worn in America, which is in danger from the horses' feet. The riding hat is the same as the gentlemen wear—crown of medium height, between the stovepipe and the flat, which gives them a stately appearance. But enough about dress.

On the 15th we left Hotel Royal, and by train arrived in Hamburg the same evening. This is an independent city, the great commercial centre of Germany. Its harbor contains an immense amount of shipping, and its railroad trains seem to move in almost every direction—all is stir and bustle. Hamburg is certainly a live city, and some portions of it very beautiful.

It was late in the evening when we arrived, but this morning, when I looked out from one of my windows which commands a good view of several much-frequented walks, I was struck with the uncommon size of the people—they seemed so very large—both men and women, young and old. After noticing them at different times, I remarked that I never saw so uniformly large people, and that I would like to see the Hamburg soldiery. This forenoon we took a ride through the city and my wish was gratified. Hamburg has but two thousand; and in passing the parade ground, a spacious square, we probably saw all of them on drill, which satisfied my curiosity. We thought those in Berlin much larger than those we saw in France, and more particularly than those we saw in Italy; but these Hamburgers are certainly more of the Goliath stamp—the tallest and stoutest military I ever saw. Their costume is of Prussian style.

I have continued to notice the size of the people in all parts of the city where we have been, and the same characteristic prevails. I made mention of it to a lady of much travel and observation—her opinion is the same; but why this distinction she failed to comprehend. We saw no reason why this city should promote an extra in the growth of humans.

The continent of Europe is a land of soldiers. We have seen so many, that we have become accustomed to the sight; but the reflection that the nations are training for war awakens at all times a painful sensation. While the Latter-day Saints are laboring to establish a kingdom of peace, the sword is the watchword among the nations of the earth.

This evening we take steamer for London. President Smith having received, through the Conference minutes, official information of his appointment as Trustee-in-trust, and feeling anxious to fulfil every obligation, he has relinquished his projected tour to Russia, which will facilitate our return. On the route, after crossing the Atlantic, my brother and I anticipate spending a few days with our relations. On the 25th is the London Conference, after which, we shall sail as soon as practicable.

ELIZA R. SNOW.

LETTER XCI.

In London—Attend Conference—Russian and Turkish Baths—Visit to Topesfield—Visit From the Marquis of Sligo.

London, May 24th, 1873.

President Brigham Young:

Your very welcome and interesting letter of April 28th is received. Previous to leaving Berlin, in Germany, I wrote to you our expected programme, dated May 11th.

Elder Erastus Snow and Erastus W. are visiting the conferences in Scandinavia. President Carrington returned from Vienna to England direct, and is looking after the emigration business; will send out a company June 4th. He is now in London.

President Lorenzo Snow, Eliza, Wm. C. Staines, and Thomas Jennings and myself have passage engaged on the *Wisconsin*, to sail May 28th. Brother Schettler and wife were expecting to accompany us, but I learn by letter, that his visits to the Moravians, in Silesia, attract so much attention that it is doubtful whether he will get through in time to do so, though his berths are engaged conditionally.

The Moravians were glad to hear him talk, and would like to hear him preach, but the Prussian laws prohibit it. Dr. Schleiden told me that he did not expect any change that would amount to an increase in religious liberty sufficient to enable us to preach in Germany at present.

We attend conference at the Royal Amphitheatre, Holborn, three meetings being advertised for Sunday, 25th.

Brother Lorenzo and Eliza will probably stop in Ohio to visit their brothers, and other kindred. I expect to reach home within ten days after landing, but will telegraph.

Our voyage across the German Ocean, or North Sea, was pleasant, considering the very cold weather. We suffered very little from sea-sickness.

I have been annoyed with rheumatism in shoulder and arm, which caused me much pain, especially while railroad riding. Since in London I have taken three vapor baths, half Turkish, half Russian, and the result is I am much better.

I visited Topesfield, in Essex, believed to be the parish from which the Smith family emigrated to Topsfield, Massachusetts. Reverend Charles Gooch agreed to search the records in his possession as soon as I should furnish him the data—dates and names—which I am to do by letter after I get home. He showed me the safe which he said contained the parish records to Elizabeth's time, in the chancel of his church. Upon the wall is a monument of marble, skilfully wrought, to the memory of "Guil Smyth," who died December 18th, 1633, aged 76. The lengthy inscription is in Latin. It was a description of this beautiful monument, which I had received from Dr. Gould, that induced me to visit Essex, and it may induce me to call at Topsfield, Massachusetts, on my way home, in search of further information. If I do so, it will probably take four or five days.

Junius F. Wells has been with me since my arrival, and has shown me as much of London as my time and strength would permit me to see.

We all sincerely hope that the efforts you have made to liberate yourself from burdens may have the desired effect—to lengthen your days and greatly increase your usefulness. Nothing shall be wanting on my part, with the help of the

Lord, and without his help we are as nothing. I regard my very existence as a live man, since I received my endowments at Nauvoo, as one continued miracle.

Regards to Brother Wells and the brethren in the office. May the Lord bless you.

GEORGE A. SMITH.

P. S.—The Marquis of Sligo has just called, and has arranged to take me and Junius through Parliament, which is in session, on Monday evening. G. A. S.

LETTER XCII.

On the Atlantic Ocean—Hamburg—London Conference—Leave for Liverpool—Embark on the "Wisconsin."

STEAMER "WISCONSIN," June 5th, 1873.

EDITOR WOMAN'S EXPONENT:

MY DEAR LULA:—We are seven days out from Liverpool—have had smooth sea, and, thus far, a very prosperous passage. Our steamer affords the best accommodations of any we have patronized on our tour—the staterooms are more commodious and the berths and lounges broader and less pent up, giving sufficient latitude for an ordinary-sized person, at least, to move. Captain Freeman is a sociable, cheerful man, apparently much liked by crew and passengers, and we are as well satisfied as possible with our home in the midst of the waters.

I wrote you last at Hamburg in Germany, the 16th of May; that evening we took steamer for London, where we arrived on the evening of the 18th and put up at "Cook's Boarding House," Great Russel Street, where we stopped on our outward tour, and experienced quite a home-feeling on our return, especially when joined, as we were, in the course of the evening by our excellent mutual young friend and brother, Elder Junius F. Wells. Here President Smith received a letter from Brother Paul A. Schettler, who parted with us at Berlin to visit his relatives, and to collect genealogies, expecting to join us at this point, stating that his old acquaintances gathered around him in great numbers, and were so anxious to hear him converse, that he should require more time than he had anticipated, unless President Smith particularly counseled otherwise. The party now consists of President George A. Smith, my brother Lorenzo Snow, T. W. Jennings and myself, being highly favored with the company of Emigration Agent, W. C. Staines, who is returning from Europe to New York.

In London we attended Conference with the Saints, on Sunday, in the Grand Amphitheatre, Holborn, where their meetings were held and well attended—President Carrington remarked that the assemblies in the afternoon and evening were larger than he had seen at any previous Conference. The Spirit of the Lord was free and powerful and the Saints rejoiced much on that occasion—testimonies were borne of a very interesting nature, and it is to be hoped that some seed fell on good ground—suffice it to say, the Saints had a refreshing time. Here I met Sister Mercy R. Thompson, whom we left in London on our way East.

On the 27th we left for Liverpool, where we experienced much kindness from President Carrington, who accompanied us from London, and also from Brother George F. Gibbs, of the *Millennial Star* office; and on the 28th went on board the *Wisconsin*. We now feel that we are on our way home, although my brother and I anticipate spending a few days in the Eastern States with our relatives. Since abroad, I have neither had time, nor allowed myself to think very much of home, except in those seasons of devotion and holy aspirations, when highest interests, and dearest objects are ever present with us! but when I shall be permitted to reach that point, I feel it will supersede every other in interest.

Woman's Exponent, of which I have received a few numbers, is to me the best representative of Utah, for in that I see many familiar names, and repeated testimonies of the continued energies and steadfastness of many of the mothers and daughters of Zion, in promoting her welfare, in which I shall be most happy to rejoice with them, and reunite my weak efforts in the great common, glorious cause.

* * * * *

We've sailed on many an ocean,
    And entered many a port—
View'd many a Princely Palace,
    And many a Lordly Court.

Seen many mosques and churches,
    And witness'd service there;
And how unlike the Gospel
    Their modes of worship are.

How long shall superstition,
    Priestcraft and ign'rance bind
In chains our fellow beings,
    And dwarf their powers of mind?

By undisputed tokens,
    His favor'd people know
That God again has spoken,
    From heav'n, to man below.

And that the glorious Gospel
    Meets every mortal need;
While Truth Eternal triumphs
    O'er every human creed.

By faith and works united,
    Through Jesus' blood made free;
How noble, pure, and Godlike,
    The lives of Saints should be!

Safe from the fierce destroyer
  That on the water rides,
And "terra firma" dangers,
  The Lord our pathway guides.

From many a stranger country,
  And many a foreign strand,
We now are sailing homeward,
  Towards our native land.

To those who have an eye to see and a heart to understand, the hand of God has been manifest in dispensing blessings to us as tourists: From calamities and dangers by storms at sea, in front and rear, we have escaped; and without any interruption worthy of note either by sea or land, for which we feel truly grateful. We expect but a short stay in New York, which you will accept as an apology for my writing as I am doing, trying to make the movements of my pen correspond with the undulating motion of the ship, which is not the easiest thing imaginable, as you will perceive by my tremulous scribbling.

ELIZA R. SNOW.

LETTER XCIII.

At St. Louis—Fine Scenery—Visit Relatives.

St. Louis, June 20th, 1873.

Editor Woman's Exponent:

Dear Lula:—When writing you last, which was on the ocean, I did not anticipate either time or opportunity for communication with you again while on my way home, but, in consequence of the extreme piety of this infidel age, we are in this great, live city, detained over Sunday. We arrived here yesterday morning from Kansas, where we found our youngest brother, whom we had not seen for more than twenty years—he was then a boy, now the father of a large and promising family, and located on a farm one half mile square, in a beautiful rolling prairie country, commanding a view, both grand and magnificent, extending as far as the eye can reach. I think I never saw a finer or more picturesque landscape scenery, while the soil is rich and very productive, situated five miles from Osage Mission, the railroad station for that section.

But more about St. Louis. We, *i. e.*, my brother Lorenzo and I, intended leaving last evening, but are detained till 10 to-night, the hour admitted as the close of the Sabbath, which, despite the sacred rest allotted the railroad trains, is decidedly a day of bustle, recreation and hilarity. While writing, my ears are saluted with almost every sound imaginable—bands of instrumental music playing in various directions—the rumble of street cars, which are loaded to their utmost capacity, constantly on the track, conveying gay pleasure-seekers to different points—picnics by land and picnics by water being a prominent order of the day—groups of people are promenading the side-walks, while processions are marching on the streets; but the railroad trains must not profane the Sabbath.

When we left New York, my brother and I proceeded directly to the place, in the State of Ohio, where he was born, and where both were brought up—the place of our childhood and our youth—also neighboring towns and counties. I had been absent thirty-seven years; my brother had returned once within that time. Very many of our relatives and friends have "gone the way of all the earth" since we left, and everything of remembrance has yielded to the strokes of the battle-axe of changeful Time.

Our former loved associates
Have mostly passed away;
While those we knew as children
Are crowned with locks of gray.

We saw Time's varied traces
  Were deep on every hand—
Indeed, upon the people,
  More mark'd than on the land.

The hands that once with firmness
  Could grasp the axe and blade,
Now move with trembling motion,
  By strength of nerve decay'd.

The change in form and feature,
  And furrows on the cheek,
Of time's increasing volume,
  In plain, round numbers speak,

And thus, as in a mirror's
  Reflection, we were told,
With stereotyp'd impressions,
  The fact of growing old.

Those of our relatives and acquaintances who remain, received us with affectionate cordiality—indeed it was one continued ovation, from first to last, through the counties of Portage, Geauga, Cuyahoga and Loraine, where we went: even children born since we left that country came distances to see and converse with us, the former friends of their deceased parents. Having been so long abroad, we felt anxious to return home; at the same time, being desirous of seeing as many of our friends and relatives as possible, we visited night and day—going from place to place in rapid succession. I am inclined to think that so much visiting was never before done in so little time.

We succeeded in gathering many genealogies both of the dead and the living; and we think, in many instances, have renewed friendships—revived and created associations that will extend into eternity. We feel that God is with us, and humbly trust that his blessing will attend our efforts.

                    ELIZA R. SNOW.

[TELEGRAM.]

SALT LAKE CITY, June 12th, 1873.

GEORGE A. SMITH, Sherman House Chicago.

All well—family and friends—glad of your speedy return.

BRIGHAM YOUNG.

[TELEGRAM.]

PRESIDENT GEORGE A. SMITH'S RETURN,

EVANSTON, W. T. June 18th, 1873.

EDITOR DESERET NEWS:

Presidents Brigham Young and Daniel H. Wells, accompanied by a large number of ladies and gentlemen, left Salt Lake City at five minutes past six o'clock this morning for Evanston, to meet President George A. Smith.

They reached Evanston all safe, at twenty minutes past one, and met President Smith and Thomas W. Jennings.

They were well received amidst warm, and cordial greetings.

The weather is delightful, and the trip has been very pleasurable.

D. W. EVANS,
A. M. MUSSER.

LETTER XCIV.

Home Again—Reception by Friends.

Brigham City, July 8th, 1873.

Editor Deseret News:

About 7 p. m. yesterday, President L. Snow, on his return from the "Holy Land," was met at Brigham Junction, four miles from here, by Judge Wright, Bishop Nichols, the Mayor and the City Council, together with a large company of ladies and gentlemen, with the Brigham City brass band; also a representation of the Sunday school, the Superintendent and associate teachers bearing a magnificent banner with appropriate mottoes. On arriving at the station, the Central Pacific train shortly appeared. On President Snow alighting from the cars, welcome strains of music were poured forth from the brass band. As he approached, the gentlemen took off their hats and warmly greeted him. The passengers on the Central Pacific train seemed to be inspired with the spirit of the occasion, as they waved hats and handkerchiefs in concert with those of the reception party.

After President Snow had shaken hands cordially with each one of the company, Judge Wright, in behalf of the citizens, delivered an appropriate address, welcoming him home, &c.; to which he briefly responded, returning thanks for this unexpected honor, and alluded to his tour through many countries, and journey of some twenty-five thousand miles without a single accident; had seen much, and often highly gratified with various scenes and objects of curiosity, but nothing had impressed his feelings so pleasantly as this meeting with his Brigham city friends.

The vehicles were presently in motion, under the soul-stirring music, which loudly echoed along the Wasatch Mountains; the procession proceeded for three quarters of an hour in the bright moonlight evening, when it reached President Snow's residence. He was here met by a large concourse of citizens of all ages, anxious to manifest personally, their earnest feelings of welcome. The ceremonies of reception were here closed by an appropriate tune from the brass band, when all dispersed to their homes.

A. CHRISTENSEN.

LETTER XCV.

SALUTATION TO THE LADIES OF UTAH.

SALT LAKE CITY, July 14th, 1873.

BELOVED SISTERS IN THE FAITH OF THE GOSPEL OF THE SON OF GOD:

It is impossible for me to express the joy and gratitude of my heart, in being once more in your midst—in the gathering place of the honest of heart. While absent, I have ever felt a degree of pride and thankfulness, that my home was in Utah—in the Valleys of the Rocky Mountains of America. Whatever others, in their ignorance, might imagine, we "know" that in Utah are associated the best and noblest spirits that are tabernacled in the flesh—that here, the highest order of intelligence is obtained, and society organized in a purer and more perfect form than anywhere else on earth.

With what sacred feelings I now realize that I am at home, surrounded by, and associated with, the Saints of God, many of whom I have already met with warm, affectionate greetings, and now avail myself of the medium of the *Exponent*, our excellent household paper, for extending to many others, with whom opportunities may not soon admit of personal interviews, my most cordial greeting, accompanied with love and blessing.

Thanks, my dear Sisters, for your faith and prayers, through which, in a great measure, I attribute the blessings of God in the wonderful prosperity which, from first to last, attended the party of tourists of which I have the honor of having been a member. We have traveled twelve thousand miles by water, and nearly or quite thirteen thousand by land, without accident, and without a single failure in making connection, either with steamer or railroad; and are now safely home.

Here let me beg acceptance of my thanks, and acknowledgment of my appreciation of the kind and generous feelings that prompted arrangements for my reception, which I very innocently frustrated by a "quiet arrival."

What an honor, to be associated with those who are coworkers with God in establishing a government of peace and purity! The more I see of the world, the more I realize the necessity of a more perfect form of government than exists among the nations of the earth; and how gratifying it is to a sympathizer with oppressed humanity, to know that God has now introduced His own authority, and is establishing His Kingdom, and that all who will, have the privilege of assisting in this great work. A work of the most important interest to the living and the dead—one which confers on living men and women the highest possible responsibilities.

While abroad, I often encountered the absurd idea, which many seem unwilling to relinquish, that here, woman is held in a state of vassalage—"down-trodden," etc., etc., to which I invariably opposed, from the fact that nowhere on earth has women as large responsibilities, and wields as much influence as with the Latter-day Saints. You, my Sisters, who are awake to your callings and your duties, will readily subscribe to the foregoing; while perhaps a few, who have no other thought of the object of their present existence, than that they are born to be idle curiosities, or playthings of human life—to trifle away time in selfish vanity, can see no good and noble position for woman to qualify herself to fill and make light of the most important labors.

We know that inasmuch as we labor for the Kingdom of God, our reward is sure, though all else should perish. Let us work on—laboring for "the things which make for peace," faith, hope, charity and perseverance in the path of perfection, until we shall be prepared for the presence of holy beings.

Your Sister in the New and Everlasting Covenant,

ELIZA R. SNOW.

www.ingramcontent.com/pod-product-compliance
Lightning Source LLC
Chambersburg PA
CBHW051247300426
44114CB00011B/925